GLOBETROTTER

GLOBETROTTER

HOW ABE SAPERSTEIN SHOOK UP THE WORLD OF SPORTS

Mark Jacob and Matthew Jacob

ROWMAN & LITTLEFIELD
Lanham • Boulder • New York • London

Published by Rowman & Littlefield
An imprint of The Rowman & Littlefield Publishing Group, Inc.
4501 Forbes Boulevard, Suite 200, Lanham, Maryland 20706
www.rowman.com

86-90 Paul Street, London EC2A 4NE, United Kingdom

British Library Cataloguing in Publication Information Available

Library of Congress Cataloging-in-Publication Data
Names: Jacob, Mark, author. | Jacob, Matthew, 1962– author.
Title: Globetrotter : how Abe Saperstein shook up the world of sports / Mark Jacob
    and Matthew Jacob.
Description: Lanham : Rowman & Littlefield, [2024] | Includes bibliographical
    references and index. | Summary: "The Harlem Globetrotters weren't from Harlem,
    and they didn't start out as globetrotters. Globetrotter is the fascinating biography of
    Abe Saperstein, a Jewish immigrant who took an obscure group of Black basketball
    players from Chicago's South Side, created the Harlem Globetrotters, and turned
    them into a worldwide sensation"—Provided by publisher.
Identifiers: LCCN 2024015434 (print) | LCCN 2024015435 (ebook) | ISBN
    9781538181454 (cloth) | ISBN 9781538181461 (epub)
Subjects: LCSH: Saperstein, Abe. | Basketball coaches—United States—Biography.
    | Harlem Globetrotters—History. | African American basketball players. | Jews—
    Illinois—Chicago—Biography. | Chicago (Ill.)—Biography.
Classification: LCC GV884.S355 J34 2024 (print) | LCC GV884.S355 (ebook) |
    DDC 796.323092 [B] —dc23/eng/20240508
LC record available at https://lccn.loc.gov/2024015434
LC ebook record available at https://lccn.loc.gov/2024015435

♾™ The paper used in this publication meets the minimum requirements of American
National Standard for Information Sciences—Permanence of Paper for Printed Library
Materials, ANSI/NISO Z39.48-1992.

To Inman Jackson, Abe Saperstein's friend, who was the epitome of the Black talent that made the Globetrotters go.

CONTENTS

FOREWORD by Mannie Jackson   ix

INTRODUCTION   xiii

1   THE DISRUPTOR   1

2   THE IMMIGRANT   15

3   THE ENTREPRENEUR   25

4   THE BARNSTORMER   35

5   THE BOSS   47

6   THE BASEBALL PROMOTER   59

7   THE CHAMPION   73

8   THE GROUNDBREAKER   91

9   THE PEOPLE PERSON   103

10   THE TEAM PLAYER   113

11   THE SHOWMAN   131

12   THE FREQUENT FLYER   147

13   THE DIPLOMAT   163

CONTENTS

14   THE COMMISSIONER   177

15   THE INNOVATOR   189

16   THE PERPETUAL MOTION MACHINE   199

EPILOGUE   213

ACKNOWLEDGMENTS   219

PHOTO CREDITS   223

NOTES   225

SELECTED BIBLIOGRAPHY   275

INDEX   279

ABOUT THE AUTHORS   303

FOREWORD

Mannie Jackson, former Harlem Globetrotters
player and the first Black owner of the team

I met Abe Saperstein when I was twelve years old. His Globetrotters played outdoors at Sportsman's Park in St. Louis in 1951. I was in the stands, and I was fascinated. I had never seen players and the game move so quickly and effortlessly. In fact, I'd never seen up close the masterful passing and dunking, and, of course, the Trotters basketball wizardry was full of joy. To get a closer look, I worked my way down from the stands and eventually reached the edge of the court. Abe walked past me, we said hello to each other, and I said, "Sir, I want to play on the team." He put his hand on my head and said, "I'll tell you what. That's possible. We'd like to have you play with us. But first you've got to go to school. You've got to get through college." And I remember walking away thinking, "What does college have to do with playing Globetrotters basketball?" But that encounter never left my mind; I studied harder and received a full scholarship from the University of Illinois, where I became captain of the basketball team, All Big Ten, a National Science Fellow, and winner of the coveted NCAA Theodore Roosevelt Award.

Soon after graduation, I went to New York City to work and play in the National Industrial Basketball League. My best friend and college teammate Gov Vaughn invited me out one night to see him play with the Trotters. I marveled at his skills and the atmosphere created by this all-Black team playing a game I thought I understood better than most. After the game I was reunited with many familiar players and, of course, Abe. Following a long night of conversation, I signed up and joined his organization. I told Abe I

Mannie Jackson

planned to play basketball for only a short time, and I wanted to learn how a business like his operated, because I planned to one day end up in the corporate world. Paul Cohen, owner of Technical Tape Corporation and my employer and mentor, simply said, "Go for it." He greatly admired the integrity and work of Abe Saperstein.

My time with the Globetrotters was a revelation. I had never been outside the United States, but, with the Trotters, I visited dozens of countries. Throughout my travels, Abe was explaining the business, even showing me sales figures to better help me understand how everything worked. The team spent four months nonstop playing against some of the best athletes in the world before the largest crowds I'd ever seen at a sporting event. This all-Black American team was very popular, and Abe was a master leader. He always spoke proudly of democracy and capitalism. When players struggled with racism and discrimination, Abe stepped in with messages of hope and progress. In those moments it was easy to see why the State Department had honored Saperstein's team with the coveted title of America's Ambassadors of Goodwill.

When I moved on to corporate assignments (General Motors, Honeywell, six Fortune 500 boards of directors, and chairman of the Basketball Hall of Fame), I had been well served by Abe Saperstein's lessons in leadership, corporate values, and brand management. He was a tireless professional and the greatest promoter and quality control executive I've ever seen. For example, Abe left no one behind. When you joined his team, you were part of the family. And he made sure you knew the Globetrotters' values: to be on time, to be courteous, and to work the details. Abe cared about all people. It didn't matter what age, gender, politics, or color you were, he simply cared. Like every great leader, he had the ability to put his arms around people and issues—in the right way.

In 1993, I stepped into the role once held by Abe: I acquired the Harlem Globetrotters. In an amazing experience through two decades, I benefited not only from the lessons he taught me, but from the reputation he had built for his team. He took the American game worldwide. He was a marketing genius who promoted a classy style of play that made the sport a popular sensation in nations and cities around the world. He would say, "Superstars come and go quickly, as do titles. Our purpose is in our uniqueness, excellence, and values. The Globetrotters are going to be around for several generations. We want help creating a better world for us all. We want our game to be fun and an inspiration of goodwill."

The entertainment and marketing value of pro basketball is obvious now, but it wasn't so clear in the days prior to television and highlight clips and certainly not when Abe first set off in a Ford Model T with five Black players to sell the sport in towns far and wide.

Abe doesn't get nearly enough credit for what he gave to the world and to sports. He created an appetite for this game we call basketball, which most people in the world had never heard of before. He made it his game, and then he made it a global game—a game for all of us to enjoy.

INTRODUCTION

Sports editor Alan Ward of the *Oakland Tribune* wrote in 1949: "When the history of American sports is compiled, the name of Abe Saperstein should be written in large, bold letters into the document."

But that hasn't happened. Saperstein is far less famous today than he deserves to be.

If Saperstein is remembered, it is for founding the Black basketball team known as the Harlem Globetrotters, but not for much more. Yet Saperstein wasn't just a major force in the popularization of Black basketball—he was a major force in the popularization of basketball, period, at a time when it struggled in the United States and was virtually unknown in some parts of the world. He pioneered the three-point shot, which has dramatically changed the character and style of the game.

And Saperstein's impact went well beyond basketball. His promotional savvy helped keep baseball's Negro Leagues alive, and he was an early force knocking down the color barrier in the major leagues. He's the reason one of the greatest pitchers of all time, Satchel Paige, finally got his shot at the majors. And Saperstein was a great promoter of international sports. When Olympic star Jesse Owens fell on hard times, Saperstein was among the few who stepped forward to befriend him.

Beyond sports, Saperstein and the Trotters were international symbols of Americanism during the Cold War. To the US State Department, they were key instruments of diplomacy at a time when the Soviet bloc was pointing to the US civil rights struggle as a sign of America's moral hypocrisy. And

along with the achievements in foreign affairs and sports, Saperstein and his comic basketball team gave the world a gift that was both immeasurable and immense: they made millions of people laugh.

Yet this is the first full book about Saperstein, a Jew born in a London slum who emigrated as a child and built a most remarkable American life. Why no biography before this? Well, his legacy is complicated. Although he empowered many Black people, he also promoted the racial stereotypes of his day. And though the clownishness of the Globetrotters was viewed by some as delightful, it was seen by others as demeaning.

Until the 1940s, the team's nickname, Globetrotters, was two words: Globe Trotters. To avoid distracting the reader, we have used the modern version in most references. In all other matters, we have tried to tell the truth as accurately as possible. That's a challenge because Saperstein sometimes invented and embellished details of his own life. This human dynamo who helped shape American sports didn't make it easy for biographers, but he sure made it interesting.

1

THE DISRUPTOR

*After two decades of struggle, a basketball game launched
Saperstein and his team into superstardom*

Chicago Stadium was stuffed with humanity, bathed in tobacco smoke, scented with popcorn, serenaded by a pipe organ, and filled with the dreams of a sports promoter named Abe Saperstein.

It was the night of February 19, 1948, and Saperstein's all-Black Harlem Globetrotters basketball team was facing off against the all-white Minneapolis Lakers, a squad that most sportswriters considered the best in the world. The Lakers had the greatest basketball player around, bespectacled giant George Mikan. But Saperstein had a weapon of his own: his irrational optimism. Saperstein was an outsider, the Jewish immigrant owner of a Black team in a white-dominated sports world. But he had silenced the doubters for two decades, and he figured he would silence more of them tonight.

As Saperstein stood on the stadium's hardwood floor, he took stock of the fans filing into the three-tiered arena. He always estimated the crowd size to make sure he was getting his fair share of the take. As one player recalled, "He was the only guy I ever met who could count the house in thirty-two seconds."[1]

Saperstein had seen a lot of crowds in his time, and he knew this one was special. It was as close as his ever-traveling team came to a home game, since the Harlem Globetrotters were born in Chicago.

The Minneapolis Lakers' George Mikan is sandwiched by the Harlem Globetrotters' Nathaniel "Sweetwater" Clifton (left) and Babe Pressley in 1950, two years after the first contest between the teams showed the competitiveness—and sometimes superiority—of Black basketball players.

Yes, the Harlem Globetrotters were born in Chicago. They weren't from Harlem, and they weren't globetrotters. That name was Saperstein's invention, his smoke and mirrors, his fake-it-till-you-make-it style.

Saperstein had come a long way from those early days. When he first took his team on the road in the late 1920s, he wore a basketball uniform under his suit in case he needed to go in as a substitute. But now his signature black mohair suit was his only uniform, covering his pudgy, five-foot-three, forty-five-year-old frame. Sportswriters frequently commented on his roly-poly shape, perhaps because he was often surrounded by tall, athletic ballplayers. He was "a man whose physical features resemble a basketball." He was "the rotund Barnum of sports." He was a person who "reminds you a lot of those little, fat salt and pepper shakers that won't fall over."[2]

Saperstein didn't seem to mind the descriptions, as long as they also noted that he was the owner of a major box-office attraction. At 3:00 a.m., seventeen hours before tipoff, fans began lining up for tickets at Chicago Stadium. As game time approached, the noise level inside the arena steadily rose, as if someone had turned up the volume on a giant radio. People used to say the stadium on the city's Near West Side was so loud that you felt like you were inside a tin can—a tin can built with more than three thousand tons of steel.[3]

The place had weight. It had history. Frank Sinatra performed here. Cowboy actor Roy Rogers proposed to cowgirl actress Dale Evans here. Franklin Roosevelt first uttered the phrase "New Deal" here. But the crowd at Roosevelt's 1932 nominating convention cheered more loudly for another Democratic initiative: a platform plank calling for the repeal of Prohibition. The Blackhawks played hockey here. Bicyclists competed in six-day marathons here. Tony Zale knocked out Rocky Graziano here, and Graziano paid him back later with a technical knockout here. The Bears captured a National Football League title here on a shortened indoor field when ice and cold made it impossible to play outdoors at Wrigley Field.[4]

Tonight, when all the paying customers had made it into the arena to see the Globetrotters face the mighty Lakers, the stadium would welcome 17,823 spectators, thanks to both heavy pregame promotion and "a benevolent smile from the fire marshal," as the *Chicago Sun-Times* put it. The enthusiastic throng, paying $3 for the best seats and $1.20 for general admission, formed the biggest audience yet for a basketball game between two professional teams in Chicago.[5]

The crowd was more racially mixed than usual in Chicago. "There were a lot of Black people there," said Abe's nephew Frank Rose, who was sitting behind the Globetrotters bench and recalled the game seventy-four years later at the age of ninety-two. "They came to see their heroes play."[6]

White fans outnumbered Black fans slightly, but just slightly. Chicago didn't have sweeping Jim Crow laws like in the South, where the Globetrotters sometimes had to play separate games before white fans and Black fans. But Chicago was segregated and deeply racist in many ways.

Less than a decade earlier, the *Chicago Tribune* had referred to a Black murder suspect as a "jungle beast" and added, "His hunched shoulders and long, sinewy arms that dangle almost to his knees; his outthrust head and catlike tread all suggest the animal." The *Tribune* said the suspect had "none of the charm of speech or manner that is characteristic of so many southern darkies."[7]

The idea that Black people were a notch or two down the evolutionary scale was fairly common among white people of the era, and part of that prejudice included the view that Black people lacked the intellectual capacity to prosper at complex tasks—like playing basketball. Around the turn of the century, Luther Gulick, the mentor of James Naismith, who invented the game of basketball, wrote that "games demanding team play are played by the Anglo-Saxon peoples, and by these peoples alone."[8]

Saperstein saw himself as an exploder of that myth. His Globetrotters often played in places where the townspeople had never seen a Black American in person before. The Trotters had met all comers and defeated them at a clip of more than 90 percent. For Saperstein, it was both a business and a crusade. He was smart enough to appreciate Black talent when others didn't. That allowed him to turn a profit and expose the folly of prejudice at the same time.

Saperstein sympathized with the plight of Black people, being a member of a minority group who had experienced ignorance and discrimination. But whereas Saperstein saw himself as trumpeting the Black cause, he was no white savior. In fact, the skill and creativity of Black Americans rescued him from a somewhat aimless early adulthood and ultimately turned him into a millionaire. In many ways, Saperstein was the one who got saved and then made the most of it.

That didn't stop the white press from describing him with such ridiculous terms as the "Great White Father"—a concept that even a self-promoter like Saperstein would have found to be over the top.[9] Sure, Saperstein was paternalistic toward his players, but it was more of a conventional boss-employee setup than a race-related relationship. And Saperstein was perfectly willing to put Black people in positions of responsibility in his organization, among them Inman Jackson, an early Globetrotter who became Saperstein's best friend and trusted coworker.

But being a self-promoter, Saperstein couldn't help presenting himself to the white community as a sort of Negro whisperer. "I honestly feel I know the Negro better than any white man in this country," he once said.[10]

For many of tonight's Black spectators, this was their first visit to the man-made cavern called Chicago Stadium. Like the regulars, they found the place accommodating but not fancy. A. J. Liebling wrote that the arena was "not a stadium but a large shed." Even so, it respected the fans enough to offer 100 percent unobstructed views, unlike many stadiums of the time.[11]

Saperstein would have the best seat, on the Globetrotters bench. And the game that unfolded before him, Trotters versus Lakers, would be a classic.

The Lakers, nicknamed after Minnesota's many bodies of water, would later move to a city with major water problems, Los Angeles. But for now, the Lakers were famous for their dominance of opponents with the help of the first superstar in the history of the National Basketball Association (NBA): the six-foot-ten Mikan.

Mikan was a hero in Chicago, having grown up an hour's drive south in Joliet, Illinois, and then starring at DePaul University on Chicago's North Side. When he entered DePaul, he was far from a finished product. But DePaul coach Ray Meyer hired a dance instructor to refine his footwork and helped him develop a virtually unblockable hook shot. Mikan's poor eyesight forced him to wear eyeglasses, which gave him a geeky appearance. But opponents quickly learned that appearances were deceiving. As DePaul won the nation's top college basketball event, the National Invitational Tournament, Mikan scored a record fifty-three points in a semifinal game, matching the total for DePaul's opponent.[12]

The Lakers had another star, Jim Pollard, who like Mikan was a former All-American and a future NBA Hall of Famer. Pollard was six-foot-five with jumping skills that earned him the nickname "Kangaroo Kid." He once injured his elbow by leaping so high that he slammed it against the backboard.[13]

Both Mikan and Pollard were taller than the tallest Globetrotter, Reece "Goose" Tatum, at six-foot-three-and-a-half. Tatum was a countrified Arkansan with a loping gait and an impressive wingspan of about eighty-four inches. He could almost touch his knees without bending down.

Saperstein had first noticed Tatum's athletic skills and his ability to entertain the fans with ball tricks when Goose was a professional baseball player. The Trotters boss had improbably converted Tatum to basketball and made him into his team's "clown prince." Tatum was a fine ballplayer, but the main skill he had over the Lakers' Mikan and Pollard was the ability to make people laugh. This was not going to be a lighthearted game, though. In that, it was far different from the Globetrotters' usual appearances, which were part basketball competition and part comedy sketch.

Over their first two decades, the Trotters had developed a repertoire of tricks and bits, such as a football dropkick skit, in which a player booted the basketball through the hoop, and a hidden ball trick, where a player pretended to pass the ball but instead tucked it under his jersey. The Trotters would climb on one another's shoulders to make baskets, put a pair of glasses on the referee to cure his "blindness," and dazzle the audience with trick shots, wacky passes, and showy dribbling. The clowning was sometimes racially stereotypical. In one routine, a few of the Trotters played regular basketball against the other team while their teammates sat in a corner of the court and engaged in a dice game.[14]

Saperstein explained the hijinks this way:

At the start of the game we go out and get the crowd google-eyed with rapid-fire passing and shooting. After ten minutes we're so far ahead it's no longer a ball game. The crowd is getting restless, see, so we make a quick switch and go into the five-minute comedy routine. . . . My idea has two advantages: It saves wear on the players and it keeps the crowd always interested. We play the longest schedule in the country, but the boys never go stale.[15]

The Globetrotters' comedy delighted fans and set Saperstein's team apart from other barnstorming squads. Over decades, it made millions of people laugh. But the hijinks also brought them criticism for racist minstrelsy, for depicting Black adults as mischievous children.

The idea that the Globetrotters were bad for the image of Black Americans was far from universal, though. After all, the Trotters outsmarted their opponents and the refs. They had the last laugh. "I think they've been a positive influence," said civil rights activist Jesse Jackson in 1978. "They did not show blacks as stupid. On the contrary, they were shown as superior."[16]

But tonight against the Lakers in Chicago Stadium, the clowning was neither demeaning nor uplifting. Instead, it was virtually nonexistent.

Some people thought the Globetrotters were a mere "show team" that would be easily dispatched by the Lakers, but Mikan knew better. "I'd watch them every chance I got, and I admired the way they played," he said decades later. "But because of . . . the funny stuff, people had no idea how good they were. That's why I wanted to play them. There was a lot of pride at stake."[17]

Saperstein set up the game with his friend, Lakers General Manager Max Winter, and they had a side bet on the outcome, though the stakes were not disclosed.[18] There was little or no public talk beforehand about the significance of an all-Black team playing an all-white team. Abe's cousin Gerald Saperstein, who watched the game from the mezzanine, said the Globetrotters boss "saw it as a game of two teams playing basketball and the best team wins. It wasn't 'Black against white' then."[19]

The matchup was a natural. Arch Ward, the legendary *Chicago Tribune* sports editor famous for inventing baseball's All-Star Game, had declared the Globetrotters to be "the best-known team in professional basketball."[20] The Lakers, meanwhile, were dominating the National Basketball League (NBL), a forerunner of the NBA. A contest in Chicago Stadium seemed like a good way to establish which team was best and make the owners a few bucks too. It also fit the image that Saperstein fostered—a team of upstarts disrupting the status quo. But Saperstein hated to lose and expressed annoyance when the Lakers "demanded their own referees, their own rules, and their own balls" for the game.[21] There was grumbling among the Lakers players, too, because they wouldn't get paid extra for the exhibition match.

Still, Mikan knew it would be a draw for the fans and a challenge for his team, saying, "I'd like to see that one from the stands myself."[22]

The Lakers–Trotters contest was the opener in a doubleheader, to be followed by a league game between the Chicago Stags and the New York Knicks in the Basketball Association of America (BAA), another NBA forerunner. That BAA game counted in the standings; the Lakers–Trotters game did not. But everyone knew which game mattered more.[23]

Both the Globetrotters and the Lakers came into the game with impressive momentum. The Trotters hadn't lost in more than two months despite a busy schedule with two separate units of the team on tour. The group that Saperstein brought to Chicago Stadium was a combination of the best players from his east and west squads. The Lakers were on an eight-game win streak and held a 9.5-game lead in the NBL's Western Division.[24]

The bookmakers' line was Lakers by eight.[25] And the Lakers made that look good at the start, jumping out to a 9–2 lead.

Goose Tatum found the game very unfunny. He was unable to handle Mikan, who poured in shot after shot. On offense, Saperstein insisted the team run its usual three-man weave, in which players ran in a figure-eight pattern beyond the free-throw line, passing the ball to each other as they crisscrossed. Besides being a feast for the eyes—a shell game in human form—the tactic was designed to bamboozle the defense, with the ball often going into a post player closer to the basket and one of the weavers breaking to the basket for a pass and easy layup or dunk. Except that Mikan's defense dominated Tatum so thoroughly in the post that the Trotters couldn't make it work. For the Trotters, the weaving was peeving but not achieving.

By halftime, Mikan had racked up eighteen points and the Lakers led 32–23.[26]

It was never pleasant in a Globetrotters locker room when Saperstein's team was losing. Canadian sportswriter Pete Sallaway witnessed a halftime rant in 1941 when Saperstein accused his players of dominating weak teams but folding against a tough one: "What's the matter with you fellows out there? . . . You bunch look like a million dollars against some ham-and-egg team. That doesn't count. But here I am in a spot where we should put on a good show and you work like a gang of bushers."[27]

After the players ran back onto the court that day in 1941, Saperstein turned to the sportswriter: "Pete, why is it that such fine athletes are so dumb? They just can't think for themselves. I wonder just how far they would get if they didn't have me around to figure out such situations."

But here at Chicago Stadium in 1948, with the Trotters in a halftime hole, it was obvious that Saperstein was the problem, or at least his pregame get-it-to-Goose strategy was. Player-coach Babe Pressley was doing most of the actual coaching by this time in the Trotters' evolution, and he gave the team its second-half instructions, which diverged from Saperstein's pregame plan. It had three prongs:

- Run, run, run.
- Get the ball to the best outside shooters.
- Mug Mikan.[28]

Roughness was a part of the game that Saperstein liked just fine. He favored giving every advantage to the defense, and once called for a change in basketball's rules to "eliminate fouls in the backcourt, except for bad sportsmanship."[29] That might have created a game that looked a lot like rugby as teams tried to bring the ball up-court. But no one tried out Saperstein's idea to find out.

Although Saperstein was tolerant of roughness, he became infuriated with physical play that might put his "clown prince" out of action. One time in Detroit after an opposing player knocked Goose Tatum into the third row of the stands, Saperstein ran across the court, shouting, "If I had a gun I'd kill that guy!"[30]

As the second half got underway at Chicago Stadium, the Trotters started double-teaming and hacking Mikan. "We said, 'If they're gonna call a foul, be sure and make him bleed.' And that's what we did," said Trotters player Vertes Zeigler. "We went to beating on him and slapping them glasses off him." As teammate Sam Wheeler put it: "If we'd had hatchets in our hands, he would have had scars on him—they would have taken 100 stitches."[31]

The goal was to foul Mikan before he had a chance to shoot, since the rules at the time gave players only one free throw for non-shooting fouls. Mikan, whose foul-shot ritual included making the sign of the cross and then tossing the ball at the basket underhanded, was a career 78 percent free-throw shooter but missed seven of his eleven free throws in this game.[32]

The generally calm Mikan got angry at the Trotters' rough treatment. His former DePaul coach, Ray Meyer, was sitting at the scorer's table and noticed Mikan's slow burn getting hotter fast. "Goose was really roughing up Mikan," Meyer said. "I saw Mikan's face get real white and I thought, 'Omigod, there it comes,' and Mikan leveled Tatum with a vicious elbow."[33]

Mikan was charged with a technical foul. "I tried to beat the Trotters all by myself, completely forgetting that I was but one cog in a great basketball machine. I was ashamed of myself," Mikan said decades later.[34]

The Trotters also took advantage of their speed and quickness with fast breaks, including what were then called "sleeper plays," in which a player would be slow getting back on defense and therefore would be open for a long pass if there was a turnover or rebound.[35]

More importantly, the Trotters' outside shooters started hitting. One of them, Ermer Robinson, had been recruited by Saperstein during a West Coast swing by the Globetrotters when they played Robinson's Fort Lewis military team. During that game, Saperstein had started out ridiculing Robinson's unusual running one-handed shot and reminding his players that they had to stick to two-handed set shots. But Robinson kept scoring, and Saperstein ended up saying, "Jeez, I better get that kid."[36]

Robinson, whose nervous chain-smoking and fear of airplane travel earned him the nickname "Shaky," coolly hit long bombs to help the Trotters outscore the Lakers 10–2 to start the second half. The contest was close the rest of the way.

Another star player for the Trotters was Marques Haynes, a dazzling ballhandler who once closed out a game by dribbling away the entire fourth quarter, taking advantage of the lack of a shot clock in that era.[37]

As the third quarter neared an end in Chicago Stadium, Haynes and Mikan battled for a loose ball and Haynes fell hard to the floor. He got up slowly and kept playing. A few minutes later it happened again, except that this time Mikan fell on top of him. The crowd went silent as Haynes lay on his back and grimaced.[38]

Eventually Babe Pressley and Ermer Robinson helped Haynes to his feet, and Saperstein rushed to his side.

"You want to come out?" Saperstein asked.

"No," Haynes answered, explaining that he was warmed up and wanted to stay that way.

"What is it, your back?" Saperstein asked.

Haynes nodded.

"You better come out," Saperstein told him.

"On the bench I'll stiffen up."

"I think you should come out."

"On the bench I'll stiffen up," Haynes repeated.

"I think you should come out," Saperstein repeated back.

"No! If I keep playing, I can stay warm."

And so he did.[39]

The score was 42–42 going into the fourth quarter, and it stayed tight. The suspense kept building, made ever more intense by the stadium's enormous pipe organ, which only encouraged the fans to shout louder. The music from the organ's six separate keyboards wailed from four boxes installed in the steel trusses a hundred feet over the court. The organ lent an almost religious intensity to the events. As one stadium organist put it, "It's like God speaking from the ceiling."[40]

Cigarette and cigar smoke hung like incense over the throng, further creating an otherworldly atmosphere. And the fans were about to see a miraculous ending.

With about two minutes left to play, the Trotters held a 59–58 lead. By this time, many fans seemed to be cheering for *both* teams, Haynes recalled. "Most people came thinking the Lakers would beat us by plenty. Then they saw how much talent there was on both sides, and started cheering every basket. And by the end, most of them were just cheering for overtime."[41]

They almost got it.

Mikan was fouled by Tatum and hit a hook shot anyway, but the referee ruled that the foul came before the shot and disallowed the basket. Mikan missed a free throw that would have tied the game. But the foul was Tatum's fifth. He fouled out. The next time Mikan came down the court, the Trotters' Sam Wheeler fouled him. This time Mikan hit the shot to tie the game.

The crowd was standing and shouting. Fans of the Globetrotters called on their team to play for the last shot, for victory or overtime. "Freeze the ball!" they chanted. "Freeze the ball!"[42]

Haynes, still smarting from those two hard falls earlier in the half, displayed his outstanding ballhandling skills for about a minute, playing for the last shot. With about ten seconds left, a defender knocked the ball out of bounds, cranking up the tension. As Haynes got the ball back inbounds, the crowd fell silent. Haynes passed to Ermer "Shaky" Robinson, who smoothly took a one-handed set shot from a distance that was about where the three-point line is now. Witnesses remember the shot's high arc, the blast of the horn ending regulation play, and then the ball swishing through the net. The final: 61–59, Globetrotters.

The crowd went "mildly insane," in the words of the *Chicago Herald-American*.[43] The Trotters lifted Robinson on their shoulders as the Lakers protested that he hadn't released his shot before the horn sounded—an appeal that was quickly rejected.

"Owner-Coach Abe Saperstein headed the parade to the locker room," according to the *Chicago Defender*.[44] Once there, the players hoisted Saperstein on their shoulders too. The moment of comradeship might have reminded Saperstein of the very earliest days, when he was more of a team-mate than a boss, and they were just six guys riding a Model T from one jerkwater town to the next.

It didn't take Saperstein long to resume the boss role, though. He handed out bonuses, with most players getting $100 but Robinson pocketing $150 and Tatum $200.[45] Savoring their victory, the players partied at the South Side's Pershing Hotel, eating lobster and listening to Lionel Hampton and his band.

One player skipped the festivities, though. Marques Haynes found his way back to Ma Piersall's rooming house on the South Side and went straight to bed. The next morning, he wasn't feeling any better, so he went to the hospital for X-rays. Doctors diagnosed him with a fracture of his fourth lumbar vertebra. Placed in a cast from his armpits to his hips, he was able to walk out of the hospital and head home to Sand Springs, Oklahoma, to recover.[46]

Chicagoans who had not attended the game pored over the exciting newspaper accounts of what they had missed. *Chicago Herald-American* reporter Edgar C. Greene led his story this way:

The sign on the marquee mentioned the Stadium boxing show tonight and read FIGHT but it applied last night as surely as it can ever apply. You had to fight your way into the arena, fight your way to a seat and fight your way out while on the basketball court the Harlem Globetrotters and Minneapolis Lakers put on a show that made the battle worth it.[47]

The sportswriter had no way of knowing that the Chicago Stadium boxing show, just one night after the Lakers–Trotters bout, would include far too much fight. A series of blows to the head by Ezzard Charles knocked out Sam Baroudi in the tenth round, and the twenty-year-old died a few hours later in the hospital from a cerebral hemorrhage.[48]

Yes, the sports business could be cruel, violent, even fatal. It was often a brutal way to make a living. But it was also glorious for the victors, and for Saperstein it was vindication.

Marques Haynes said that for the players, the game "was more about pride than a black-and-white thing."[49] But in retrospect, the game is remembered as a key step in convincing the white basketball world that Black athletes could compete at the highest levels. That, in turn, raised the pressure two years later for the new NBA to admit its first Black players. Modern-day sportswriter Eric Nusbaum has called the 1948 game "the pivotal moment in basketball's integration."[50]

For the Black fans who had witnessed the Globetrotters' triumph that night, "it was a great evening," said Chicago historian Timuel Black. "We went back to our various bars or taverns and talked about it. It was more than just a victory of the Trotters; it was also a victory of the Black community over the hostile white community."[51]

There were a lot more struggles ahead, of course. On the same night as this triumph of Black talent, President Harry Truman gave a speech in Washington supporting his civil rights initiatives. Some Southern Democrats boycotted the address, including the wife of South Carolina Senator Olin D. Johnston, who declined to attend "because I might be seated next to a Negro."[52]

Saperstein, who had been seated next to Negroes for decades, savored the victory, but he wasn't as giddy as some of his players. His nephew Frank Rose recalled Saperstein's strange reaction after the victory. Believing his own hype, Saperstein had fully expected a victory—but an easier one than he got. The game seemed to disappoint him a bit.

"I thought he was pretty nonplussed by it, to tell you the truth," Rose said. "I think he was surprised that the game was as close as it was. He thought the Globetrotters were going to walk all over Mikan's team, and that just didn't happen. . . . He seemed nonplussed by the whole thing, like, 'this is just the way it goes.'"[53]

Marie Linehan, who ran Saperstein's Chicago office, recalled enjoying the game from a courtside seat. "I couldn't talk for a week, I screamed so hard," she said.[54] But Saperstein and his organization didn't linger for long on the triumph. They would keep moving—to the next game and the next and the next.

More than two-thirds through his life, Saperstein was still not a wealthy man, but that was about to change. And only Saperstein might have been overconfident enough to predict all the achievements that lay ahead, including his contribution to ending baseball's color line, his revolutionary change in basketball's rules, and his burnishing of America's image overseas during the Cold War.

The whole time, Saperstein was something of a cipher, wheeling and dealing both in public and in secret with his friends and his adversaries. Rumors always flew around him, some of them likely started by him. You never knew what Saperstein would come up with next.

Asked a few years after the Trotters–Lakers game how his team became such a box-office sensation, he answered, "I don't know exactly, but you can go along with a show for twenty years and nothing outstanding will happen and then, boom, you're a hit."[55]

Saperstein was indeed a spectacular hit, but also a paradox.

He exploded stereotypes about Black people, but he promoted stereotypes as well.

He encouraged on-court clowning that made many people laugh but made others cringe.

He left some players grateful for the opportunity but left others feeling mistreated.

He was bluntly honest with some sportswriters but spun elaborate fictions for others.

Abe Saperstein's story is a tangle of contradictions, myths, mysteries, mistakes, and triumphs. It's the story of a force of nature who crashed through life, making a spectacular impact.

2

THE IMMIGRANT

Born in London, Saperstein found his passion
on the playgrounds of Chicago

A braham Michael Saperstein was born in a slum. London's East End neighborhood of Whitechapel was a murder scene for Jack the Ripper, a workshop for prostitutes, a clubhouse for criminals, a last stop of the desperate, and a way station for poor immigrants like Saperstein's parents, Jews who had recently arrived from Poland.[1]

A few years before Saperstein's birth, an American visitor described Whitechapel: "Tiny boys and girls, their shoeless little feet in the gutter, gnawing a dry crust; drink-sodden old women reeling along between others not so much less intoxicated than themselves; knots of shabby, broken-down men around the public-house doors."[2]

Saperstein was born in 1902 on the Fourth of July, which was not a day of celebration in London, of course. But the next day was. Soon-to-be-coronated King Edward VII threw a dinner for half a million slum dwellers, who drank to his health from coronation cups given away as souvenirs.[3]

Abe's parents, Louis and Anna Saperstein, were from Lomza, a city in northeastern Poland that was occupied by the Russian Empire. They married in 1900, honeymooned in London, and decided to stay. Louis was a twenty-year-old tailor who could read and write Hebrew and Yiddish. Anna was illiterate.[4] They were among two million Jews who left Russian-held

Confident teenager Abe Saperstein (right) with his mother Anna, sister Leah, and brother Jake in 1916.

areas between 1881 and 1925.[5] The incentives were obvious: economic opportunities abroad and an escape from anti-Semitism under the czar and the risk of being drafted into the Russian army. The Sapersteins' reasons for emigrating are unknown, but the decision saved them and their descendants. Four decades later, Nazi invaders took the Jews of Lomza by cattle car to their mass murder at Auschwitz-Birkenau.[6]

London was a new, forbidding world to the young Saperstein family and certainly wasn't free from anti-Semitism. A visitor to Whitechapel in the summer of Abe's birth was author Jack London, who passed himself off as a stranded American sailor in order to hang out with the homeless, get admitted to a workhouse, and then write a book about London's poor titled *The People of the Abyss*.[7] The author recalled overhearing workmen talk about Jews taking their jobs.[8]

One of them said: "But 'ow about this 'ere cheap immigration? The Jews of Whitechapel, say, a-cutting our throats right along?"

Another responded: "You can't blame them. They're just like us, and they've got to live. Don't blame the man who offers to work cheaper than you and gets your job."

In 1906, the Sapersteins decided to move again. By that time, Abe had two younger siblings with a third on the way. His father, Louis, traveled across the Atlantic, was processed through Ellis Island, and took a job as a tailor in New York City's garment district, with the idea of the family following once he was established. Louis soon found New York unsatisfactory and moved on to Chicago, where an aunt had offered to put him up.

Louis joined his aunt on the West Side's Jackson Boulevard and began looking for work. He spotted a newspaper ad for a tailor shop in the North Side's Ravenswood neighborhood, populated by people of German, Irish, and Swedish descent. The ad specified "No Jews allowed," but that was only a minor obstacle for Louis, who decided to pass himself off as German and rename himself "Schneider," the German and Yiddish word for "tailor." It worked.[9]

Not only did Louis get the job, but the shop's owner soon decided to move to California. Before leaving, the owner shared his equipment and helped Louis set up his own Ravenswood shop specializing in ladies' dresses. The son of Lomza, with passable English from his time in London but no ability to write in English beyond his name, became an instant entrepreneur in America.

And Abe became a globetrotter at the age of five when his mother took him and his siblings on a long trek to Chicago in 1907. Abe's arrival began a love affair with Chicago, which he always considered his home base despite spending the vast majority of his life elsewhere.

The city that young Abe encountered was a messy metropolis that gained half a million residents during the first decade of the twentieth century. The Chicago River had recently been reversed in an audacious engineering project to prevent cholera outbreaks caused by waste flowing into Lake Michigan. The stockyards on the South Side were busy turning the Midwest's livestock into the nation's dinners, but the work conditions were facing new scrutiny because of a muckraking novel called *The Jungle* by Upton Sinclair. And it was a sports-mad city, with the Chicago Cubs winning baseball's World Series the year that Abe arrived. That victory took place at the West Side Grounds; the Cubs wouldn't move to the North Side's Weeghman Park (later renamed Wrigley Field) for another eight years.

The Saperstein family's first Chicago home was in a predictable place for Jewish immigrants to settle, a West Side house on Roosevelt Road, not far from the Maxwell Street Market. But it was even farther away from Louis's work than his aunt's home had been, so the family soon moved much closer to Louis's tailor shop, becoming one of the few Jewish families in the Ravenswood neighborhood.[10]

The family eventually had to find room for nine children—in order, Abe, Leah, Morry, Rocky, Jacob, Frances, Harry, Katherine, and Fay. Guy Saperstein, son of Abe's brother Harry, said the family's size made it difficult for them to secure housing and keep it. "My dad would tell me stories about how they would lie to rent an apartment," Guy said. "And the landlord would find out three months later that they had nine kids and not the three kids that Grandpa had told them about and toss them out. So they were constantly being evicted."[11]

"We had a helluva time staying in one place," Harry once recalled, claiming that the family lived in nine homes in his first seven years of life. The family was visited by social workers bringing charitable aid, then known as "relief."[12]

Louis "was constantly working. He worked seven days a week, twelve hours a day," recalled Leah's son, Roy Raemer, who lived with his grandparents for a time. Though mostly a ladies' tailor, Louis made clothes for all his children.[13]

The Sapersteins were struggling but resilient, showing the optimism and ambition that would be among Abe's most noteworthy traits. "That family, they were dirt poor, but that family had so much fun," Guy said. "And they did it collaboratively."[14]

Guy cited a regular chore that his father, Harry, did with two of his brothers. "My dad was four years old, and he was hopping on the train with two of his brothers and going to Indiana at 4:00 a.m. on a Saturday morning to buy potatoes to bring back," Guy said. "They would hawk the potatoes in the alleyways of Chicago, just to make a few quarters."

The Sapersteins of Ravenswood were fairly secular Conservative Jews who attended services for the High Holidays but rarely for the rest of the year. Louis maintained ties to Jewish culture by taking the children to the Maxwell Street Market to buy weekly groceries and treat each kid to a corned beef sandwich. Anna, who spoke to the children in Yiddish, cooked such old-world favorites as beet soup, cabbage soup, and chicken soup with kreplach.[15]

Abe's sister Leah said the children had trouble as the only Jews in their public elementary school, enduring taunts of "Christ killers." Abe's fights on the playground increased his interest in boxing—and in other sports that seemed to give him an opportunity to compete on even terms. "Abe was crazy about sports," said his sister Fay. "He lived for sports."

Abe found his joy on the ballfields and basketball courts of the Wilson Avenue YMCA and Welles Park, and even in front of the mirrors in his father's tailor shop, where he practiced his basketball moves.[16] He shot baskets with a boy named Bob Elson, whose parents operated a grocery store next to his dad's shop. Like Abe, Elson had a brilliant sports future ahead of him: he became the radio play-by-play man for the Chicago White Sox baseball team.[17]

Abe's sister Fay said her brother "made friends easily and kept them."[18]

"Our house was the headquarters for the boys in the neighborhood," Fay said. "One baseball season, I remember, Abe played second base for a Catholic parochial school even though he was a student in the public school down the street. After a game, he would bring the other boys home with him for supper. The noise was deafening."

Whether the Catholic school's Jewish second baseman dwelled on his ethnic outsider status or not, he battled a stereotype of Jews as bookish and physically weak. Henry Ford, the automobile pioneer and rabid anti-Semite, wrote in 1921:

> Jews are not sportsmen. This is not set down in complaint against them, but merely as analysis. It may be a defect in their character, or it may not; it is nevertheless a fact which discriminating Jews unhesitatingly acknowledge. Whether this is due to their physical lethargy, their dislike of unnecessary physical action, or their serious cast of mind, others may decide; the Jew is not naturally an out-of-door sportsman; if he takes up golf it is because his station in society calls for it, not that he really likes it; and if he goes in for collegiate athletics, as some of the younger Jews are doing, it is because so much attention has been called to their neglect of the sports that the younger generation thinks it necessary to remove that occasion of remark.[19]

So, according to Ford, Jews were getting into sports in a sneaky plot to hide the fact that they didn't like sports.

Abe's winning personality often defeated such irrational prejudice, and at the age of twelve he almost broke into motion pictures. A movie theater on Clark Street held a contest to pick the most popular youngster in Ravenswood, with the winner getting a two-week tryout at Chicago's Essanay Studios. Movie patrons wrote Abe's name often enough on their ticket stubs that he made the finals along with four others. The final vote would come after each of them gave a speech. Abe's sister Leah helped him write and practice his address, but when it came time to give it at the theater, he clutched up. A few embarrassing seconds later, Abe got over his stage fright—a condition he never seemed to experience again for the rest of his life. Either the patrons were impressed by Abe's belated delivery or they felt sorry for his shyness. Either way, he won.

Essanay Studios was a big deal in the days before Hollywood dominated moviemaking. Named for the initials of its owners S and A—George Spoor and Gilbert Anderson—Essanay featured some of the greatest film stars of the era, including Gloria Swanson, Ben Turpin, and Charlie Chaplin. On his first day, Abe rode his bike to Essanay and came home bragging that he'd spotted Swanson. On his second day, he lost control of his bike going over railroad tracks and broke his arm en route to the studio. His movie career was over, but not his show business career, as it turned out.[20]

Abe held a variety of jobs in his youth, including delivering newspapers and setting pins at a bowling alley. But he still found time for mischief. He once competed with friends to see who could drink the most Italian red wine. Abe won but got so sick that it turned him against alcohol for the rest of his life. At Lake View High School, he was active in the Reserve Officer Training Corps and ended up wearing his ROTC uniform to graduation because his father didn't finish sewing his dress suit in time. But Abe preferred sports to the military at Lake View, playing intramural baseball and basketball his first three years but making the varsity as a senior.[21]

On the diamond, Abe was a classy infielder, but his slight build and short stature made him no kind of slugger. After Abe became famous, Globetrotters publicity materials included a story about Abe's baseball exploits that seems improbable but can't be altogether discounted. He supposedly went one-for-two at the plate—along with twenty-three walks.[22]

High school basketball in that era was divided into three levels: heavyweight, lightweight, and bantamweight. Abe went into the smallest division, bantamweight, with a limit of 115 pounds. Abe didn't play in some early games but was a starting guard by the time Lake View reached the city playoffs and lost in the semifinals. His high school yearbook declared: "Abe is the fastest little bantam in Chicago. He can play rings around his opponents and his man never breaks loose." Abe's high school athletic feats were embellished in later-day Globetrotters publicity, such as a claim that Abe had made all-city and all-state, even though Illinois didn't even have an all-state basketball team until the 1930s.[23]

Another point of dispute is whether Abe ever went to the University of Illinois, as he claimed. Family lore has it that Abe attended for a time—perhaps six weeks, perhaps six months—but was called home by his father, who needed Abe's tuition money to help pay for a house. Abe claimed that he attended college for a year, and he offered a different reason for dropping out: the Illini basketball team wouldn't give him a chance because he was five-foot-three. A check with the University of Illinois Transcript and Verification Unit shows no record of Abe ever attending the school, though an official there said it's possible that if he was there for a very short time—say, six weeks—his name might not survive in the records.[24]

The story about Louis Saperstein taking his son's college money is made more plausible by the fact that Louis bought the family's first house in the same month that Abe graduated from Lake View High. Louis was compelled to make the purchase because the family was being evicted again. Abe's sister Leah, then sixteen years old, found a house for sale at 3828 Hermitage Avenue at a price of $4,500, with a $500 down payment. "Papa never had $500 to his name," said Abe's brother Harry, but Louis managed to assemble the down payment by borrowing from friends and family.[25]

The home was not only the first that the family owned, but also the first with electricity. There weren't enough bedrooms to go around, so Abe slept on the living room couch or an enclosed porch. That sort of treatment might have prodded some older children in big families to move out on their own, but Abe stayed in the family home for the next ten years.[26]

If not a college career, what was Abe going to do? He didn't seem to know. But he was certain he didn't want to work for his father. Instead, he delivered flower arrangements for Schiller's Florist and talked the owner into sponsoring an industrial-league basketball team, with Abe serving as player-coach. Abe went on to jobs at the Victor Adding Machine Company and the Chicago & Northwestern Railroad, getting those employers to sponsor his sports teams too. At one point he hitchhiked to the Pacific Northwest, where he picked apples and harvested wheat.[27]

Abe would later make the dubious claim he was "a regular with the Cleveland Rosenblums when that team was national professional cage champions." The early pro basketball team, sponsored by Cleveland clothing store owner Max Rosenblum, won championships in 1925–1926, 1928–1929, and 1929–1930. Abe couldn't have played with the Rosenblums in those last two seasons because he was touring with the Globetrotters, and a search of newspaper archives finds no mention of Abe being a member of the Rosenblums during that first season either. In one game during the 1925–1926 season, the Rosenblums got eight men into the game. None of them was named Abe Saperstein. Abe made the apparently bogus Rosenblums claim with sportswriters far from Cleveland and dropped it from his résumé when his team became a national sensation.[28]

In his mid-twenties, Abe was still sleeping on his parents' couch, still searching for his place in the world. But his lack of defined goals didn't mean he was lazy. In fact, he always had a highly disciplined lifestyle.

Guy Saperstein said his father, Harry, raved about his big brother's work habits. "My dad would tell me that Abe had everything timed," Guy said. "He knew it took one minute and forty seconds to brush his teeth. Everything he did was timed and extremely efficient. My dad used to tell me how amazingly efficient he was and how he could accomplish the work of three people."[29]

Lanier Saperstein, Abe's grandson, said Abe was known to take "one day off a year, which was Yom Kippur. And that whole day he was unable to sit still. He'd be washing and sweeping."[30]

Abe had plenty of energy alright. He just needed a focus, which he would soon find, spectacularly.

3

THE ENTREPRENEUR

The birth of the Globetrotters is cloaked in mystery,
some of it created by Saperstein himself

A be Saperstein didn't want to work in the adding machine business or
with flowers or railroads or apple orchards. He had tried those things
before moving on to a job that would set his career's course. At age twenty-
four, he was hired as a public employee at Welles Park, the North Side rec-
reation area where he had played sports in his youth. One of his duties was
to coach the Chicago Reds, an amateur basketball team he had previously
played for.[1]

The job was a godsend to Saperstein, allowing him to hobnob with sports
figures throughout Chicago, including members of the city's fast-growing
Black community. The Great Migration from the South doubled Chicago's
Black population in the 1910s and then doubled it again in the 1920s, creating a culturally vibrant South Side neighborhood known as Bronzeville. But
the newcomers met bitter resistance in Chicago. Twenty-three Black people
and fifteen white people had died in a 1919 race riot triggered by the drown-
ing of a Black swimmer who was attacked by rock-throwing white people.[2]

Saperstein, an outsider in many situations, found he got along well with
Black people, especially those who shared his love of sports. One of them
was Walter Ball, who had been a highly regarded spitball pitcher in the
Negro Leagues. By the time he and Saperstein met, Ball was in his forties

The Globetrotters of the 1930–1931 season. Standing from left: Saperstein, Walter "Toots" Wright, Byron "Fat" Long, Inman Jackson, and William "Kid" Oliver. Seated: Al "Runt" Pullins.

and headed a baseball team called the Walter Balls, which was looking for someone to help set up a tour for them in Illinois and southern Wisconsin. Ball wanted to hire a white person who would be trusted by white folks in small towns. Saperstein eagerly agreed to make the arrangements, and he did a good enough job that it appeared to be his "in" for Black sports promotion.[3]

Saperstein became acquainted with other prominent Black sports figures on the South Side, including former pro football players Fritz Pollard and Dick Hudson. Unlike Major League Baseball, the National Football League (NFL) allowed Black players in the 1920s and early '30s, before an unofficial color line was in force from 1934 to 1945.[4]

Hudson, who had been a fullback with the NFL's Minnesota Marines and Hammond (Indiana) Pros, was a familiar face in Bronzeville's nightclub scene, with a reputation as a terrific dancer.[5] Pollard was a halfback who led

Brown University to victories over then-powerhouses Harvard and Yale, once outgaining the entire Harvard team 269 yards to 226. He went on to become a player-coach with the NFL's Akron Pros, Milwaukee Badgers, Hammond Pros, and Providence Steam Roller. The NFL's only Black head coach in the league's first six decades, Pollard was named to the Pro Football Hall of Fame posthumously.[6]

Saperstein, on the other hand, was a young North Side Jewish man with almost no credentials who would show up and chat with the Black sports luminaries. Decades later, after Saperstein became world famous, Pollard recalled the three of them dreaming big in his office at the Pollard Coal Company:

> It was in that office that the idea for forming an all-colored basketball team was conceived. Could Dick Hudson possibly have dreamed at the time that a young fellow in his early twenties, by the name of Abe Saperstein, who happened to drop in at the time to see the outstanding athletes that come to see me, would someday capitalize on his idea and make an all-Negro basketball team the sensation of the country?[7]

The formation of the Harlem Globetrotters is one of the fuzziest aspects of the Abe Saperstein story. No one was keeping close track of the names, places, and dates at the time. After all, basketball was a minor sport back then, well behind baseball and football in popularity. Teams came and went over the years with little notice, and no one knew at the time that the birth of the Trotters would matter. There was also a concerted effort by Saperstein to embellish the story later on, which contributed to today's confusion.

Here's how Saperstein described the Globetrotters' origin two decades later:

> It was back in 1926. A Negro basketball team in Chicago needed a coach and I got the job because I was the only one to apply. The team was named the Savoy Big Five and was sponsored by a dance hall. We didn't do so well. At the end of the first season, the owners of the Savoy dance hall dropped the sponsorship. Said they were tired of losing money. Well, there we were without jobs, eight players and little Abie. Figuring we had nothing to lose anyway, we agreed to barnstorm the country after changing our name to the Harlem Globetrotters.[8]

In Saperstein's later years and even today, the Globetrotters have told the Savoy Big Five origin story and claimed that the team's first road game as the Harlem Globetrotters was in Hinckley, Illinois, on January 7, 1927. But that date is almost certainly wrong.

For one thing, the Savoy Ballroom didn't even exist then, so the Savoy Big Five didn't either. A *Chicago Tribune* article in February 1927 detailed plans to build a "big darktown ballroom" at Forty-Seventh Street and South Park Way. The Savoy Ballroom opened on November 23, 1927, and the *Chicago Defender* ran an account of the Savoy Big Five basketball team "playing its first game" on January 3, 1928.[9]

Another point of uncertainty involves Saperstein's role with the Savoy Big Five. A March 1928 article in the *Savoyager*, a newspaper published by the Savoy Ballroom, said Hudson was the team's manager and Bob Anderson was assistant coach. A team photo from the time includes the players in uniforms and two men in suits—Hudson and Anderson—but not Saperstein. Even so, Fritz Pollard confirmed that Saperstein was involved with the team, writing that Hudson persuaded the Savoy's white owner, I. J. (Jay) Faggen, to sponsor the team and took "Saperstein along with him as a partner."[10] And a February 1928 article in the *LaCrosse (Wisconsin) Tribune* identified Saperstein as the team's "manager."[11]

It's possible but not documented that Saperstein had helped Hudson with a previous all-Black team, the Giles Post American Legion squad, which was composed of former Wendell Phillips High School stars and was based at the Eighth Regiment Armory at Thirty-Fifth Street and Giles Avenue. Giles Post toured Wisconsin in a successful road trip in the winter of 1926–1927, but afterward Hudson came under fire from *Chicago Defender* sports editor Fay Young for not getting the legion commander's permission to make the tour and for claiming some of his players were former college stars when they weren't.[12]

The Savoy Big Five was Hudson's attempt to re-create the Giles Post team without legion oversight, and it included some of the same Wendell Phillips stars, such as Tommy Brookins, Randolph Ramsey, and Walter "Toots" Wright, plus a tall but inexperienced player from Lane Technical High School named Inman Jackson, who would become a leading light in the Globetrotters' story. Saperstein even appeared in a game in La Crosse but didn't score. Like Hudson's tenure with Giles, his time with Savoy was tumultuous. By April 1928, Brookins, Ramsey, Wright, and Jackson had quit the Big Five "because they were unable to reach an agreement with manager Faggen," as the *Defender* put it.[13]

Enter the Globetrotters, though probably not according to the official story.

Brookins, one of the Savoy Big Five stars who had quit, started his own team. Brookins was a colorful character, talented as a singer as well as a basketball sharpshooter. In November 1928, the *Defender* announced the founding of a basketball team called Tommy Brookins' Globe Trotters.[14] The name "Globe Trotters" was not unique. At least two white basketball teams with that nickname had toured the Midwest in previous years: the Minneapolis Globe Trotters—sometimes known as Waldron's Famous Globe Trotters—and Basloe's Globe Trotters, who hailed from upstate New York.[15]

Nearly half a century after the events, Brookins told a vivid story about how his Globe Trotters led to Abe Saperstein's Harlem Globetrotters.[16] It's a story that clashes sharply with Saperstein's account, and Brookins didn't share it publicly until after Saperstein had died, leaving no opportunity for Saperstein to issue a rebuttal. Here's how Brookins's story came to light.

In the early 1970s, *New York Times* sportswriter Michael Strauss was on the island of St. Martin, part of the Lesser Antilles in the Caribbean Sea, to visit his daughter. He ran across a local restaurant owner named Tommy Brookins, and they got to talking. Brookins told him he was from Chicago and had worked with promoter Dick Hudson to start a team called the Globe Trotters that became the Harlem Globetrotters. Brookins said he got to know Saperstein because his team wanted to barnstorm in Wisconsin and Michigan, and Hudson told him: "I've got a man who I think can help us. His name is Abe Saperstein. He has booked baseball teams in both those states and he can help us—because he has a white face."

According to Brookins, Saperstein was strictly a booking agent, charging a 10 percent fee on the profits of any games he set up. Brookins said he and his players gave Saperstein $100 up front to travel north and arrange the tour. And everything went well on the road trip, Brookins said, until a fan came up to them in the locker room after a game in Wisconsin and said: "I also saw you guys the other night in Eau Claire. You fellows are great."

Problem was, the team hadn't played in Eau Claire. Brookins said teammate Randolph Ramsey afterward revealed that Saperstein had set up a
second Globe Trotters team, using "all the players we didn't want." Ramsey
said he hadn't told Brookins earlier because, "I was waiting until you were
in a good mood."

Brookins said he later confronted Saperstein, who told him there was
nothing to be done about it, since the second team was already on tour.
The idea of having two teams barnstorming at the same time with the same
name would later become standard operating procedure for the Globetrotters; some years they even had three teams of Globetrotters on the road
simultaneously.

According to Brookins, his initial anger with Saperstein soon cooled off.
"Actually, the news didn't come as much as a shock as it might have," he
recalled. "I had considered leaving my team anyhow because I received an
offer to sing at the Regal Theatre in Chicago for $75 per week. That was
pretty good money then, even for a basketball player."

Also, he said, his mother was sick and he wanted to stay close to home.
Brookins said his only request was that Saperstein give the members of
his disbanding team a chance to make Saperstein's squad, and Saperstein
agreed. Brookins ultimately had a nice career in show business, touring
Europe as part of a dance, song, and comedy duo with Sammy Van. Later
he opened a Chicago nightclub called Cabin in the Sky with his lover, singer
Ethel Waters.[17]

Sometime after the breakup, Saperstein felt comfortable enough to ask
Brookins for any spare uniforms he had. Brookins gave him three. "They
were lying in my closet collecting dust anyhow," Brookins said.

Hudson quickly exited the Globetrotters picture too. Fritz Pollard
recalled that Saperstein "began playing with the idea of taking the team on
a western tour and, over some negligble thing, got into a controversy that
severed their partnership."[18]

Brookins's account of the birth of the Globetrotters is not particularly
well known because it appeared in a freelance piece by Strauss in *Sports
Quarterly Basketball Special, 1973–74* rather than in Strauss's own newspaper, the *New York Times*.

The sequence of events that created the Harlem Globetrotters is unlikely
to ever be known with certainty, but the fact is, Brookins's story lines up

better with the available evidence than the Globetrotters' official version does. And it's clear that the Trotters knew they had problems with their official account. An unsigned, undated, two-page report in the team's office files titled "'Very Special' Notes Regarding Origin of Harlem Globetrotters" admitted that the January 7, 1927, date for the supposed first road game in Hinckley, Illinois, was "very debatable."[19]

"The actual year the team was formed was known only to Abe Saperstein and probably Inman Jackson," the Trotters' internal report said. "In the years following (let's say) 1929 so much of the Globetrotter history became 'lore' and retelling of the story through publicity releases, conversations, and actual fabrication finally evolved into an acceptable myth which has been well nurtured down through the years."

Two lists in the Globetrotters office files said Saperstein's first Globetrotters squad included Al "Runt" Pullins, Byron "Fat" Long, Walter "Toots" Wright, William "Kid" Oliver, and Andy Washington. One of those lists said the "#1 Harlem Globetrotters team" played in the "1927–28 season," which contradicts the claim of a January 7, 1927, start.[20] To cast further doubt on the official story, the unnamed writer of the origin report noted: "Runt Pullins, alleged to have been on the first team, tells me that he couldn't have played in 1927 or 1928 because he was still in high school in Chicago."

But why stick with a myth that the team knew was false? Or as the Globetrotters' own report put it: "Why all the shenanigans?????"

The writer speculated that it was related to lawsuits the Globetrotters filed in the late 1940s and '50s to protect their brand, the implication being that Saperstein had settled on a set of origin facts as part of his legal arguments and wasn't inclined to acknowledge that he had misled the courts. Ben Green, who wrote an exhaustive 2005 history of the Globetrotters, *Spinning the Globe*, noted that Saperstein didn't publicize the alleged January 7, 1927, start date until 1947. Green speculated that the adoption of that date may have been a simple "marketing ploy" to promote the team's supposed twentieth anniversary.[21]

So when did the Harlem Globetrotters play their first road game, if not on January 7, 1927?

It could have been a year or two later.

A local newspaper, the *Hinckley Review*, wrote in 1959 about taking a look at a scrapbook kept by Carlos Powelson, a member of the Hinckley

Merchants team that defeated the Globetrotters in the game believed to be the first. The *Review* printed a box score, listing the same Globetrotters players who were on the Globetrotters' official first-team list. Saperstein's squad had traveled by train to Aurora, west of Chicago, then gotten rides from the Merchants players to and from the Hinckley High School gym.[22]

The *Hinckley Review* said the first game took place on January 21, 1928, but other newspaper articles suggest the first game was on January 21 of the next year—1929. On January 19, 1929, the *DeKalb (Illinois) Chronicle* wrote about the Hinckley Merchants' plans to play a New York team called the Harlem Globetrotters two days later. There's no mention of any previous contest against these "colored athletes of the east," leaving the impression that the Trotters were new to this area. A few days later, the same newspaper ran a story and box score from the game, and the outcome is very similar—but not identical—to the game described in the 1959 *Hinckley Review* article. The DeKalb paper gave the score as Merchants 43, Trotters 35. The Hinckley article gave it as 43–34. The same eleven players appear in both box scores. Six have the same point totals, whereas five others vary by a point or two. Either the battling box scores are from the same game or it's a most unusual coincidence.[23]

J. Michael Kenyon, a Seattle sportswriter who undertook extensive research to compile his own list of the Globetrotters' game dates and outcomes, believed the Globetrotters' debut was on January 21, 1929. Having pored over thousands of newspaper stories about the team, Kenyon may have come to that conclusion based on the lack of stories before that date and the steady stream after. Indeed, the authors of this book sifted through multiple newspaper databases for contemporary accounts of Harlem Globetrotters games in 1927 and 1928 and found none. But starting with the game in Hinckley on January 21, 1929, there are plenty.[24]

What appears most likely is that Saperstein organized the team in 1928 and it started barnstorming as the Harlem Globetrotters in January 1929. Two newspaper articles in late 1928 showed Saperstein trying to line up games for his team. Portland's *Oregonian* reported in November 1928 that manager A. M. Saperstein wanted to tour the Pacific Northwest with "an all-colored basketball team, the Harlem globe trotters of New York city." The article shared Saperstein's outrageously false claim that the team had "played the Atlantic seaboard as the Harlem big five for the last four seasons." The next month, a *Minneapolis Tribune* story cited tentative plans for the Harlem Globetrotters to play a local team there in early January 1929. But it doesn't appear that either the Minnesota or Oregon feelers led to actual games.[25]

In a 1952 interview, Runt Pullins confirmed that he was on the original Globetrotters team: "Each of us chipped in $15 apiece to get to the first town, Hinckley, Illinois, on our first road trip. That was twenty-three years ago." If you do the math, "twenty-three years ago" is 1929.[26]

Another reason to think Saperstein's Globetrotters didn't start touring until 1929 was that he had another job in 1928—a Chicago patronage position as a forester, hiring tree surgeons to maintain the foliage of Lincoln Park.[27]

But by 1929 he was done with forestry and branching out as a sports entrepreneur.

4

THE BARNSTORMER

Saperstein's new team overcame snowstorms, fisticuffs,
and the Great Depression to win Midwest fans

A be Saperstein, who would one day boast that he had traveled five million miles by air, began his barnstorming career bouncing down country roads in a Ford Model T, trying to get from one small Midwestern town to the next before his jalopy gave out.[1]

It must have seemed like a fool's errand to some: a Jewish guy and five Black athletes rolling into predominantly white rural towns where some residents had never even seen a Jew or a Black person face-to-face. Would the townspeople actually pay good money to watch them play basketball?

Not so much, at first.

"The terms were very meager—maybe a twenty-five-dollar guarantee plus ten percent of the gate," said Abe's brother Harry. "They were lucky to get thirty-five bucks."[2]

One game in the early 1930s took place in Waterloo, Iowa, on "a cold, bitter night. No one came to see the game. I mean no one," recalled Dell Raymond, a player on the opposing team. The Globetrotters had been promised whatever was left after expenses, but the gym rental fee and the referee's pay took everything.[3]

"They didn't have anything and begged us to give them $5 although we had no contractual obligation," Raymond said, and indeed his team's

Inman Jackson, Abe Saperstein's closest friend, was one of the Globetrotters' early stars but by the time of this cartoon in the early 1940s was considered an "old man" on the team.

manager gave them the $5. Raymond felt so sorry for them that he handed over another sixty cents from his own pocket.

Housing was not guaranteed. Sometimes the team slept in the car. Or in small-town jails. Or on the floor of a local Black family's home. Finding hotels that would accept the Black athletes was a challenge. One time in Des Moines, Saperstein got a room at a whites-only hotel, and the players quietly climbed up the fire escape and slept in his room.[4]

To avoid hassles at local restaurants, the Trotters would buy roasted corn and vegetables from roadside stands. Another common dinner was salami and crackers, "with canned sardines for dessert—sometimes," Saperstein said. "Once we had so little to spend that the team played three games in two days with only a single meal of hamburgers to keep us going."[5]

"We never missed a meal," he said, "but we sure postponed a lot of them."[6]

They played in some ridiculous venues, including an empty swimming pool. And then there was the hayloft incident.

"One night in Wheatland, Iowa," Saperstein said, "we're playing in a hayloft upstairs in a barn. The big door at the end, where they load the hay through, was boarded up. There was some pretty fair body contact in those days, and somebody hit one of our boys, Lester Johnson, and Lester crashed right through the boards and into the night. We thought he was killed for sure. We all ran outside. He wasn't hurt, but he wasn't happy."[7]

Johnson had landed in a pile of manure, earning the lasting nickname "Luscious Lester."

In the Chicago suburb of Des Plaines, the Globetrotters were booked in a converted ballroom featuring six pillars in the playing area. The Trotters "changed their style to fit conditions," according to *Esquire* magazine. "They caromed balls off the posts, threw curves around them, and finally disconcerted the home team completely by hiding the guards behind pillars nearest the basket and popping out as the forwards came confidently past."[8]

The barnstormers' cars took a beating as they toured Illinois and Iowa at first, then added Minnesota, Wisconsin, Michigan, the Dakotas, and the Canadian province of Manitoba during the next several years. Their primary ride, purchased by Saperstein from a funeral parlor, was described as a Model T with side curtains. "The car looked like it had come out of a meat grinder," he said. "Six of us traveled in it and carried all the baggage too."[9]

According to one account, they graduated to "two rickety autos" instead of one. Saperstein called one of them the "baggage car" and the other the "club car." Another newspaper story recalled them touring in a Model A, and yet another said they used an old truck that couldn't go more than fifty miles without breaking down. It's likely that they ran through a number of vehicles during those first few years.[10]

By the mid-thirties, when Saperstein married, his in-laws chipped in. Saperstein's nephew Frank Rose recalled: "My dad had an automobile wrecking yard . . . and when Abe married my aunt, he was a pretty poor guy, and he asked my dad if he could borrow a car. My dad loaned him a car for a couple of months and finally he gave the car to Abe. . . . It was an old Essex. It was about an eight-passenger automobile. It was like a big hearse. I remember seeing it. It was an old, long car."[11]

The team's revenue, accommodations, and transportation were pitiful, and their timing was even worse. The Great Depression soon descended upon the nation, leaving a quarter of the workforce unemployed. It was not a good time to persuade people to shell out hard-earned money on a traveling show. Decades later, Saperstein had a shoestring framed in his office with the words: "This is the shoestring I started on."[12]

But from the start Saperstein was upbeat, energetic, optimistic. Not because of the circumstances, but because he knew himself and what he could accomplish. Saperstein had faith in his product and in himself.

At the start, his team's full name was the New York Harlem Globe Trotters. "New York" was apparently intended to make the team seem big-time. Saperstein put "Harlem" in the name as advance notice to white people that a Black team was coming to their town. "Globe Trotters" was a way to convey experience and sophistication. ("Globe Trotters" gradually morphed into the single word "Globetrotters" in the 1940s.)[13]

Saperstein soon dropped "New York" from the name. Saperstein's brother Harry said he did that to reduce the word count for the Western Union night letters he sent out to coordinate appearances. Harry, then in high school, was the team's secretary, and their office was in Saperstein's coat, where he kept scraps of paper, and in a bedroom of the family's home on Hermitage Avenue, where Harry typed out contracts. Harry said he was taking a typing class at Lake View High School, and "I needed the practice."[14]

The operation rested on the force of Saperstein's personality and the talent of his team.

The Trotters' early star was Runt Pullins, a skinny, five-foot-nine player with great speed and shooting skills. Pullins was the first Globetrotter to perform a routine that would later become a staple for Marques Haynes and others—dribbling around and through the entire opposing team. The Trotters' big man, who joined the team in December 1930, was Inman Jackson, a former Savoy Big Five second-teamer who seemed to get better with every game.[15]

Jackson was born in Chicago in 1907, the son of a railway porter also named Inman Jackson and his wife Sarah, who was sixteen when she gave birth. Both parents were part of the Great Migration, the father from Virginia and mother from South Carolina. The 1910 census listed the elder Inman as Black, whereas Sarah and her son were designated as "mulatto," or racially mixed. In subsequent censuses, both were designated Black or Negro.[16]

Often described as likable, Jackson would soon become Saperstein's team captain, most trusted assistant, and closest friend. Newspaper accounts called "Big Jack" a "giant" even though he was only six-foot-three and two hundred pounds, small by today's basketball standards.

Though genial off the court, Jackson held his own in the post. Against the Barnsdall Millers in Minneapolis in January 1933, rough play near the end of a 36–32 Globetrotters victory led to a postgame fight between Jackson and opposing center Bill Roberts. Witnesses told a local newspaper that Jackson "pushed Roberts and when the Barnsdall player turned, Jackson struck him in the nose, breaking it. One of the spectators stepped into the breach and as he did so, Jackson swung again, and then started for the dressing room on the run. A riot threatened until police stepped in and separated the players from the milling crowd."[17]

Saperstein later insisted that Roberts hit Jackson first.[18]

A year later, Jackson threw some verbal punches against racism in an interview with a radical leftist farmers' newspaper, the *Producers News*, run by the United Farmers League. Jackson offered his opinion on the Scottsboro Boys case, a rape prosecution in Alabama involving nine Black teens and young men in which a warped system of justice was evident. "Of course I cannot believe the Scottsboro boys are guilty," said Jackson. But he emphasized that the problem went well beyond the South.[19]

"Jim Crowism doesn't stop at the Mason-Dixon line," he said. "In Great Falls, Montana, we were refused service at almost every restaurant in town. In Minneapolis, the team was denied hotel rooms and were eventually sent to a flophouse down by the railroad tracks." He recalled similar prejudice in Nebraska, North Dakota, and Colorado.[20]

If the happy-go-lucky court presence of the Globetrotters suggested that they weren't outraged by the racism of their time, Jackson's interview showed otherwise. It also revealed the independent streak of a player who sometimes seemed stuck in Saperstein's shadow. It's unlikely that Jackson asked permission—or would have gotten it—to give such a controversial interview to a radical newspaper, and Saperstein would no doubt have been relieved that the remarks got limited circulation. In general, the Globetrotters took great pains to be friendly and nonthreatening to their mostly rural, overwhelmingly white customers. The goal was to beat the local teams—but not too badly. After all, Saperstein wanted the locals to like his Trotters enough that they'd welcome them back for another beating later. But whether the locals treated the Trotters like friendly visitors or bitter foes, it was always top of mind that they were ethnic outsiders. Former Trotters recalled that children would walk up and touch them to see if their blackness would rub off.[21] A South Dakota sportswriter may have thought he was paying the team a compliment when he wrote: "They are more at home with a basketball in their hands than a Southern plantation darkey is with a watermelon."[22]

Saperstein's Jewishness wasn't ignored either. A Minnesota newspaperman wrote that Saperstein acknowledged that the Globetrotters were a money-making enterprise and "when a member of a race known far and wide for its ability to make money breaks down and confesses, it must be true."[23]

Beyond the obvious racism, Saperstein was challenged to maneuver around the crosscurrents of small-town politics. According to an oft-told Saperstein story, he and the Globetrotters stopped in Shelby, Montana, to play a local all-star team, and the mayor asked Saperstein how much money he wanted in order to throw the game. Saperstein told him his team always played to win, and the mayor left angry. An hour later, the county sheriff showed up and said he'd heard there was a lot of gambling on the game and the "wise guys" expected the Trotters to lose on purpose. If that happened, the sheriff warned, he'd throw the whole team in jail. The team went out and ran to a 30–6 lead by halftime, winning easily and staying out of jail.[24]

The Globetrotters had the advantage of operating in an entertainment desert. Many small towns had movie houses and library lectures but not much else. Commercial radio was only a decade old. Commercial television wouldn't exist for another two decades.

Mostly the Trotters played local teams, with names like Servus Rubber Company, the Maytag Washers, the Waldorf Cafe Five, and the Eastern South Dakota State Teachers. But sometimes they matched up with other professional touring teams. A frequent opponent was the House of David, a beard-wearing squad from a religious commune in Benton Harbor, Michigan, that toured with both baseball and basketball teams to raise funds and publicize their faith.[25]

In Minnesota, the Globetrotters faced off against Babe Didrikson's All-Stars, a team helmed by the most famous woman athlete of the era, who had won two gold medals at the 1932 Olympics. With the Trotters leading by a wide margin, Inman Jackson tossed the ball to Didrikson, but she tossed it back, saying, "I don't want my baskets that way." A sportswriter reported that "Didrickson before the game told me she hated to play the colored boys but after the game one could see that she really had developed an admiration for them."[26]

Another national sports star, Bronko Nagurski, was also an early opponent of the Trotters. A fullback and tackle who later made both the college and pro football halls of fame, Nagurski was a member of the Barnsdall Millers basketball team that fought with the Globetrotters in Minneapolis. But there were no reports that Nagurski tangled with Inman Jackson.[27]

What set the Globetrotters apart in the Midwest was their blackness and the flashiness of their on-court clowning. Some other teams displayed trickery but not like the Trotters.

It's unlikely that there was a "Eureka!" moment when the Globetrotters adopted their role as a comedy act, featuring trick passes and shots, teasing opponents and referees with the ball, rolling the ball between opponents' legs, and whatever else would amuse the crowd. Very early on, newspapers praised their "fancy ball-handling" and called them "good stars at comedy." When Saperstein sought games in the Pacific Northwest in 1928—likely before they'd played a single road game—the Portland *Oregonian* wrote that the Globetrotters "color their style of game with burlesque and comic antics."[28]

The development of the Globetrotters' clowning repertoire was a process in which they saw what worked with the audience and incorporated elements into their game over time. That didn't stop Saperstein from inventing different stories about when the clowning started and setting those origin stories in various Iowa towns, including Williamsburg, Algona, Swea City, and Newton.

According to one version, Saperstein told the players, "Let's clown it up," and they responded: "We're not a minstrel show." He said he persuaded them by saying, "Look, this place is so quiet. The only sound in the place is our stomachs growling."[29]

The creative origins of the Globetrotters' showy style have been explained in a variety of ways. Some baseball teams, both Black and white, engaged in clowning and showboating in the same era when the Trotters emerged, so perhaps they borrowed from each other. The Globetrotters' routine known as the "Magic Circle"—six players at center court doing fancy pregame dribbling and passing—bore more than a slight resemblance to the "game of pepper" warmup originated by baseball's House of David.[30] Some social scientists trace the Globetrotters' routines back to the tradition of the "trickster," a fascinating character in African folklore that was brought to North America by enslaved people. Damion L. Thomas, sports curator at the Smithsonian National Museum of African American History and Culture, explained the trickster tradition this way: "African Americans relied upon widespread perceptions of them as ignorant, lazy, and childlike to create spaces to confront white supremacy through guile, trickery, subterfuge, and deception."[31]

Of course, the Globetrotters' aim was not to "confront" their mostly white fans but to entertain them for money. The vibe was playfully subversive, flouting basketball conventions but always recruiting the audience as an ally. The vast majority of ideas for routines sprang from the players, not Saperstein, though he had veto power and paid bonuses to players who came up with new trickery that he liked.[32]

Not all spectators appreciated their basketball seasoned with clowning. At a 1932 game in Rochester, Minnesota, the Globetrotters "began to pull some comedy, which half the crowd ate up and the other half booed," according to a local report.[33] But Saperstein had a grip on the public's preferences, and the comedy became synonymous with Globetrotters basketball early on. Inman Jackson described how he came up with a lasting routine mimicking a football play with a dropkick of the basketball:

> We were playing in Iron Mountain, Michigan, in the early '30s and the local team, out to show us up both by beating us and out-comedying us, was doing all kinds of little tricks like palming the ball, spinning it on one finger, and the like. They had one player—an Indian named Tony Wapp—who was especially good and started doing all the tricks that we had worked so hard on and was stealing the show from us. This worried me, so I felt I had to come up with a topper. Then next time I got hold of the ball well beyond the middle of the court I let it drop to the floor and drop-kicked it. Lo and behold, it went right through the hoop. The crowd let out a wild whoop and the stunt was in our repertoire to stay.[34]

Jackson became the team's research-and-development department. "Inman's the guy who transformed the Trotters from a bunch traveling around playing basketball like everybody else to the great show they are," said Charlie Eckman, who refereed early Globetrotters games. "He gave them all the fancy-dan stuff, rolling it around his back, the figure eight, the weave, all their little acts. A new guy would join up and Inman would take him aside and make a ballhandler out of him."[35] Eckman said Jackson also had the ability to "drive a bus and go for days without eating," both valuable skills in the early days.

Jackson's most vivid memory as a Globetrotter had nothing to do with playing, clowning, or coaching. "It happened in the '30s, somewhere in Iowa," Jackson recalled. "We were nowhere, in the middle of a blizzard, when the car broke down. I figured we were going to freeze to death. I got out of the car and lifted the hood like I knew what I was doing. I reached in and shook something and said, 'Please, Lord.' Got back in the car and it started."[36]

The Globetrotters kept expanding their footprint, building their fan base and actually making a living by playing basketball. Demand was so great that Saperstein started a second Globetrotters team that stayed close to home in Chicago, and he also fielded an all-white traveling team called the New York Nationals, coached by his brother Rocky.[37]

When Saperstein and his Globetrotters toured the Midwest, the take was split seven ways, with each of the five players getting a share and Saperstein getting two shares, for coaching, gasoline, car upkeep, and booking expenses.[38] The players were generally pleased by the arrangement, though player Byron "Fat" Long once accused Saperstein of shorting the players then punched him and quit. But Fat returned soon after, and Saperstein took him back.[39]

Saperstein played occasionally in a pinch, but he didn't help much on the court. Bernard Duffy, a Minnesota sportswriter, recalled a game in Arcadia, Wisconsin, in which Saperstein subbed for a player with a sprained ankle and "showed the skillful ball-handling and clowning for which his teams made their fame and fortune."[40] But Duffy, a Saperstein booster, shared that recollection decades after the fact. Contemporary reviews were not nearly as laudatory. When the Globetrotters' sharpshooting George Easter suffered from appendicitis and Saperstein had to play a full game in Great Falls, Montana, "his shooting and passing was not up to the standard of the other four members of the team," according to a local newspaper. Saperstein also had to step in and play for the New York Nationals because of an unspecified emergency in St. Cloud, Minnesota, and "his lack of practice and training was apparent," wrote a local sportswriter.[41]

Saperstein couldn't play in the pivot, but he was a master at pivoting away from business crises. His Globetrotters were in Minot, North Dakota, in March 1933, when panic due to the Depression compelled President Franklin D. Roosevelt to order a "bank holiday"—a suspension of bank transactions for a week.

"We were getting a lot of cancellations so I stayed up for seventy-two hours booking towns that were not affected by the bank holiday," Saperstein said. "I just took those little towns . . . where people didn't put their money in banks, where they buried it out in the backyard instead. They had money available when nobody else did."[42]

Saperstein never seemed to sleep. Duffy, the friendly Minnesota sportswriter, recalled a morning in March 1931 when Saperstein "got me out of bed" at 2:00 a.m. to say he had seriously considered sending a couple of players back to Chicago to show his dissatisfaction with how his team had played the night before.[43]

No one outworked Saperstein and his players. Their schedule was stuffed with about 150 games per season, and they once played sixty-one days in a row. Saperstein claimed to have won 136 out of 146 games during the 1930–1931 season, and that seems plausible, given the uneven local competition, Saperstein's astute assembly of talent, and the fact that the players on the Trotters had played together for years.[44]

Beyond the team's record, other aspects of the growing Globetrotters legend were embellished to ridiculous proportions. But sportswriters seemed to buy it.

In 1929, when the team had hardly started, the *Davenport (Iowa) Democrat and Leader* was passing on the absurd claim that the Globetrotters had stopped there on their way from Washington, DC, to the Pacific Coast, "and when their schedule is finished sometime in May, they will have played to practically every state in the Union."[45]

Even the *Chicago Defender*, which knew the team was dominated by former Wendell Phillips High School players and should have known it was Chicago based, reported that the Globetrotters were from New York. "Pullins, an all-city selection during his days at Phillips, went at once to New York when offered a fat contract at the conclusion of his prep days," the *Defender* wrote in November 1930. "Before going, Pullins persuaded his old chum Wright, also a former Phillips luminary, to go east with him, which Wright readily did."[46]

By that time, the Trotters had "gone east" very rarely and never to New York. Virtually all of their games had been north, south, and west of Chicago.

Saperstein claimed that his players "are all college negroes," as one South Dakota newspaper put it.[47] They weren't. Inman Jackson was described as "a grad of Knox College" and "a former captain of the City College of New York squad," but there's no evidence he ever went to college.[48] It's unclear why Saperstein spread false claims about his players being former college stars. Perhaps he wanted to allay rural white people's concerns about Black people coming to their town, but it also may have been an attempt to cast his players as amateurs rather than professionals so that the Trotters' amateur opponents wouldn't run afoul of Amateur Athletic Union rules banning games against pros.[49]

In 1930, Saperstein got the *Mason City (Iowa) Globe-Gazette* to repeat his claim that the Globetrotters were "world champion." But as he kept expanding the Globetrotters' territory and developing national aspirations, he must have known a claim like that wouldn't play with more sophisticated audiences. Nonetheless, he pushed an equally untrue boast: that the Trotters were "co-claimants of the world's colored basketball championship." In fact, the best Black team was obviously the New York Renaissance, known as the Rens, a genuinely New York–based unit. The Rens, who were named after the Renaissance Casino, their home base in Harlem, dominated East Coast basketball, routinely defeating white teams.[50]

Showing his great promotional instincts, Saperstein cooked up a rivalry with the Rens based on nothing more than his ability to get sportswriters to print what he said. By 1933, two Black newspapers were playing along with Saperstein's growing talk of the "rivalry." The *Pittsburgh Courier* called the Globetrotters "a glaring challenge to the brilliant record of the New York Renaissance." The *Defender* ran a headline reading: "Fans Want Rens and Globe Trotters Game" and reported that many "fans," all unnamed, were writing the newspaper demanding a match between the teams.[51]

The Rens would ignore the talk—at first. But Saperstein would keep suggesting that his Trotters could beat them. "Only the New York Renaissance team can rival the colored club when it comes to playing basketball," wrote the *Breckenridge (Minnesota) Gazette Telegram*, "and manager Saperstein believes his team could win the world's colored basketball championship could he sign the Renaissance team for a series of games."[52]

It was an outrageous claim when Saperstein made it, but like much of his bombast, he would ultimately turn it into a reality.

5

THE BOSS

*Saperstein claimed sole ownership of the Globetrotters
and led them to celebrity status*

By the winter of 1933–1934, Abe Saperstein was seeing encouraging signs of success. Midwestern towns were welcoming the Globetrotters back year after year. Local newspapers were turning them into celebrities. And they weren't begging for meal money after games anymore.

Saperstein was increasingly putting a personal brand on the team, with the front of the uniforms reading "Saperstein's Harlem New York" and later "Saperstein's Harlem Globe Trotters."[1] The players may not have minded Saperstein's self-promotion as long as he continued to operate the team as a partnership, with two shares for him and one for each of the players.

But Saperstein grew tired of that arrangement and laid down the law in January 1934: From now on, he was the boss, and they were his employees.

Henceforth, players would be working for Saperstein at the rate of $7.50 per game—the equivalent of about $177 in today's dollars. This was a pay cut, and some of the players were incensed.[2]

"We kept doing a little better every year," said Runt Pullins. "After five years we were averaging about $40 apiece per night. . . . Then one night in Butte, Montana, Abe told us he was going to put us all on salary. We felt as long as we had all started out as equal partners we should stay that way. So we split up."[3]

Abe Saperstein was thirty-one and his bride, Sylvia Franklin, was twenty-two when they wed in the living room of Abe's parents' home.

Gone were Pullins, George Easter, and Fat Long, while Inman Jackson and William "Razor" Frazier stayed with Saperstein. Pullins later indicated that he and the others left by choice, whereas Saperstein told sportswriters he had fired them to improve the product—a questionable notion since Pullins was one of the team's star players.

As Saperstein's sportswriter friend Bernard Duffy put it, "Pullins gradually started causing Saperstein trouble and the break finally came last week when Saperstein realized that if things progressed any further he would merely be the booking manager. Pullins did not think the mild-tempered Abe would ever fire him, but that's just how it happened."[4]

With most of his team gone, Saperstein canceled upcoming dates. A Montana newspaper sympathetic to Saperstein said he "took his entire squad into Chicago and there reorganized the team, eliminating some of the boys who were getting a bit too routine in their work. He added some of the finest players in America and rebuilt the squad around Inman Jackson, the great captain and center, who had all the good stuff shown here last time."[5]

Saperstein added two players from Detroit, Harry Rusan and Gus Finney, and completed the squad with forty-one-year-old Lawrence "Rock" Anderson, a former Savoy Big Five player who had subbed for the Trotters in the past. Rusan took the Pullins role and was described by the Montana newspaper as "one of the smallest men in the game, weighing but 135, and incidentally one of the fastest."[6]

Pullins wasn't done barnstorming. He formed his own team to tour the areas established by the Trotters and called his squad the Harlem Globe Trotter All-Stars. That infuriated Saperstein, who threatened to seek a federal injunction. It's not clear whether Saperstein ever actually filed suit, but the threat may have been enough. Pullins changed his team's name to the New York Globe Trotters, then the Broadway Clowns, and later to the Harlem Clowns.[7]

Within three weeks, Saperstein's team was back on the road, described by a sportswriter as "once more just one, big, happy family." As would often be the case, Saperstein's media-charming skills shaped how newspapers described this transition. The *Billings (Montana) Gazette*, which called the players' departure an "insurrection," helped Saperstein frame his team's image around Inman Jackson. "Jackson, to my way of thinking, is the finest star the Negro race has developed," Saperstein said. "He has been playing for days now with a blood clot in his left arm. He won't go on the bench."[8]

It's unknown whether Saperstein had planned for a long time to take over the team or whether he did it on the spur of the moment. Perhaps it was his attempt to get his personal finances on firmer footing because he was preparing to get married.

His bride, Sylvia Franklin, came from a Jewish family in Chicago and was known by relatives and friends as a warm, caring person. Nine years younger than Saperstein, Sylvia was an attractive young woman with dishwater blond hair and blue eyes. According to family lore, when a movie was made about Saperstein and the Globetrotters in the 1950s, Sylvia was annoyed that the actress who portrayed her had more stereotypically dark Jewish features. The filmmakers supposedly told the family that if they had cast an actress who actually looked like Sylvia, the audience wouldn't have believed she was Jewish.[9]

Sylvia finished three years of high school but then dropped out, suffering from depression.[10] She helped out in a family business in which her uncle worked as a "song plugger," an early-twentieth-century job in which people performed songs to help sell sheet music. With Sylvia's help, her uncle entertained the audiences at movie theaters, according to Joyce Leviton, Sylvia's niece:

> She was a beauty queen. In those days, you would go to the movie and in between the double feature they would have different shticks, and one would be a beauty contest, and Aunt Sylvia would always be entered into this beauty contest. Of course it would be fixed, and she would always win. And [her uncle] would also have a bingo game, and my father and my cousins would go to the bingo game and as soon as five numbers were called, they would yell "Bingo!" and they would take the same set of dishes next week and bring it to the next place.[11]

Leviton emphasized that "Aunt Sylvia was in several not-fixed beauty contests, and she won. At least that was what I had heard. If you see pictures of her, you see she was very beautiful."

Abe and Sylvia were married on May 5, 1934, when he was thirty-one and she was twenty-two. The ceremony in Louis and Anna Saperstein's living room was attended by family and friends, including Inman Jackson. Afterward, the wedding party dined on corned beef sandwiches.[12]

According to an oft-told Saperstein story, his new wife got a taste of life on the road months later when she joined the team in the most harrowing experience in its history, a winter trip through Montana in two old cars, a Ford sedan and a Pierce-Arrow limousine. Saperstein recalled:

> The morning we left Jordan [Montana] the natives warned us that a snow-storm was brewing and that instead of cutting across country we should stick to well-traveled routes. . . . But we were from Chicago and knew more about weather than country bumpkins did. . . . We cut across country. A blizzard began. Drifts piled up. We stalled, and we pushed and pulled. We tore the clutch from the Ford trying to get it [out of] a roadside drift. A sheep herder on horseback told us to head for cover fast or we'd freeze to death. He pointed over the broad expanse of white and said we'd find a sheep camp somewhere over there. We loaded everything into the Pierce-Arrow. Inman Jackson, our center, rode on one running board. I rode on the other. . . . When we hit a drift, we'd hop off and give a push. . . . We stalled in one big drift and had to huff and puff. As the car lurched forward, I fell flat in the snow. Jackson hopped on the running board and away they raced as I hollered into the wail of a Montana blizzard.[13]

"I thought then that I'd had it," Saperstein said. He tried to follow the tire tracks before the falling snow covered them up.[14]

> The Trotters didn't miss me until they checked in at the camp with the sheep herders, other marooned travelers, and several sheep. My wife became hysterical. A search party went out. When they found me, I was on hands and knees trying to crawl along the dim tracks left by the car. I've never been so close to heaven.[15]

For the next three days, conditions in the tiny cabin were close but not heavenly. More than a dozen people and nine sheep were holed up there.

> Probably we never would have been found except that a fellow from Glasgow [Montana] was along and after three days his wife got worried and sent out a search party that found us. They got us into Glasgow around noon and the superintendent of schools, who was promoting the game, said we'd play that night. The town's telephone operator called everybody in the district to tell 'em about it, and we must've had 1,500 at the game.[16]

To Saperstein, it was a triumph over adversity. But to Sylvia, it was a traumatic ordeal. "She never was very enthusiastic about making winter trips with us after that," Saperstein said.[17]

Bouncing back from both the "insurrection" and his vacation with the sheep, Saperstein took his team farther west than ever before, to the Pacific Northwest in early 1935. He planned to play a robust schedule against opponents that included about thirty-five college teams. But that plan ran up against the region's Amateur Athletic Union (AAU) boss, Aaron Frank, who declared that the Globetrotters were professionals and therefore barred from games against amateurs. The Pacific Northwest district was apparently more of a stickler for the rules than AAU officials elsewhere, who had let the Trotters play college teams for years.[18]

Saperstein, of course, rarely let reality get in the way of his ambitions, and this would be no exception. He insisted the Trotters were true amateurs whose AAU membership cards had just expired. And he argued that the money he paid his players fell below the AAU-allowed $8.50 travel daily expense allowance. But the AAU also banned amateurs from getting those expenses for more than twenty-one days in a year, so Saperstein was still in a fix. Nevertheless, he had one of his brothers send a telegram to a Washington State AAU official declaring that Midwest AAU leadership had approved the Globetrotters as "goodwill ambassadors for the national AAU."

Frank wasn't buying it, and he checked with AAU officials in Chicago who stated: "The Harlem Globetrotters have played all season without a permit. . . . A permit to travel was denied them."[19]

Saperstein had lost. The college teams were off-limits. But he would come back to the Pacific Northwest the next season, finding noncollege teams to play against and turning the region into one of his most welcoming destinations. Later in his career he recalled his first stop in Seattle, where he and his players got hotel rooms in a rundown neighborhood, and he bought a knife to protect himself. "That hotel was so rough, I was afraid to go down the dark hall to wake up my players," Saperstein said.[20]

Vancouver, British Columbia, in particular was a hotbed for Globetrotters fandom, and the team would come back year after year. Globetrotters road manager Chuck Jones said Inman Jackson had a pranking ritual he pulled on his teammates when he drove them through Vancouver Island's

Cathedral Grove, a stand of old-growth Douglas fir that could be spooky at night.

"Driving back to Nanaimo after an exhibition in Port Alberni, he always stops the car in the heart of Cathedral Grove, turns off all the lights, and offers $5 to any member of the team who will get out and walk one hundred yards up the road in front of the car, alone," Jones said. "He's been doing it for six years and hasn't had a taker yet."[21]

Jackson was the second-in-command and ran the team on those occasions when Saperstein made trips home or elsewhere during barnstorming. Saperstein said he paid Jackson $90 a week—$1,900 in today's dollars—but it's unclear whether that pay was year-round or just during the season.[22] Though Jackson was much more low key, he shared Saperstein's talent for public relations. In a letter to the editor he wrote after a game in Iron River, Michigan, Jackson said the Trotters "never had a more interesting game than we had with your young team."[23]

In the second half of the 1930s, the Trotters stayed mostly in the Upper Midwest and Pacific Northwest, revisiting their already established fan base and becoming more financially healthy.

Sportswriter James Enright later recalled a wintry night in 1938 when Saperstein showed him a $1,000 bill. "See this?" Saperstein said. "It's the first one I've ever had, and it's all mine—every cent of it. I've worked hard for this one, and I'm going to work a lot harder because I want to get some more to keep it company."[24]

The hard times were not over, however. During a trip to the American Southwest, Saperstein and six players showed up almost an hour late for a game in Las Vegas, New Mexico. Saperstein had a good excuse: his team had tried and failed to secure hotel rooms but had eventually found a place to eat. When they returned from the restaurant to their touring car, they discovered their baggage and best uniforms had been stolen. But the fans of the home team, the New Mexico Normal University Cowboys (now New Mexico Highlands University) showed no sympathy and booed them lustily. The referee was free with his whistle, and one Globetrotter fouled out. Then another was shoved against a wall and suffered a knee injury, leaving the Trotters with only four available players. Saperstein was no longer serving as a substitute by this time, so he asked if the player with the fouls could return. The answer was no. But the team's depleted status changed the sentiments of the crowd, which started cheering every Trotter basket. When Saperstein's team won, the fans lavished them with a rousing ovation. Glory was fleeting, however. The Globetrotters returned to their car to find that someone had let the air out of the tires. And because they had parked in a no-parking zone in their haste to get to the game, the car had a parking ticket. Saperstein caught one break, though: the mayor fixed the ticket.[25]

Though the Trotters continued to drub their mostly local competition, their status as a national basketball power existed mostly in Saperstein's imagination. Even Runt Pullins's team, now known as the Broadway Clowns, was undercutting the Trotters' image by continuing to play in the same areas and playing well. "It is said that they threaten to dislodge the Trotters from their position of kings of the hoop world," reported the *Vancouver Province*.[26]

Among the teams more famous than the Globetrotters were the all-Black New York Renaissance, who were still ignoring Saperstein's calls for a game, and the all-white New York Celtics, whose best days were behind them but who still commanded attention. The Celtics had no direct connection with the modern-day Boston Celtics, a team that wasn't formed until 1946.

The *Chicago Defender* noted that Saperstein "has been trying to match his team against the New York Renaissance without any success. Then he went after, taunted the Celtics manager, and got a game against the Celtics."[27]

That game was set in March 1938 at the White City Amusement Park on Chicago's South Side, a location that in past decades had featured an attraction called the African Dip, a dunk-tank game in which a Black man sat on a platform with a target over his head and white fairgoers threw baseballs at the target. If they hit it, the platform collapsed and the Black man splashed into a tub of water, amusing the white patrons.[28]

But the continued influx of Black Southerners was changing the face of the South Side, and plenty of Black fans came out to White City for the Trotters–Celtics game. Saperstein's team started out flat, trailing 14–2 at the end of the first quarter. Then Harry Rusan "went crazy," in the *Defender*'s words, and began hitting from long range. Saperstein put in Jackson, who by this point in his career was an assistant coach and substitute player, and Jackson led the team back. The Trotters jumped to a 36–34 lead, and then the Celtics tied it with one minute and ten seconds left, making the crowd think the contest might be headed for overtime. But the Celtics walked off the court, claiming "the game had ended and there would be no overtime period because they had a train to catch," the *Defender* reported.[29]

The Black newspaper was openly skeptical of this explanation, suggesting the Celtics were trying to protect their bets. "As regards to 'catching a train,' the Celtics left town early Saturday morning," the *Defender* said. "Some were around the White City business office as late as 12:45 a.m."

The result may have been disappointing to Saperstein, but it raised the Trotters' profile and thus ratcheted up the pressure on the Rens to agree to a game. Saperstein kept issuing challenges, and in January 1939 the Rens finally responded. "In a pointed letter written by Road Manager Eric Illidge, it was definitely stated that not only are the Rens unafraid of Abe Saperstein's 'Trotters' but they would play them at any time, at any place, for nothing," reported the *Pittsburgh Courier*. The Rens called the Globetrotters "clowns of the courts," which surely offended Saperstein, who had the twin goals of fielding an entertaining team that would sell tickets and also producing the best basketball team in the world.[30]

Before a head-to-head matchup between the Trotters and the Rens could be arranged, both teams were invited to the first World Professional Basketball Tournament in Chicago in late March of 1939. Saperstein's team warmed up for the tournament by playing a rematch with the New York Celtics, beating them easily, 37–24.[31]

By this time, the Trotters had added beefy Ted Strong Jr., who had "the biggest hands in basketball," according to Saperstein, along with rookies Babe Pressley and Bernie Price. Just before the tournament, Saperstein had fired sharpshooter Bill Ford for disciplinary reasons but had picked up the man regarded as the best player in Detroit, Larry Bleach. The Trotters seemed to be in the best shape in their history.[32]

This 1939 tournament was the biggest stage yet for the Globetrotters. Sponsored by William Randolph Hearst's *Chicago American* and *Chicago Herald-Examiner*, the event would crown a national champion from a disorganized pro basketball landscape in which many teams claimed dominance without having to prove it. The tournament commissioner was George Halas, founder of the Chicago Bears football team. The referee was Pat Kennedy, who was sometimes accused of upstaging the players with his shouts of "No-no-no-NO!" when calling a foul and who would later in his career referee for the Globetrotters overseas.[33]

Along with the Trotters and the Rens, the tournament featured the Celtics, the bearded House of David, the New York Yankees (yes, they were once a basketball team too), and a handful of other squads. The Rens and the Celtics got first-round byes. The Trotters didn't, despite their recent ravaging of the Celtics, and had to play two games on the opening day.[34]

The first was against the Fort Wayne Harvesters, former college players from Indiana. The Trotters handled them easily, 41–33. The second was with a local team, the Chicago Harmons, who featured six-foot-nine Mike Novak, a former All-American at Loyola University who specialized in goaltending, which was legal in that era. But the Harmons didn't have much else, and the Trotters won, 31–25. A sign of the Trotters' limited fame was the fact that the *Chicago Tribune*, which had a distant relationship with the city's Black community, labeled the Harmons as "the only Chicago entry in the pro meet," not realizing the Trotters had local roots.[35]

Next up in the semifinals: the Rens. The matchup attracted a Chicago Coliseum crowd of eight thousand fans, many of them Black. The *Courier*'s Wendell Smith grumbled about the tournament's only two Black teams being put in the same bracket so they met in the semifinals, but Saperstein and his players were getting the game they had demanded for six years.[36]

The Rens, featuring such future Hall of Famers as Charles "Tarzan" Cooper and William "Pop" Gates, tore into the Globetrotters, jumping out to an 11–2 lead. Either the Trotters were getting bottled up or they were breaking free and then missing their shots. They didn't score for a full fifteen minutes in the first half. The Trotters finally brought it to 15–10 by halftime, but a five-point lead was significant in an era when there was no shot clock and a team as accomplished as the Rens was handling the ball. The Rens pushed the lead to eight points with about four minutes left, but Pressley and Bleach hit outside shots, and Strong managed a layup with forty-eight seconds on the clock. The Trotters were within two points, on the edge of a miracle. And then they weren't: the Rens' Tarzan Cooper streaked down the lane, caught a pass, and scored for the final 27–23 score.[37]

Saperstein had asked for it, and he had gotten it—defeat at the hands of the mighty Rens. He probably didn't take it well. "My father was a very poor sport," his daughter Eloise recalled decades later. "When he won, we celebrated, he took everyone out to dinner. When he lost, we had to wait a long time for him to walk around the stadium, until he walked off his anxiety attack."[38]

The Rens won the next night's final against the Oshkosh All-Stars, a game played to three thousand fans, a fraction of the previous night's crowd. The Trotters won the 36–33 battle with the Sheboygan Redskins for third place, collecting $400. It wasn't first-place money—$1,000—but it wasn't bad. To many observers, the Trotters had acquitted themselves well and made a good argument that the two best pro basketball teams in the country were Black.

That wasn't good enough for Saperstein, though. He wanted to be the best. He offered his excuses in a letter to a Washington State newspaper:

> Following a most successful tour of the Pacific Northwest, the boys developed a little "prima donna" trouble among themselves and I had to release the stellar shooting guard Bill Ford and send Harry Rusan, the long-shooting mite forward, home for discipline. . . . Rusan was ordered back to the team just before the opening of the rich prize event, but he never returned to shape, proving the disappointment of the tourney. Another tough break found us getting two games on the opening day, which tired the team out.[39]

On the positive side, Saperstein said the Trotters "were picked as the team with the most appeal and the best ballhandling." That sounded a little like the Miss Congeniality prize at the Miss America Pageant, but it was better than nothing. Saperstein was undeterred. Although the Globetrotters were his main passion, he was diversifying into new teams and sports as well. Maybe Inman Jackson's able assistance with the Trotters gave Saperstein the freedom to freelance. Or perhaps Saperstein simply never ran out of energy.

In 1937, he managed a women's basketball team called Helen Stephens' St. Louis Caging Co-Eds, which went up against men's teams. Stephens was a two-time gold medalist in the 1936 Olympics in Berlin, winning the 100-meter sprint and anchoring the 400-meter relay. In a world often hostile to women athletes, Stephens was accused by a Polish sportswriter of being a man in disguise, and Olympic officials insisted on a physical exam. A news report said they were able to "ascertain her true sex" and let her compete.[40]

Saperstein told a sportswriter that his new basketball star was "a girl who's so full of color that she makes my Trotters look like albinos by comparison. She's bigger than the average man—and faster, ever so much faster. On the track, I mean, of course. She's not a bit 'fast' otherwise."

Saperstein owned and promoted other traveling basketball teams in the 1930s, including the all-Chinese Hong Wa Kues from San Francisco.

Saperstein noted the players' short stature and said they "amazed fans with their ability to cope with giant teams."[41] Then there was an all-Black team managed by Saperstein's brother Morry, which served as a sort of farm club for the Trotters. It bore a name that is jarring today but was casually accepted then: the Boston Brownskins.[42]

Saperstein also helped create a Midwestern lacrosse league that flopped in 1936. "A four-team league functioning around Chicago and Milwaukee went flooey," according to a sportswriter. "The promoters couldn't give tickets away as game after game drew nothing but players' families and the referees' mothers-in-law."[43]

Saperstein explored opportunities in boxing as well. "He holds a contract on a colored featherweight by the name of Joe Law," reported a sportswriter, adding that "Abe expects him to go places in the fight racket." Law didn't, losing about two-thirds of his bouts.[44]

Saperstein got into soccer, too, promoting a visit by England's Charlton Athletic squad to Chicago in 1937. As it turned out, the soccer club's visit required Saperstein to moonlight as a sportswriter too.

"Abe's office had to do the publicity on the club for the Chicago papers, so he was in pretty close touch with the situation," reported a Vancouver newspaper. "The *Chicago Daily News* had a soccer writer, an expert, but he was at home with a terrific case of influenza on the day of the game. None of the other sportswriters on the paper had ever seen the game, so they asked Abe to do the story. As it happened, Abe didn't know whether they played the game with a stick or a pair of dice."[45]

That didn't stop Saperstein, though. Neither did the birth of his first child, daughter Eloise, on the same day as the game. "I dashed from the soccer game to the hospital to welcome our baby girl," Saperstein said.[46]

Then, according to the Vancouver paper, Saperstein "bought a stack of English newspapers at a newsstand. After studying their soccer stories for style, tone, and literary quality, he wrote his soccer epic and took it down to the sports editor. Four days later, he called in there again, and was informed that his story of the game was termed by Chicago readers from the Old Country the best soccer story they had ever seen in a Chicago paper."[47]

Saperstein was always writing his own story in one way or another. And he was always looking for new worlds—or sports—to conquer.

6

THE BASEBALL
PROMOTER

Saperstein served as an enthusiastic but controversial
pitchman for the Negro Leagues

Building the Globetrotters into a juggernaut should have left Abe Saperstein with little time for anything else. But he also made his mark in an entirely different sport: baseball.

Saperstein's first foray into baseball promotion came in 1927 when he booked games for the Walter Balls, a Chicago semipro Black team. During the 1930s, he plunged deeper into the sport, working as a promoter, publicist, and agent for Negro Leagues baseball teams and their star players. Saperstein's most frequent job was booking barnstorming games—contests between teams that were not in the same league and, therefore, were not counted in the official standings.[1]

In 1932, Saperstein began booking barnstorming games for a team called the Cleveland Black Friars. The reason he chose a Minnesota city for a 1932 barnstorming game, a local sportswriter wrote, was "because of the crowds which have always turned out to see his basketball teams play here."[2] By the end of the decade, he would become the top baseball booking agent in the Midwest, negotiating the terms of most nonleague games played by Negro American League (NAL) teams.[3]

Saperstein checks out the pitching arm of Satchel Paige, whose baseball barnstorming was a bonanza for both men. In back is Walter Dukes of the Harlem Globetrotters basketball team.

Saperstein's greatest fame in baseball came from serving as business agent for Satchel Paige, a Black player who pitched himself into the Hall of Fame. It proved to be a win-win relationship.

Long before baseball's era of free agents, Paige acted like one, seizing every opportunity to monetize his talent. This made him a good client for Saperstein. The hard-throwing pitcher was willing to moonlight or play offseason games to raise his income.

Saperstein and Paige clicked because they had much in common: audacity, a restless nature, and a reputation among journalists for being quotable. Paige once told a reporter the secret of his success: "Diet. I eat only fried foods." Like Saperstein, Paige was adept at spinning a fanciful tale—such as the claim that his green convertible had previously belonged to actress Bette Davis.[4]

In 1933, Saperstein recruited Paige and other Black players to join white semipro baseball teams in North Dakota—a state with 377 Black residents out of a total population of nearly 681,000. The deal that Saperstein negotiated for Paige brought the righthanded hurler to a team in the capital city of Bismarck. Neil Churchill, an automobile dealer who owned the team, had heard that a rival team was recruiting Black players, so he responded in kind. When he asked Saperstein to recommend "the greatest colored pitcher in baseball today," Saperstein had a quick answer: Paige. Churchill signed the hurler to a contract and lent him the fanciest cars from his Chrysler dealership. But he warned Paige not to be seen "riding white girls around in broad daylight."[5] Paige pitched well for the Bismarck nine and helped the club draw excellent crowds.

Paige returned to play for the Bismarck club in 1935, and his Saperstein-facilitated contract paid the pitcher $8,600 in salary and fringe benefits—more than seven times the per capita income of Americans.[6]

By this time, news was spreading far and wide about Paige's amazing arm. A sports columnist wrote that Paige's fastball "looks as if it could beat a bullet to the plate."[7] Saperstein was impressed by Paige's raw talent but also captivated by his theatrical demeanor. Paige engaged in pantomimes with fans, rotated his arms like a windmill before throwing a pitch, made warm-up throws while seated, and sauntered his way from the dugout to the pitcher's mound at a snail's pace.[8] Paige talked trash to hitters, Black *and* white, so loudly that fans could follow the banter. "Get ready for a smoker at your knees," he would bark at a player who stepped into the batter's box.[9]

Paige was notorious for breaking business agreements, and Saperstein enabled him. "[Paige] would walk out on more signed contracts than any player in history," wrote biographer Larry Tye. "When he came back it was generally on even richer terms than before."[10] Paige's decision to join the Bismarck team ignored the contract he had with the Pittsburgh Crawfords of the Negro National League (NNL). Alan Pollock, son of longtime baseball promoter Syd Pollock, recalled that no team could predict "when Satchel would miss a game for a girlfriend or a nearby lake stocked with fish."[11] One team owner told Paige he would offer him the shortest contract in baseball: "No show, no dough."[12]

The pitching phenom didn't stay in any city for long. In 1938, Paige and the NNL's Newark Eagles could not agree on a contract, so he left the country to pitch in the Mexico League. Taking the mound nearly every day there, Paige developed a severely sore arm, prompting a physician to give him the bad news: he would never pitch again. Although the NAL's Kansas City Monarchs knew about the condition of Paige's arm, they signed the thirty-two-year-old anyway—perhaps with Saperstein's reminder that Paige remained a fan favorite. Eventually, Paige came back to form, and he developed a curveball and hesitation pitch to ease the stress on his arm.[13]

Once Paige regained his mastery, Saperstein eagerly booked him for one event after another. In 1942, Saperstein arranged games in three cities featuring a Black team, anchored by Paige, squaring off against an all-white squad of stars led by pitcher Jay Hanna "Dizzy" Dean. Years earlier, Dean had boasted that a team with Paige and him on its roster would "clinch the pennant mathematically by the Fourth of July and go fishin' until the World Series."[14]

Paige knew his financial future benefited greatly from Saperstein, and the Alabama native dubbed the sports agent "Abraham Lincoln-stein." Paige appreciated the "real big money" he earned from barnstorming, and Saperstein took a healthy cut from many of these games.[15]

Both men could drive a hard bargain. Before the 1943 East-West All-Star game, Paige insisted that league officials pay him a $200 bonus to participate. It's unclear whether Saperstein supported this demand, but Paige was insistent. "Without me, that East-West game wouldn't draw two-thirds the people it would if I was playing," he reasoned. And he got his bonus.[16]

Paige was not just a good draw for Black fans. He helped draw many white patrons to Negro Leagues games. Whites made up nearly one-quarter of the crowd at a May 1941 doubleheader at Yankee Stadium in which Paige pitched.[17]

During the mid-1940s, Paige saw only limited action with the Monarchs' league games, instead pitching mostly for a squad that the Monarchs organized for barnstorming games. Saperstein, who was the booking agent for many of these games, designated Paige as "an individual proposition." This meant the Monarchs' opponent was required to pay an additional fee to book a game when Paige was in the lineup.[18]

Saperstein's booking and publicizing of barnstorming games made a vital contribution to Black baseball. Even in good times, the Negro Leagues faced financial pressure, but the Great Depression threatened to sink them, and barnstorming revenue was a key reason these teams stayed in business.[19]

Saperstein supported other barnstorming teams, too, such as the multiracial, multiethnic All-Nations baseball club. Organized and promoted by Saperstein in 1933, All-Nations featured players who were Native American, Black, British, Austrian, Czech, Estonian, French, German, Irish, Italian, and Mexican. In advertisements, Saperstein hailed the team as a "true product of the American melting pot."[20] Saperstein threw an odd wrinkle into the All-Nations games. "It is Saperstein's custom," wrote a sportswriter, "where the team plays more than one game in a town, to use his catcher for one inning in every position on the club." The catcher did a good job of playing every other position, the sportswriter added, except for pitcher "where his offering is little better than mediocre."[21]

In the early 1940s, Saperstein managed publicity and bookings for the House of David. He was well acquainted with the athletes from that religious community because his Globetrotters had played its basketball squad for years. The bearded House of David baseball team often played against Black teams, and sometimes the otherwise white club asked Paige to pitch. When Paige did so, he called his teammates "Jesus boys."[22]

Although scheduling and promotion were Saperstein's bread and butter in baseball, he occasionally assumed the roles of executive and co-owner.

In 1938, Saperstein was elected president of a semipro white league called the Tri-State Baseball League, featuring eight teams from Illinois, Indiana, and Wisconsin. The teams were organized by cities to promote their hometown companies; the South Bend (Indiana) Studebakers, for example, plugged the local automaker. From the start, the Tri-State teams faced financial strain. In the spring of 1939, the league shrank to only six teams. By 1940, the Tri-State was no more. Saperstein's attempt to revive the league in 1941 failed.[23]

Around this time, Saperstein became a Negro Leagues co-owner by providing funds to help Black hotelier Tom Hayes buy the Birmingham Black Barons—the NAL team for which Paige pitched in the late 1920s. Hayes was a businessman but not much of a baseball fan, so his partnership with Saperstein worked well.

Saperstein strengthened the Black Barons' roster by bringing in Ted Radcliffe, who earned the nickname "Double Duty" by sometimes catching one game of a doubleheader and then pitching all nine innings of the second game.[24]

Saperstein also reaped a publicity bonanza by signing pitcher Frank "Groundhog" Thompson, whose nickname came from his five-foot-one frame and his cleft lip. In an era when people were far less sensitive in describing people's physical features, Saperstein turned Thompson's "homely" appearance into a sales point. But Saperstein knew Thompson also had talent. When the Black Barons' new pitcher first took the mound, fans laughed, but their attitude changed after he retired the first six batters he faced.[25]

Saperstein's association with the Black Barons led to his discovery of one of the most famous players in Globetrotters history. Reece "Goose" Tatum, who grew up in rural Arkansas, was a baseball player for Birmingham when Saperstein first laid eyes on him. Tatum was a good hitter but an exceptional fielder. His long arms, spindly torso, and height of six feet, three and a half inches meant that a baseball rarely got past him at first base. And Tatum's defensive skills came with a dose of humor. An Oklahoma sportswriter wrote about a game in which Tatum "juggled the ball until it appeared he had it on a string" and "did everything last night but make the ball talk."[26] Saperstein knew immediately that Tatum's height and showmanship would make him perfect for the Globetrotters. Tatum joined the Globetrotters basketball team in 1942, but he continued playing baseball during the summer months.

The Black Barons gained a national profile partly because Saperstein booked them to play barnstorming games far from Alabama. "Saperstein was a smart man," Radcliffe recalled. "He'd book us in those big four-team doubleheaders in Yankee Stadium. Every time the Yankees would leave, Birmingham would be in Yankee Stadium with twenty-five to thirty thousand people."[27]

But Saperstein's aggressive marketing of the Black Barons once got him in trouble. In July 1945, the Lafayette Red Sox, a white semipro baseball team in that Indiana city, should have been pleased to beat the barnstorming Birmingham team. Instead, the Red Sox were angry after learning that Saperstein—who booked this game—had not sent the regular Birmingham players to Lafayette. Instead, he had split the Black Barons, sending some of its players to Lafayette and the remainder to play in Michigan the same night. Players with less skill and experience donned Birmingham uniforms that evening to fill the vacant positions. After the game, a Lafayette newspaper columnist was furious. The quality of Red Sox games, he promised, was "not going to be torn down by individuals, such as Saperstein, who blandly declared over the phone that 'it isn't the first time I've scheduled one team in two towns on the same night.'"[28]

Saperstein's baseball and basketball worlds constantly intermingled. He arranged for several Black Barons players to join the Globetrotters basketball squad or perform other jobs to support the Trotters' tours—enabling these athletes to earn money outside of baseball season. Radcliffe played with the Globetrotters one year, whereas another Birmingham player drove the Trotters' team bus. Winfield Welch, manager of the Black Barons, worked for a few years as a road manager for the Globetrotters basketball squad.[29]

The Black Barons weren't the only example of Saperstein's overlapping basketball and baseball enterprises. Ted Strong Jr. played basketball for the Globetrotters but spent several summers with the Monarchs, helping the club win the 1942 Negro League World Series.

In 1944, Saperstein launched the Harlem Globetrotters *baseball* team, which played barnstorming games. Again, Paige was a crucial ingredient. He sometimes pitched for the baseball Globetrotters, occasionally played for their opponent, and later served as a player-manager for the Trotters squad. The rest of the team was made up mostly of players with experience in the Negro Leagues. One of them was Radcliffe, who, like Paige, had grown up playing ball on the sandlots of Mobile, Alabama. The Globetrotters baseball team never achieved the fame of its basketball cousin, but it played America's pastime as late as 1954.[30]

Saperstein told a sportswriter in 1946 that Black baseball was drawing more of his attention than basketball. At the top of his agenda was launching a new professional baseball league on the Pacific Coast. The original idea for the West Coast Negro Baseball Association (WCNBA) came from two firefighters in Berkeley, California. Saperstein embraced the concept, viewing the region as fertile territory because no Major League or Negro Leagues ballclub existed west of St. Louis. And thousands of Black workers had migrated west during the Depression and World War II.[31]

Teams in the WCNBA were based in six cities: Los Angeles, Oakland, Portland, San Diego, San Francisco, and Seattle. Besides serving as WCNBA president, Saperstein owned the Seattle Steelheads. Olympic track legend Jesse Owens, a friend of Saperstein, assumed ownership of the Portland Rose Buds and served as WCNBA's vice president. Owens was optimistic about the new league's prospects. "I don't see how we can miss," he said. "I have had numerous dealings with Saperstein and owe most of my success in my diamond activities to his generous and astute direction."[32]

Unfortunately for Saperstein and Owens, attendance wasn't strong enough to sustain the WCNBA, which folded after playing only thirty games.

Saperstein always seemed to have a fallback plan. After the WCNBA failed, he converted his Seattle team into a barnstorming club that played under various names. Goose Tatum played on this club, which inserted razzle-dazzle elements into games and used the seventh-inning stretch to stage a race between Owens and one of the team's ballplayers.[33]

Saperstein made a few moves during the 1930s and '40s that created friction with Black baseball owners and journalists. One was booking games for a team called the Zulu Cannibal Giants.

Formed by former Negro Leagues pitcher Charlie Henry in 1934, the Cannibal Giants wore costumes, not uniforms—dressing in grass skirts, face paint, and nose rings. Some played in their bare feet. Each Cannibal Giants player was given a supposedly African name, such as Wahoo, Impo, and Moki. Saperstein booked games for the team in the Midwest, while his friend Syd Pollock scheduled their games in the Northeast.

Although some newspapers accurately reported the team's origins, others reinforced a ridiculous caricature—probably encouraged by the publicity materials from Saperstein and Pollock. *The Indianapolis News* described the

Cannibal Giants as "real natives of the Zulu colony who have been brought to America and schooled in the American national pastime."[34]

In 1937, Henry decided to sell the team, and Saperstein and Pollock bought shares. Although the Cannibal Giants attracted fans mostly through a demeaning spectacle, the team did have some talented players. One of them was John "Buck" O'Neil, a future Hall of Famer. O'Neil recalled feeling demoralized on a team "acting like a bunch of fools to draw white folks" to the ballpark. O'Neil went on to an impressive career with the NAL's Monarchs and later became the first Black coach in the major leagues.[35]

Saperstein also raised the ire of Black leaders and journalists by booking games for the Ethiopian Clowns, a team initially based in Miami. Its players wore face paint and took supposedly African names but eschewed the grass skirts that had been worn by the Cannibal Giants. Although the Clowns' appearance was less outlandish, their on-the-field antics offended many Black baseball officials. Cumberland "Cum" Posey, who owned the NNL's Homestead Grays, complained that using "Ethiopian" in the team's name insulted Blacks by making light of "the downfall of the only empire which really belonged to the Negro race."[36] Black sportswriter Wendell Smith decried the Clowns as a "fourth-rate Uncle Tom minstrel show."[37]

Saperstein and Pollock, an owner of the Clowns, were frequent targets of these criticisms. Black team owners were also angry at Saperstein when some of their scheduled games were canceled because the opposing team had signed a deal with him to play the Clowns that same day for more money.[38]

The Cannibal Giants and the Clowns played barnstorming games and did not participate in the Negro Leagues during the 1930s. Although several of the Clowns' players were talented enough to later join the rosters of Negro Leagues clubs, the team's comedy antics were the primary draw for fans. Fay Young of the *Chicago Defender* conceded that "whether some of us like the white chalk on the players' faces or not, the Clowns prove from the crowds they draw that they have something the public wants."[39]

One of Saperstein's biggest breaks in baseball came in 1939 when he was chosen as publicity agent for the Negro Leagues East-West All-Star Game in Chicago. Saperstein was paid 5 percent of the gate receipts. The East-West games attracted Black fans from many cities, and one sportswriter called it "the single, regular galvanizing event for blacks otherwise limited by Jim

Crow laws." Historian John Holway said, "It was more of a World Series than the World Series was."[40]

The 1939 East-West game promoted by Saperstein drew about forty thousand fans to Chicago's Comiskey Park. It was the largest crowd yet for an East-West game. The attendance was roughly double the crowd for the season's second East-West game, played weeks later at New York's Yankee Stadium without Saperstein's publicity.[41]

Despite the positive metrics from the East-West game in Chicago, Saperstein's role as a promoter placed him at the center of an intense debate among Negro League owners about whether his fees were excessive. While the *Defender*'s Young chided NAL and NNL owners for not devoting more attention to publicity, he took aim at Saperstein for "making his living off Negro activities." However, Wendell Smith criticized efforts to end Saperstein's role in promoting the East-West game, applauding him as "one of the sports world's most liberal men, and a square shooter from head to foot."[42]

Saperstein's compensation rate for booking or promoting games varied. In 1941, he arranged for three NAL teams to play a series of games in Cincinnati, receiving 35 percent of the total gate receipts and charging each team an additional 5 percent booking fee. Posey had once defended the use of booking agents by Negro League teams, who would be in an "awful fix" without these agents' services.[43] But Posey grew irritated at Saperstein's lucrative deals. "There should be no place in Negro or any other kind of baseball for a man like this," wrote Posey.[44] A sportswriter for a Black Virginia newspaper lamented that "Jews have taken over" the Negro Leagues.[45]

Yet other Black journalists defended Saperstein's work as a booker. "He has more friends among Negro baseball players than any other man in the game," wrote Dan Burley. "No player who has a contract with him squawks about not getting paid or mistreated."[46] Burley, who later became associate editor of *Ebony* magazine, also defended Saperstein's booking fees. "There might be a profit to Saperstein on one game," he wrote, "but what about expenses lost on rainouts, small crowds, etc."[47]

Because of Saperstein's connections in the Midwest—the NAL's backyard—he was a favorite booking agent for that league. Even though the NAL had "the anti-Sapersteins and the pro-Sapersteins," as Posey put it, the league was supportive enough of the controversial promoter, which created a point of conflict with the NNL.[48]

The 1941 East-West All Star game set an attendance record as 50,256 fans filled Comiskey Park, validating the support from Black team owners who had pushed successfully for Saperstein to promote the game. The attendance was only four thousand less than the crowd drawn by that year's MLB All-Star game.

The next year, Saperstein and Pollock co-launched a six-team league called the Negro Major Baseball League of America that included the Clowns. Posey, the NNL's secretary, attacked the new league as "a personal threat of Saperstein directed toward his former associates of the Negro American League." Wendell Smith was more measured in the *Pittsburgh Courier*: "I know [Saperstein] and think he is sincere and honest. But I do object to the league he has organized and tried to peddle as one on par with the Negro American and National Leagues."[49] The Saperstein-Pollock league lasted only one season.

Despite the failure of the league he had co-launched with Pollock, Saperstein prospered as the financial situation for the Negro Leagues improved during the war years. "Colored baseball has done so well this summer, has made so much money, that it scares me," he told a sportswriter.[50]

In 1943, the Clowns joined the NAL, retaining a dose of comedy but ditching their most controversial elements: the face paint and African-style names. That year, the Clowns slowly transitioned from "Ethiopian" in their name to "Cincinnati," where they were based.[51]

Saperstein tried to reshuffle the deck of Black baseball a year later. He persuaded Pollock to move the Clowns from Cincinnati to Indianapolis, where the team had always drawn good crowds—and where Saperstein had exclusive booking rights. He also sought to give his brother Morry a chance to acquire the NAL's Chicago American Giants and move them to Cincinnati. This scheme failed.[52]

Meanwhile, relations between Saperstein and the NNL deteriorated. In June 1944, NNL owners voted unanimously to forbid their teams from playing any game booked or promoted by Saperstein. Yet the rule had little effect on Saperstein's revenues for two reasons: he worked primarily for NAL teams, and not all NNL teams complied with the rule. Saperstein booked at least one game each in 1944 and 1945 for the NNL's Newark Eagles, whose co-owner had been among his leading critics.[53]

In 1947, Saperstein asked the NAL to admit the Cincinnati Crescents, a Black team he had organized. Instead, league officials opted to accept new franchises in Detroit and St. Louis.[54]

As he did with basketball, Saperstein had plenty to say about ways to improve the fan appeal of baseball. The Negro Leagues began playing night baseball in 1930, but, heading into the 1938 season, only two MLB clubs had hosted a game under the lights. Saperstein told a sportswriter why more MLB teams should play night baseball. "People can't afford to lay off work to go to afternoon ball games anymore," he said. "But they like to get out at night and what better place to spend a warm evening than a ball park."[55]

During the late 1940s, the relationship between Saperstein and Pollock soured. Pollock's son blamed the chill on Saperstein's failure to repay $10,000 that his father Syd had loaned the Chicago promoter. After 1950, the two baseball mavericks never spoke or exchanged letters. But the Clowns—the two promoters' key collaboration—flourished for many years despite frequent criticism. In 1951, the Clowns' most famous player appeared, and he stayed with the team for just twenty-six games. His name was Henry Aaron, and he delighted the fans by swinging his bat, instead of clowning around.[56]

For more than twenty years, Saperstein raised the profile of Black baseball and its stars. "In many departments, says Abe, the Negro professionals are equal to anything the white major leagues have to offer," a columnist wrote in 1938.[57] Yet Saperstein's remarks sometimes reinforced racial myths. Explaining baseball's popularity among Black Americans, Saperstein said, "The Negro has more money than he ever had before, and you know how baseball is inborn among them."[58] Despite occasional eyebrow-raising comments like this, Saperstein built close relationships with some Black baseball players.

Besides Paige, Radcliffe was another star who considered Abe a good friend. Radcliffe recalled that Saperstein bought him a new car almost every year. There was one rule: when Saperstein was in town, Radcliffe agreed to drive him to meetings or appointments. Radcliffe also credited Saperstein for getting him a job as a Cleveland Indians scout in the early 1960s. He called Saperstein the "most generous owner" for whom he played.[59]

Still, Black baseball officials were divided over Saperstein's roles and contributions. Effa Manley, a co-owner of the NNL's Newark Eagles, accused him of exploiting Black baseball. But J. B. Martin, NAL president, defended Saperstein and said the promoter carried out an agreement with his league "to the letter."[60] Decades later, Manley's views softened considerably. She said the white booking agents who worked with Negro Leagues teams were "a legitimate business. They weren't doing anything wrong."[61]

7

THE CHAMPION

The Globetrotters kept vying for the national title, and
Saperstein thrived despite wartime challenges

A be Saperstein hated to lose. And he went into the 1939–1940 basket-ball season still smarting over the Globetrotters' defeat at the hands of the New York Renaissance in the first-ever national pro tournament in Chicago.

When Saperstein didn't like the way things were going, he didn't stand by and hope for better luck in the future. He shook things up.

First, he tried to get the players on the Rens to abandon owner Bob Douglas as a group and join him. As former Rens player John Isaacs told author Ben Green, "When that didn't work, he decided to go individually—and he wanted me. He even had Harry Rusan contact me and try to get me to come play. I told him, 'OK, but first put my money in escrow, then I'll consider it.' Rusan looked at me like I was crazy. I decided, I'm not going to get caught up in this."[1]

Having failed in his effort to recruit the Rens, Saperstein set out to beef up his own team. That meant dumping aged Rock Anderson and five-foot-nine sharpshooter Rusan, who had been suspended the previous season and whose lack of height had been badly exploited in the pro tournament. Saperstein picked up two outstanding players from Toledo: Roscoe "Duke"

Reece "Goose" Tatum's wingspan and athleticism made him a dominant basketball player. His comedic instincts made him a fan favorite.

Cumberland, a six-foot-three inside banger, and Sonny Boswell, who was skinny but six-foot-two and—most importantly—one of the best outside shooters in the country.

With Boswell aboard, the Trotters started scoring more points than ever before, sometimes doubling their opponents' total. In previous seasons, the Globetrotters had tried to leap to a safe lead then shift to tricks and comedy to entertain the fans and avoid embarrassing the opposition with a lopsided score. Saperstein had even experimented with the idea of spotting the opponents points at the start of the game, but that didn't leave any time for clowning and the fans didn't like it.[2] Now, during the 1939–1940 season, the team was performing its usual tricks, but it was also making the score into a joke.

Perhaps Boswell's presence didn't fully explain the scoring surge, though. Saperstein seemed determined to run up the score and prove his team's dominance, aiming the entire season at the next pro tournament in Chicago in March.

The Trotters' tournament run began at the Madison Street Armory against Wisconsin's Kenosha Badgers. Or rather, it was a tournament walk, as the Trotters strolled to an easy 50–26 victory. Next up were the New York Renaissance, in a bracket setup ensuring that the two Black squads—among the best teams—would not meet in the finals or even the semis.

The Rens were three-to-one favorites to win the tournament, and some bookmakers spotted them ten points against the Trotters. Last year's contest had been much closer than that, of course, and this year's would be too. With Boswell and his teammates sprinting and shooting, a departure from the methodical pass-pass-pass-pass tactics popular at the time, the Rens were thrown off their game. "Those kids just ran and chucked and ran and chucked some more," Rens owner Douglas said.[3]

The first three quarters ended with the Rens up, 31–30, in a game that would ultimately see fourteen lead changes. And then, out of exhaustion, caution, or both, the game reverted to old-fashioned ball control. With two minutes left, the Rens clung to their one-point lead, 35–34. The Rens added a free throw, and the Trotters got the ball and began to work for the final shot to tie. The Rens swarmed Boswell, who had scored eighteen of his team's thirty-four points. With about a minute left, the ball wound up with Babe Pressley in the corner. Yes, Babe Pressley, the bruiser known as "the Blue Ox," who had yet to score a point. Pressley put up a shot, and it went in. Game tied.[4]

The Rens then came back and attempted a game winner, which missed, with the Trotters rebounding. The ball went to Boswell and the Rens did one of the worst things possible: they fouled him. He hit the shot, putting the Trotters in the lead, 37–36, and with time running out, the Rens' Puggy Bell somehow got behind all of the Globetrotters and took a long pass. Luckily for the Trotters, his momentum took him too far underneath the backboard and his shot clanged off the rim. The Rens' Tarzan Cooper was following the play and went for the loose ball, but the Trotters' old man, Inman Jackson, got there first and cradled the ball so that neither Cooper nor Bell could grab it as time ran out.

Six thousand fans—and the bookmakers—were stunned. Saperstein, an irrational optimist, probably was not.

The *Dayton Journal* reported that "the New York Rens were so upset by their loss at the hands of the Globe Trotters that they broke down after the game and cried like babies."[5] *Chicago Defender* columnist Fay Young wrote that the performance of the Black teams had proven two things: "Basketball is now a game for big, tall men," and "basketball is not a white man's game. The pale faces just don't know how to play it."[6]

That was a ridiculous claim at the time, and the Globetrotters certainly weren't buying it, since they had two respectable white teams left to beat to win the title. Next came the Syracuse Reds, who were disposed of by a 34–24 score, with Boswell having an off night but his teammates picking him up. Then there was the final against the Chicago Bruins, owned by the Chicago Bears' football boss, George Halas. The Bruins featured Mike Novak, the six-foot-nine goaltending expert who had played with the Chicago Harmons when they lost to the Trotters in the previous year's tournament. The Bruins were a favorite among Chicago's white press, and the *Chicago Tribune* still hadn't figured out that the Trotters were locally based, describing them as "a Negro team from Seattle, Washington."[7]

Despite struggling with a sprained ankle, Novak was still a formidable defender, and the game was a low-scoring affair, with the Trotters leading 7–6 after a quarter. But the Globetrotters' Boswell heated up outside, and the Trotters zoomed to a 20–13 lead at halftime. Then the wheels came off, with the Trotters scoring a single point in the third quarter and Ted Strong Jr. fouling out, forcing Inman Jackson into action again. With five-and-a-half minutes left to play, the Trotters trailed 29–21, a big deficit for that era.

As *Collier's* magazine put it in the casual racist parlance of the time, "the situation was darker than the expressions on the faces of the big, black bucks."[8]

But Saperstein's team came back. He had invited Leon Wheeler, a Black coach from Detroit, to serve as his assistant for the tournament, and Wheeler finally persuaded him to replace the aged Jackson with the last man on the bench, Al Fawks, who rarely played. Within ten seconds of getting in the game, Fawks drained a long set shot, the highlight of a Trotters charge that eventually evened the score at 29–29. The mostly white crowd of 6,500 was "on the verge of hysteria," according to the *Chicago Herald-American*.[9]

Then an even more improbable play occurred. With a minute left, one of the Trotters' beefier players, Bernie Price, picked up his dribble near half court and inexplicably decided to take a shot. The long-distance two-handed set shot quieted the fans until it went in, at which time the crowd went nuts. Three Bruins missed free throws in the last minute, and the game ended 31–29. The Harlem Globetrotters were champions.

The *Defender* noted that the result was "contrary to all pre-tournament dope" and "cost many bettors money."[10] But Saperstein, who collected a $1,000 prize for this team, shared the wealth by awarding a $100 bonus to each of the Trotters players.

The Globetrotters owner, who would cite the championship in promotional materials for many years to come, publicly downplayed the accomplishment. "World champions, my eye," Saperstein said. "The world isn't one tournament held in Chicago. We're crossroads champions, that's what. We won that title by playing in every whistle-stop in the country and showing the people how this basketball game should really be played."[11]

Perhaps the greatest dividend from the tournament victory came eight months later, when the *Herald-American* launched the All-Star Classic, a game between the winner of the pro tournament and an all-star team made up of recently graduated college stars chosen by a panel of thirty-six sportswriters. At the time, college basketball drew much more fan interest than the pro game, so the pros—and Saperstein—were catching a lift from the college boys. Saperstein saw the marketing potential and knew how to exploit it. A Wisconsin newspaper said it had "learned from Chicago sources" that Saperstein had ordered the Globetrotters' training camp to start a week early because he was "impressed by the imposing array of players being selected for the College All-Stars." The "Chicago sources" might well have been Saperstein himself. The Globetrotters usually held their preseason tune-up in their hometown, Chicago, but this time they spent most of their camp in Sheboygan, Wisconsin, so they could scrimmage with the Sheboygan Redskins. Out-of-town training camps are common for pro sports teams in modern times, but this was a basketball rarity in 1940, yet another trendsetting move by the Harlem Globetrotters.[12] While the Trotters were prepping for the big game, Saperstein and his wife, Sylvia, bolstered their own team with the birth of a son, Jerry.

In the run-up to the All-Star Classic, the white media lavished attention on the all-white All-Stars at the expense of the all-Black Globetrotters. Perhaps sensitive to that, the *Defender* noted that both a Miss All-Star, who was white, and a Miss Bronze America, who was Black, would appear at the game, and "both young women will be dressed alike."[13] The Classic took place at Chicago Stadium in front of 20,583 fans, the largest US crowd to watch a basketball game up to that time. The *Defender* said the crowd "throughout the night cheered the plays of both teams, displaying no partisanship at all."

There was plenty to cheer about. The teams were knotted 20–20 at halftime and 30–30 after three quarters. "With two minutes left to play, the Globetrotters were leading 37 to 35 and 'putting on the show' to kill time," the *Defender* reported. But fancy passing and trickery didn't work. The All-Stars stole the ball and scored. Then they scored again with mere seconds left, grabbing a 39–37 lead. The Trotters desperately got the ball to their best shooter, Boswell, who heaved it from around midcourt. And it went in.[14]

The five-minute overtime period was a seesaw affair, with the teams tied 42–42 until a hometown star—but not for the Globetrotters—ended the drama. Stan Szukala, formerly of DePaul University, put up the game winner for the All-Stars.

It was "the wildest, wooliest basketball game ever seen in this section of the country," according to sportswriter Wendell Smith, who added that the entire crowd "rose as one after the battle was over and gave both teams an ovation that shook the lofty rafters of this mammoth stadium."[15]

The Globetrotters had lost on the court but won a huge publicity victory. They would never again be challenged by the Rens as America's best Black basketball team, and Saperstein would eventually buy the Rens off the bargain rack in 1949.[16] The Trotters could credibly claim they were the best team, period—Black or white—though they would fail to win a second pro championship in their four attempts. They had won once, which was enough for it to be featured on team stationery and on the side of its newly purchased team vehicle, a used army "carryall" truck.[17] And the Globetrotters' title as champs appeared in virtually every newspaper story whenever they came to town.

Saperstein entrusted the Globetrotters' 1940–1941 Pacific Northwest tour to Inman Jackson but required daily telegrams or letters detailing the team's performance. The Trotters' top man was increasingly busy with his baseball activities, plus his newly created basketball teams, such as the Chicago Brown Bombers and a new version of the Savoy Big Five. No longer operating his business with slips of paper in his overcoat, Saperstein opened a two-room office for Abe Saperstein Sports Enterprises in Chicago's Loop at 192 North Clark Street, three floors above Gibby's Restaurant, a popular hangout for the theater crowd, mobsters, and politicians. Saperstein's office featured a large portrait of Abraham Lincoln gazing at him.[18]

While serving their loyal fans in the Pacific Northwest, the much-in-demand Globetrotters expanded their footprint dramatically that season, playing extensively in California and also making an eastern swing that included Pittsburgh, New York City, Baltimore, and Washington, DC.[19]

But things turned sour with their loss to the Detroit Eagles in the third annual pro tournament in Chicago, especially due to their lackluster effort in surrendering the title. The *Defender* accused the Globetrotters of partying too hard beforehand: "On Friday night and into the wee hours Saturday morning, the boys were enjoying the floor show at Dave's. . . . Is that the way athletes train?" Columnist Fay Young said, "Abe Saperstein needs to put a guard with his boys on the eve of a tournament."[20]

It got worse. The next month, before the last game of the 1940–1941 season, Saperstein faced a player revolt over money—a repeat of the Runt Pullins incident in which he lost some of his best players. This time it was Sonny Boswell, Duke Cumberland, and Hilary Brown. Then it got even worse: all three signed with the dreaded New York Renaissance.

The Trotters still had Ted Strong Jr., Babe Pressley, Bernie Price, and of course Inman Jackson, and in Saperstein's usual over-the-top manner, he declared them "the best team I've ever shown. . . . Because this is a *team*. There isn't a prima donna in the bunch."[21]

One of Saperstein's many strengths was his eye for talent, and although he was publicly praising his depleted squad, he was looking for better. Such as a fellow who had played baseball for him and was taking up basketball. An odd, countrified young man named Reece "Goose" Tatum, who would become one of the most famous Globetrotters in team history.

Tatum joined the Globetrotters after the player revolt but played sparingly that first season. He emerged as a star in his second year, showing both athletic gifts and great comedic instincts. And the comedy was becoming increasingly important for Saperstein's marketing efforts. The Trotters were among the best basketball teams, but he knew they were by far the best *comedy* basketball team. The challenge for Saperstein and his players was to feast on the laughs of the crowd and the growing ticket revenue without losing their identity as a team of athletes.

"The thing about the clowning," Saperstein said at the time, "is to know when to stop. If you give the fans too much of the hippodroming, they get tired of it. The ball game is liable to become a farce. We try to give them enough but not too much—keep them yelling for a little more. That's just good show business."[22]

The comedy was an important part of the Globetrotters' warm relationship with the fans. Once at Gonzaga University in Spokane, Washington, a Globetrotter tried a "howitzer shot" in warm-ups before the start of the second half, throwing the ball high up to the rafters, and when it dropped, it hit the rim and tore it loose. While officials repaired the rim, Inman Jackson went out to center court with a young child from the audience and passed the ball back and forth as entertainment.[23]

Goose Tatum was terrific with the kids, too. During halftime in Wichita, Kansas, Tatum brought a young boy from the audience onto the court and tried to teach him how to shoot a hook shot. The kid wasn't getting it, so Tatum put him on his shoulders and had the boy drop the ball through the hoop. The crowd roared. Tatum escorted the boy to a place on the Globetrotters' bench, then escorted a Trotters teammate into the stands, instructing him to sit in the boy's seat, beside his parents. The audience loved it.[24]

Sometimes the comic bits were ad lib, and sometimes they were elaborate conspiracies. Saperstein recalled:

We were in Chicago once and some guy wrote that we did everything but eat the ball. So I decided that next time in, we'd do just that. First we got a chocolate ball but you couldn't handle it. Then we go to this baker and have him make two big loaves of Jewish rye bread. We scooped them out, taped them together, and they look just like a basketball. When there's a time-out, we put the bread ball in and someone throws it to Goose Tatum. So he starts peeling it and eating it. I tell you the people fell out of their seats.[25]

Though many of the clowning bits were positive and charming, others struck some Black people as demeaning. A notorious example was the craps game, when a few Trotters would break away from the game and shoot dice in the corner of the court. That recurring bit prompted Buster Miller, columnist for the Black *New York Age*, to declare that he was no longer "neutral" on the question of the Renaissance versus the Globetrotters and was backing the Rens:

> Saperstein's idea of a world's championship team of colored players appears to be a minstrel show. . . . Our peanut Barnum invented the brilliant idea of having his players cut a few capers after they had built up a fairly good lead over their opponents in the final minutes of a game. Then one of the Trotters retires to a corner of the court, produces a pair of dice, and indulges in a game of solitary crap. If the lead is big enough and safe enough, a teammate will stroll over and join in. The routine is varied sometimes with a pack of cards standing in for the galloping dominoes. Of course this bit of burlesque probably wows white spectators just about as much as it sickens the colored fans. . . . It's bad enough to have the race continually portrayed on stage and screen as inveterate clowns, crapshooters or Uncle Toms. But when this particular brand of hokum invades the sports field, this writer is going to yell—but loud.[26]

It's impossible to defend the craps routine, but even less-fraught skits rankled some people, who thought the players came across as mischievous children. But were the Globetrotters' routines racist? The answer comes down largely to whether you believe the Trotters were being "laughed at" or "laughed with." Opponents and referees were often the butts of the jokes, with the Trotters sharing the laugh with the crowd. So it's not a given that white fans thought less of the players or of Black people in general because of the clowning. On the other hand, it's not hard to understand why some people were offended that one of Black people's most prominent roles in American life was serving as jesters.

Abe Saperstein's role in shaping the Black American image was controversial then and remains so today. Where people come down on the issue depends partly on whether they think historical figures should be judged in the context of their times or by more enlightened modern standards. In his time, Saperstein was far more open-minded and tolerant than society at large. By choice, he spent more time around Black people than almost any other white American alive. He was a businessman trying to entertain fans—both white and Black—by showcasing the talent of Black Americans. He was trying to make people happy and to make money for both himself and his Black players.

But while doing so, he promoted stereotypes. "A Negro is a natural entertainer," he once said, and a Canadian sportswriter who was chummy with Saperstein echoed that notion, writing that the Globetrotters "laugh and play with the innate humor of their race."[27] Black Americans such as Buster Miller didn't want to be amusing to white people; they wanted to be respected by them. And sometimes Saperstein's comments went beyond stereotype all the way to ugly condescension.

An interview with columnist Hal Straight published in the *Vancouver Sun* in 1940 might make a modern reader wonder whether Saperstein knew he was speaking on the record. Straight asked him why Black athletes were doing so well in sports, and Saperstein answered:

> Coaches claim they can't get this generation to practice, to work. They are brought into the world to enjoy easy conditions. But the Negro is the son of a hard worker. Take [boxer] Joe Louis. Dumb as all get out. Manual labor in a Detroit auto plant . . . and just got by. . . . Even today he can't think for himself. But he had a beautiful body . . . and could do anything he was asked . . . and he had to be asked. I think you'll find for the next five years or so that the Negro will dominate sport in North America. Then after that he'll flatten out to the same level as the white man.[28]

Saperstein also was asked if Black athletes were hard to handle, and he gave this response: "They are temperamental. You have to watch yourself. My gang is all kids, all under twenty-four except for Inman Jackson. But with a Negro you either have to be boss or nothing and I'm boss and we get along swell."

Those insulting comments reflected just one aspect of a complex and contradictory man. Saperstein thought segregation was stupid, as this incident in the Jim Crow South in the early 1940s shows.

"One night we got into Atlanta late," Saperstein recalled, "and I went to a hotel on Auburn Street, in the Negro section, along with the players. I'm just dropping off to sleep when a couple of detectives crash in and tell me I gotta get out."

An officer told him: "What are you doing down here in this neighborhood?"

"Well, up to a minute ago, I was sleeping," he said.

"Well, get on up to Peachtree Street," the detective told him.[29]

On that same tour of the South, the Globetrotters played Black college teams rather than white teams because of laws against race mixing. In Alabama, Black fans and white fans couldn't even watch basketball together. Saperstein's team played for a white audience and then played a second game for a Black audience.[30]

An incident in Florida involving Saperstein's daughter Eloise showed how the family's relationships with Black people clashed with the racism that surrounded them. Saperstein's wife, Sylvia, traveled with Eloise to attend a Globetrotters game in Miami Beach in the late 1940s. Eloise recalled that she was about eleven years old, "almost developed," and wore a strapless navy blue blouse. She saw Inman Jackson, whom she had always known and who had "diapered me" as a baby. "Jackson lifted me up, as he always did, and I gave him a kiss on the cheek, as I always did." This caused a racial incident, with word spreading through the crowd that a Black man had grabbed a white woman and kissed her. Some suggested he should be lynched. The game was delayed as Saperstein got Jackson out of the arena to safety. Then Saperstein went up to his daughter and quietly explained: "You're a big girl now in your strapless blouse and you can no longer be picked up by Jackson or ever kiss Jackson, particularly down South. Tonight you almost had Jackson killed." Eloise remembered the incident as her first realization of America's racial divide.[31]

While Saperstein could seem condescending toward Black people in some interviews, he also came across as an exploder of negative stereotypes: "Negro athletes are supposed to be strictly front runners. You know, great when they're ahead but inclined to fold up when the white boys put the pressure on them. In other words, they haven't guts. The Globe Trotters have done as much as Joe Louis to show that idea is cockeyed."[32]

Don Shelby, a white Minneapolis broadcast journalist and basketball writer who saw the Globetrotters as a youth in Muncie, Indiana, in the 1950s, said Saperstein's team changed white attitudes. Though Muncie "was known as the northern headquarters of the Ku Klux Klan," Shelby said, there was "this odd paradox":[33]

White people there recognized the talent they were seeing. Watching the Globetrotters' incredible athleticism on the court started to change the paradigm of how white fans viewed Black athletes. The cultural shift might have been only by millimeters, but I think it gained momentum from there. Watching those games may have gotten some of the white fans to thinking: "Well, maybe Blacks should be playing in pro basketball."

With Saperstein starting to make real money, the issue of how much he shared with the players kept coming up. Saperstein claimed in 1942 that Babe Pressley was his top earner at $400 per month plus expenses, with the lowest pay $200 a month and the average $300. It's likely that these figures were only for the months they were playing, which would make the average annual salary about $1,800, or the equivalent of $34,500 in today's dollars for half a year's work. Saperstein wasn't inclined to say how much he made personally.[34]

But the pay issues probably shouldn't be viewed as racial as much as labor versus management during an era in which sports owners had almost all of the leverage. After all, this was a time when Major League Baseball players took jobs selling suits and hardware to tide themselves over during the offseason. And even when players walked out on Saperstein, they often returned. Sonny Boswell and Duke Cumberland, who had quit in 1941, came back during the 1943–1944 season. And Runt Pullins, who had led the 1934 "insurrection," rejoined the team for a few games in 1942.[35] Of course, their return also reflected the economy's limited job opportunities for Black people.

Pro-Saperstein members of the white press were impatient with concerns about "exploitation."

"I guess we can safely describe Mr. Abe Saperstein now as a success," wrote Stu Keate of the *Vancouver Province*. "His promotions with Negro athletes have attained such proportions that he is being charged in certain quarters as 'exploiting' the colored race. You know what that means. It means his critics didn't have the energy or ability to put across the deal themselves."[36]

Saperstein certainly had the energy and ability to make his promotion of Black athletes a smashing success. But just as the Globetrotters were making national news, the nation was focused on a far grimmer news story: US entry into World War II.

The Japanese attack on Pearl Harbor on December 7, 1941, plunged the nation into uncertainty. The next day, President Franklin D. Roosevelt gave his famous "infamy" speech to Congress, and a day after that, the Trotters played as scheduled in Decatur, Illinois. Halftime was different, though: the public address system piped in a radio address by FDR.[37]

Saperstein was thirty-nine at the time, which meant he had to register for the draft, though he was unlikely to be called. Some of his best players went into the military or took jobs in the war industry. He lost his rising star, Goose Tatum, for several years to the US Army Air Corps. Tatum even helped the Lincoln Army Air Field Wings defeat the Globetrotters in a game in Nebraska in 1944.

But Saperstein managed to keep the Trotters going, fielding not one but two teams. The main team that continued traveling widely was led by Inman Jackson. The second unit stayed closer to the Chicago area so that players could keep their defense industry jobs.

Whereas other teams such as the Rens curtailed their tours, Saperstein made sure the Globetrotters' schedule included stops at many military installations to play teams of soldiers, like Tatum's air base squad. In a late 1942 explanation that may have been a Globetrotters news release—it was worded the same way in several newspapers in different states—Saperstein defended his continued touring at a time when gasoline rationing was in effect and able-bodied men were expected to join the war effort:

> [Saperstein] was uncertain at the start of this season, due to war conditions, as to whether or not to travel his aggregation. He was left no choice in the matter, however. From all sections of the country came an avalanche of requests for games to stimulate the morale of war industry workers and help raise funds for various war fund efforts, in addition to playing various service teams at their camps.[38]

The result was that the Globetrotters maintained and even broadened their visibility during this national ordeal, and by war's end they were in an even stronger position versus their pro basketball competitors than they had been before. The frequent visits to military bases had another benefit beyond allowing the Trotters to support the war effort: the team could gas up its vehicles at the bases.[39]

Saperstein was a patriot, and he drove his team hard to entertain the troops and war workers. He recalled a day in Tacoma: "We played an afternoon game at Fort Lewis for the soldiers, moved into the Armory for a night game, bedded down there for a few hours, then got up and played a game around 2:30 a.m. for the [factory] swing-shifters."[40]

But occasionally the Globetrotters' games to support the war effort led to on-court warfare. In Northern California, the Globetrotters played an army team from the Presidio of Monterey, and Saperstein pulled his team off the court midgame because he thought the referees were calling too many fouls. When the contest resumed, the Trotters won, 39–36. The Presidio was so miffed that it issued a statement denouncing "the type of sportsmanship displayed by the Globetrotter manager" and claiming the army had won 2–0 by forfeit.[41]

At a time when American servicemen were dying overseas, some people thought the Trotters were having too good a time on the homefront. C. W. Wilson of Chewelah, Washington, wrote a letter to the editor of the *Spokane Spokesman-Review*:

How can the 'Globe Trotters,' pictured in *The Spokesman-Review*'s Sunday sports section, have the nerve to be physically fit, as they certainly look, yet not in the service of their country, just taking up travel space which could be used to better advantage surely. . . . I don't understand how such men can 'trot' around when farmer boys badly needed who really get down and grub in the earth and milk cows, feed hogs, etc., are drafted into the army.[42]

Saperstein insisted he was motivated by the soldiers serving overseas—including his brothers Harry and Rocky, who had urged him to use his team to boost morale. "They believe in sports, and therefore so do I," he said.[43]

The Globetrotters' continued touring suggested an official endorsement, at least to Canadian sportswriter Pete Sallaway. "Saperstein's high rating with the authorities in Washington is recognized by the fact that his Trotters are the only touring club still on the road, despite strict travel and manpower conditions in effect as a result of the war," he wrote in 1944. Of course, Sallaway was easily charmed by Saperstein and was still repeating the nonsense that the Globetrotters boss was "a former professional star in his own rights."[44]

Saperstein tried to allay concerns about his wartime touring by claiming that "all the players were 4-Fs," men who had received deferments from the draft for various reasons. He called them the "Psycho Five," a reference to one reason for getting 4-F status, though Saperstein clearly was joking about that.[45] When the Trotters' "old man," Inman Jackson, finally got a draft notice in late 1943, Saperstein said: "He sure had all of us fooled. We all thought he was over forty." (He was thirty-six.)[46]

The loss of so many players led Saperstein to pick up white center Bob Kartens in 1943, but he was no token hire. Kartens was a talented ballhandler who developed many of the ball-spinning and juggling tricks traditionally performed in the "Magic Circle" at the start of Trotters games. Karstens also is credited with inventing the "wobbly ball," which was weighted inside so that it rolled and flew erratically.[47]

In the 1940s, the Globetrotters retroactively made another Saperstein boast a reality, becoming true globetrotters. They already had been to one foreign country, Canada, but added two others, Mexico and Cuba, as well as venturing nearly halfway across the Pacific Ocean to visit an exotic US territory called Hawaii. Saperstein would sometimes complain about the rigors of international travel, but there was no question it fed his fascination with foreign cultures and adventure. In many ways, it defined the last third of his life.

In 1943 and 1944, the Globetrotters won the Mexico City Invitational tournament. Saperstein recalled how his team "paraded with American flags, and each player was presented with floral pieces by dazzling Mexican girls."[48]

Fourteen thousand fans filled an arena built for fewer than half that many, and the cramped conditions led to a scare. "During one exciting moment," Saperstein recalled, "a Mexican player stumbled over a spectator, and hot remarks followed. The spectator jumped to his feet, pulled a huge horse pistol out of his belt, and brandished it wildly. There might have been serious trouble but the crowd booed the fan so roughly that he subsided, and continued to boo until he left the arena."[49]

During that first visit to Mexico, Saperstein found time to pay his respects to the widow of revolutionary Pancho Villa, who resided on the estate her husband built.[50]

In April 1946, the Globetrotters toured Hawaii, arriving on the same day that a tsunami struck the islands, killing 159 people. Most of the Trotters' games were played on islands that had suffered little damage, so their itinerary was not disrupted. In two weeks facing local teams, the Trotters found that the comedy that played well on Oahu wasn't always as welcome on other islands. One fan in Hilo yelled: "Honolulu fans may go for that, but we like good basketball!" Still, the visit was a success, with a game against a US military all-star team drawing nearly twelve thousand fans. The Trotters had clobbered their opponents, often doubling their score, but Saperstein smartly left the Hawaiians with their self-respect by naming an "all-opponent Hawaii team" before departing. And he was back the next year. Hawaii would become one of the team's favorite stops.[51]

In 1947, the Globetrotters flew to Cuba for the International Cup tournament in the pre-Castro days when Havana was a wide-open party town for tourists. The Trotters' visit came two months after the later-to-be-notorious "Havana Conference" mob summit hosted by Charles "Lucky" Luciano and Meyer Lansky at the Hotel Nacional and just a couple days before the Brooklyn Dodgers arrived in Cuba for spring training with an up-and-coming minor leaguer named Jackie Robinson. Unlike the Globetrotters' visits to Hawaii and Mexico, they faced no local teams in Cuba. The Trotters went undefeated in a four-team tournament in the Palacio de los Deportes, which featured yet another Saperstein-owned farm club, the Kansas City Stars, along with the House of David and Mexico's Chihuahua Dorados.[52]

It was clear that Abe Saperstein Sports Enterprises had emerged from the war years in great shape. The global disaster had created a closer, more connected world, with the United States in the role of superpower, and Saperstein was prepared for his Globetrotters to dominate the nation's basketball and win over the rest of the world as well.

Goose Tatum had left the service and returned to Saperstein's team in time to wear a grass skirt and do a hula dance when they toured Hawaii. Another great player who would define the Globetrotters, Marques Haynes, was coming aboard. The Globetrotters encountered Haynes by accident. They were supposed to play in Oklahoma City against a team called the Professional All-Stars, which canceled on short notice. Saperstein sent a telegram to the only historically black college in the state, Langston, and asked for a game. Langston obliged and upset the Trotters 74–70, led by Haynes, a slight five-foot-eleven senior who dropped twenty-six points on them. Haynes was so impressive that the Globetrotters offered him a job immediately. "You can leave with us tonight. We're going to Dallas," Trotters traveling secretary Winfield Welch told Haynes, apparently after talking with Saperstein by phone. Haynes said he would stay in school and graduate, and even then he struggled over whether to accept an offer to teach history and coach basketball in Enid, Oklahoma, or sign on with the Globetrotters. Fortunately for the Trotters, the man who was perhaps the greatest dribbler of his era eventually said yes.[53]

In 1946, the same year that Haynes joined Saperstein's operation, so did a player who was even more amazing in some respects. Boid Buie lost his left arm in a car accident when he was thirteen. He played basketball anyway, and became a star at Tennessee A&I State College (now Tennessee State University).

"Frankly," Saperstein explained, "I signed Boid as a freak attraction on the recommendation of his coach at Tennessee State. I tried him out in what amounts to spring training for the Harlem Globetrotters, against Loyola of Chicago. I didn't expect much. But he dumped ten points from mid-court and, as you know, Loyola is no pushover in the Midwest. Buie wasn't ready for the Globetrotters but was good enough, strictly on merit, to make first string on the Kansas City five."[54]

Buie ended up playing for both Saperstein's Kansas City Stars and the Globetrotters. He also pitched briefly for the Globetrotters baseball team. Despite Saperstein's unfortunate description of Buie as a "freak," the Globetrotters owner earned praise for showcasing a player whose response to a disability was heartening to war veterans recovering from their wounds.[55]

Saperstein made another noteworthy acquisition in the mid-1940s, bolstering the lineup at his home office in downtown Chicago. He hired Marie Linehan, who was known as Saperstein's secretary but would have been more accurately described as his chief of staff. She was the person who knew everything that was happening throughout his organization and who understood his wishes better than anyone else.

Linehan, a devout Roman Catholic who was the daughter of a German American father and an Irish mother, quit high school to help earn money for her impoverished family. She developed lung problems in her early twenties that sent her to a tuberculosis sanatorium. There she met and fell in love with another patient, Bart Edward Linehan. After they were released, they married and had a son, but Bart died when the child was just a year old. Opportunities were limited for single mothers—especially those without a high school diploma—but Linehan found work as a clerk at Chicago's Kelvyn Park High School, where the basketball coach was Phil Brownstein, a friend of Saperstein who would later serve as a Globetrotters scout. Brownstein suggested Saperstein try to hire Linehan, and she eventually agreed to come aboard on a one-year trial basis. Linehan would work for the Globetrotters for the next four decades, never remarrying, while always remaining devoted to the team and to Saperstein. As Linehan's daughter-in-law Kathie put it, "Not only was she very efficient and very dedicated to Abe in the whole project, she was also kind of a mother figure for a lot of the players." Saperstein called her "the world's best secretary—every club in the major leagues has tried to steal her from me."[56]

Other full-time employees of Saperstein's ever-growing empire were his brothers Morry and Rocky. By decade's end, *Pittsburgh Courier* sportswriter Wendell Smith, who had accompanied the Globetrotters to Mexico, would move to Chicago for a job at a white-owned newspaper, the *Herald-American*, and his new wife, Wyonella, would take a job helping Linehan turn Saperstein's Chicago office into a smooth-running sports promotion machine.[57]

Meanwhile, the hands-on coaching of the Globetrotters was primarily handled by Inman Jackson and team captain Babe Pressley. Saperstein didn't get too involved except during the big moments, such as the 1948 game against the Minneapolis Lakers that catapulted the Globetrotters to greater prominence and proved that Black players belonged in the NBA. Saperstein was spending more time making another point: that Black players belonged in baseball's major leagues.

8

THE GROUNDBREAKER

*Saperstein helped erase baseball's color line, bringing
pitching ace Satchel Paige into the majors*

A be Saperstein and his fellow sports promoter and friend Bill Veeck
cooked up an audacious scheme to tear down baseball's color barrier
in 1942.

Veeck would buy the Philadelphia Phillies and fill it with Black ballplayers at a time when not a single Black person played in Major League Baseball (MLB). Veeck planned to recruit the Negro Leagues' finest players with the help of Saperstein and Black sportswriter Andrew Spurgeon "Doc" Young, whom he called "two of the most knowledgeable men in the country on the subject of Negro Baseball."[1]

Saperstein and Veeck were natural allies who shared a love for baseball. Veeck grew up in the Chicago suburb of Hinsdale, less than twenty miles from the North Side Chicago neighborhood of Saperstein's youth. Veeck's father had been president of the Chicago Cubs, and the younger Veeck worked as an office boy for the team. In 1941, when Veeck faced financial stress as owner of the minor league Milwaukee Brewers, Saperstein came to the rescue by granting Veeck regional rights to book games for the Globetrotters.[2]

Veeck and Saperstein also shared the belief that professional sports were a show as much as a game. "What a professional in sport really is is an entertainer," Saperstein told a sportswriter. As a team owner, Veeck devised

Cleveland Indians owner Bill Veeck (left), Indians executive Hank Greenberg, and Saperstein posed with a basketball for this photo, but their biggest collaboration was signing Negro Leagues star Satchel Paige to a Major League Baseball contract.

theatrical ploys to draw fans, including staging weddings at home plate and giving away a two-hundred-pound block of ice. For a 1951 game, he allowed fans to decide—by holding up "yes" or "no" placards—whether his team should pull its starting pitcher.[3]

Both men were disruptors. As Veeck put it, "I try not to break the rules but merely to test their elasticity." Saperstein was decades ahead of MLB teams when he recommended that a club's ticket prices vary based on the popularity of its opponents.[4]

Their nonconformist nature was just one factor in Saperstein and Veeck's radical scheme to remake the Phillies. Their disdain for racial barriers was another.

When Veeck's Brewers were in spring training in Ocala, Florida, in 1942, he wandered into the colored-only bleachers section, wishing to talk with

Black fans. He repeatedly defied a sheriff's request for him to leave the section and even ignored the mayor, who had been summoned to the ballpark. Veeck got his way. Hank Greenberg, a Hall of Fame player, recalled a conversation with Veeck. "When I first met him in 1947 he was talking to me about the Indians," said Greenberg. "I thought he was talking about the ball club, but, no, he was talking about the American Indians who were treated so badly by the U.S. government."[5]

Saperstein's views on race were more complicated. On one hand, he promoted Black baseball teams that fostered a demeaning, racist image by wearing face paint and using fake African names. On the other hand, Saperstein repeatedly made the case that the best Black athletes were more than able to compete effectively against white stars in basketball and baseball. In 1938, a sports columnist summarized Saperstein's view that, in many phases of the game, "the Negro professionals are equal to anything the white Major Leagues have to offer."[6] And Saperstein hosted his players for annual dinners at his Chicago home despite the annoyance of some neighbors.

"I remember one neighbor in particular being very, very, very upset that Blacks were being brought into the neighborhood," Saperstein's niece Joyce Leviton recalled decades later.[7]

Asked if she remembered what the neighbor said, Leviton replied, "I do, but I don't want to say it. . . . It was not nice. My father particularly was very upset by that. Very upset."

Did the neighbor use the N-word?

"Yes, he did. With a few other not-nice things."

To Saperstein and Veeck, the Phillies presented quite an opportunity to rattle the cages of racists. The maverick promoters knew the Phillies owners had every reason to sell the team. The Phils reportedly owed league officials $160,000 and were two years behind in paying rent for their ballpark. Philadelphia fans were growing restless, having watched the team finish in last place in 1942 for the fifth consecutive season. At a time when World War II military service was depleting baseball rosters of stars like Greenberg and Bob Feller, Veeck believed that an all-Black Philadelphia team would have enough talent to win the pennant.[8]

In the end, the scheme never came close to fruition. It isn't clear how far it got—whether it was derailed by MLB Commissioner Kenesaw Mountain Landis, as Veeck claimed, or simply an idea that Veeck and Saperstein discussed but took no further, as some believe. In any case, there are good reasons to believe that Veeck and Saperstein were serious about trying it.[9]

At Veeck's request, Saperstein compiled a list in 1942 of the Negro League players who were best prepared for Major League Baseball. That same year, Veeck met with Phillies owner Gerry Nugent—a necessary first step if he sought to acquire the club.[10] In early 1944, Saperstein told a sportswriter that he didn't expect individual Black players to be welcomed onto existing MLB teams. "Best thing they can do," said Saperstein, "is enter the big leagues as a team—not as individuals mingling with whites."[11] This assessment strongly suggests that Saperstein was on board with creating an all-Black team. In addition, Veeck recalled the Phillies scheme in a 1953 conversation with sportswriter Shirley Povich, disclosing, "Abe Saperstein, an owner in the Negro [Leagues], and I had plans."[12]

In 1954, a *Chicago Defender* article quoted Saperstein describing the Phillies scheme. "[Veeck] was going to take the Phils to spring training in Florida and then—on the day the season opened—dispose of the entire team," Saperstein said. "Meanwhile, with a team composed entirely of Negroes, who would have trained separately, he would have opened the [National League] season."[13]

It's also noteworthy that in 1943, the year after the scheme was hatched, star Negro Leagues pitcher Satchel Paige promoted the idea of an all-Black team in Major League Baseball. "I wish we could start out with a club of our own—all colored boys," Paige told a reporter. "Later, when they got used to us playing, they could mix the teams up."[14] Although the timing of his comment might have been coincidental, it's reasonable to believe that Paige, who was close to Saperstein, had been briefed on the Phillies plan and hoped that Veeck might try the same strategy with a different MLB team.

Saperstein and others who sought to integrate Major League Baseball were confronting a racist practice with very deep roots. The National Association of Base Ball Players adopted a rule in 1867 to bar "any club which may be composed of one or more colored persons."[15] But enforcement was spotty, as more than fifty Black athletes played on racially integrated teams between 1883 and 1898.[16]

In 1887, it was front-page news in the *New York Times* when the St. Louis Browns owner canceled a game against the all-Black Cuban Giants after receiving a mutinous letter signed by eight of his players. In their letter, the St. Louis players declared that they would "cheerfully play against white people at any time" but would not play the Giants.[17] In 1898, a Black team disbanded after playing half a season in the Iron and Oil Base Ball League, a semipro association of six teams in New York and Pennsylvania. As the new century arrived, historian Jules Tygiel wrote, "the national pastime was a Jim Crow enterprise."[18]

In the following decades, Black and white players played with or against each other in only a handful of games, and no MLB team was integrated. During the 1930s, Satchel Paige spent the offseason of the Negro Leagues pitching in the California Winter Leagues, in which Black ballclubs faced white teams and often won. In one game, Paige faced Rogers Hornsby, a future Hall of Famer and suspected Ku Klux Klan member, who had sworn never to smoke, drink, or go to the movie theater, fearful that watching movies would cause eyestrain. Hornsby must have questioned his eyesight as he left the ballpark that day because Paige struck him out three times.[19]

Glaring racism was exposed during a 1938 interview that Jake Powell, a New York Yankees outfielder, had with Chicago White Sox radio announcer Bob Elson, Saperstein's boyhood friend. When Elson asked Powell how he kept in shape during the offseason, the Yankees outfielder said, "I'm a policeman and I beat niggers over the head with my [nightstick] while on my beat."[20] Powell was suspended for ten days.[21]

Saperstein thought the creation of an all-Black team was the most viable path for racially integrating Major League Baseball because he had little faith that an existing team would step forward to sign one or more Black players. He also may have worried that pressuring MLB teams to add Black players could backfire on Negro Leagues teams, most of which played their games in MLB parks. A *San Francisco Examiner* columnist interviewed Saperstein in 1943 and surmised that Saperstein was reluctant to push for Major League Baseball to accept Black players out of fear that "if the majors get sore enough to bar the Negro clubs from their parks, there just won't be any organized colored baseball."[22]

Bigotry endured largely because white fans, sportswriters, and MLB officials devised clever language to rationalize it. In 1945, a Wisconsin newspaper columnist wrote that integrating Major League Baseball would actually *harm* Black athletes: "To merge Negroes with whites would destroy the individual style that is their main asset."[23]

Jackie Robinson took the first step toward shattering MLB's racist barrier in 1945 when the Brooklyn Dodgers signed him to a contract. He played his first game as a Brooklyn Dodger in April 1947, but the year before, Saperstein was skeptical that Robinson would get much playing time. He told a sports columnist that Robinson was likely to sit on the Dodgers bench for a while and then later manage a Black club. Alf Cottrell, the columnist, shared his impression that Saperstein felt "organized baseball still doesn't want colored ballplayers no matter how much they have on the horsehide."[24]

Even after the Dodgers promoted Robinson to their major league roster in early 1947, Saperstein called it a "pure accident." The event that prompted the Dodgers to elevate Robinson, Saperstein claimed, came right before the season when their manager, Leo Durocher, was suspended for associating with gamblers. "It stirred up such a hornet's nest of publicity that [Brooklyn General Manager] Branch Rickey had to grab something quick to take Durocher out of the headlines," said Saperstein. "[Rickey] grabbed Robinson and put him in a Dodger uniform."[25]

Contrary to Saperstein's theory, there is ample evidence that the Dodgers had planned to promote Robinson to the National League before Durocher's suspension. During spring training, shortly before he was suspended, Durocher told several Brooklyn players who didn't want a Black teammate "that Robinson was going to open the season with us come hell or high water, and if they didn't like it they could leave now and we'd trade them or get rid of them some other way."[26]

Months before promoting Robinson to the Dodgers' regular-season roster, Rickey had met with leaders of Brooklyn's Black community, seeking their help to make Robinson's transition to the major leagues as stress-free as possible. According to one sportswriter, Black leaders were told "there must be no gloating by Negroes when Robinson was brought up" to play in Brooklyn.[27]

If Saperstein deliberately spun his fanciful tale about the factors that elevated Robinson to Brooklyn, his motivation isn't obvious. But there are a few likely explanations.

First, Saperstein might have sought to detract from Rickey's accomplishment because he resented the Dodgers executive for maligning the Negro Leagues years earlier as being "in the zone of a racket."[28] Although some Black team owners did operate "policy" rackets that functioned like a local lottery, Saperstein may have taken offense at Rickey's denigration of a baseball organization with which he was closely associated.[29]

Second, Saperstein was probably disappointed that the player breaking the color barrier was Robinson and not a Black player whom he represented. Therefore, casting this achievement as driven by circumstance might have been his way to downplay its importance and preserve his pride. Although Saperstein wanted to see Major League Baseball integrated, he wanted to be the one who helped make it happen.

Third, Saperstein might have been looking for an excuse for why his bench-warming prediction for Robinson's future proved wrong.

Around 1970, a few years after Saperstein's death, his family asked Marie Linehan for any correspondence in the office files between Saperstein and famous people. The family even gave Linehan a list of celebrities whose writings might be there. Linehan seemed annoyed by the request and wrote a testy note back:

> Re Jackie Robinson. It is a fact that Abe despised Robinson, had absolutely nothing to do with his career. It is a fact that he discussed this with Wendell Smith—telling Wendell he thought he was out of his mind to bother with this matter. Abe did not sponsor or encourage Robinson. The one thing Abe did not want was for black players to break into the Major Leagues.[30]

It's hard to accept this statement at face value. Wendell Smith, a Black sportswriter, was close to Robinson and was hired by Rickey to travel with Robinson when he broke into baseball. Smith also ghostwrote a newspaper column for Robinson. Yet Saperstein and Smith were also close, and Smith's wife Wyonella later worked in Saperstein's office. It's unlikely the two men would have remained on friendly terms if Smith had felt Saperstein opposed the integration of baseball. Smith once wrote that Saperstein reacted to Robinson entering the majors by telling him, "I've been praying for this day." Smith declared that Saperstein "did as much as anyone we know to break down the barrier against the Negro in Major League Baseball."[31]

According to Saperstein family lore, a tearful Robinson telephoned Saperstein at home when he first broke into the majors and told him about being spit on by racist fans. Saperstein supposedly encouraged him to keep going, but there's no more independent support for that story than for how Linehan described Saperstein's views about Robinson and integration.

Clearly, though, Robinson was a revered figure in the Saperstein family in later years. Saperstein's granddaughter Abra Berkley recalled her mother Eloise—Abe's daughter, who was probably closest to him—weeping over Robinson's struggle shortly before her death in 2018. They were on a trip to California, and Abra and her children briefly left Eloise at the hotel.

"I come back to the hotel room," Abra said. "She is bawling, like she is so upset. She is still in her nightgown. And it's like 2, 3 in the afternoon. And I'm like, 'What's the matter? Did you fall? What happened?' She had watched [the movie] *42* for the first time because we were in the hotel room, and it just came on. And she was like, 'I remember the whole thing.' It just all came back to her. I don't know when I had seen her that upset. She was like, 'That was what happened. [Robinson] had called.'"[32]

Without additional evidence, it's impossible to know how Saperstein felt about Robinson. But what seems likely is that Saperstein was less enthusiastic about Black players breaking into Major League Baseball if he wasn't involved in making it happen. Yet when Saperstein could help make it happen, he did.

Several months into Robinson's rookie season, Saperstein told a sportswriter that the Brooklyn infielder was having an excellent year, adding that "his deportment off the field is perfect."[33] Saperstein said it was inevitable for every MLB team to have at least one Black player.[34] If there had been bad blood between Saperstein and Robinson, it is unlikely that the Dodger star would have agreed in 1957 to be the main speaker at a charity dinner honoring Saperstein.[35]

With the color barrier broken, Saperstein devoted greater energy to promoting other Negro Leagues stars whom he felt should be signed. In 1947, soon after Robinson's debut, Veeck—who had purchased the Indians the year before—asked Saperstein and Smith to identify the most promising prospect in the Negro Leagues. "So Wendell, Abe and I met a couple of times and we arrived at Larry Doby as the best young player in the [Negro] league," said Veeck.[36] Cleveland signed Doby to a contract, and on July 5, 1947, he became the first Black athlete to play for an American League club.

Days later, Saperstein tried to negotiate a deal for another Black prospect, Sam Jethroe, to join the San Francisco Seals, a white minor league team. Jethroe was so fast, said a teammate, that he could "outrun the word of God."[37] Saperstein couldn't strike a deal, but Jethroe eventually made it to the major leagues in 1950, and he led the league in stolen bases with the Boston Braves and was named Rookie of the Year.

Yet Saperstein's most significant contribution to the integration of baseball occurred when he helped to consummate the most important personnel decision of the 1948 MLB season—the Cleveland Indians' signing of Satchel Paige. Once again, he worked behind the scenes with Veeck.[38]

Soon after Veeck bought the team, he telephoned Saperstein and asked whether Paige's pitching abilities remained solid. It was a reasonable question for the Indians owner to pose. Only three years earlier, Saperstein told a sportswriter that Paige's pitching skills had diminished: "He has lost his high, hard one."[39] But by 1946, Saperstein told Veeck that Paige remained talented. Still, Veeck was not ready to give the pitcher a shot, perhaps worried that Paige was too old. Although historians now agree that he was born on July 7, 1906, Paige encouraged speculation about his age and claimed he didn't know his birth date because a goat had eaten the family Bible in which this date was recorded.[40]

Two weeks into the 1948 season, Veeck hired Saperstein as a special representative of the Indians. He was charged with organizing a scouting program to identify Negro Leagues players who had the skills to join Cleveland or its farm clubs.[41]

At the start of June 1948, the Indians were only one game behind the first-place Philadelphia Athletics. That month, Saperstein joined Veeck at a Cleveland ballgame in which the team's relief pitchers took a beating. Afterward, Saperstein recommended Paige as the solution for the Indians' bullpen woes. Paige recalled that "there still wasn't anybody in the Negro Leagues who could throw better than me. Abe knew that."[42]

With Veeck's team in the thick of a pennant race and growing concerns about the bullpen, the Indians owner invited Paige for a tryout. Saperstein and the hurler arrived in Cleveland on July 7, 1948—Paige's forty-second birthday. As Veeck and Saperstein watched, Paige fired pitch after pitch to Indians player-manager Lou Boudreau, who caught the righthander's throws.[43]

Minutes after the tryout, Veeck signed Paige to a contract that paid him $25,000 for the final three months of the season. It instantly made Paige the oldest MLB rookie in history. As part of the Paige deal, Cleveland gave

$15,000 each to Saperstein and the owner of the Kansas City Monarchs, the team that had contractual rights to Paige. Saperstein's financial interest in the Cleveland Indians went beyond the Paige acquisition; he owned stock in the club.[44]

The publisher of *Sporting News* criticized the Paige signing and argued that acquiring a player at such an advanced age "is to demean the standards" of professional baseball.[45] Some sportswriters and MLB players viewed Paige's signing as a publicity gimmick. Years later, Paige offered his take. "Maybe Mr. Veeck did want some publicity," he wrote, "but he wanted a pitcher, too. There was only one guy around who could fill both orders."[46]

When Paige joined the team, it was a boon for attendance—and not only at Cleveland's Municipal Stadium. When he first pitched in Chicago, Comiskey Park recorded its third-highest attendance ever: 51,013 fans. Paige was brilliant, hurling a shutout as the Indians won, 5-0.[47]

Saperstein could have relaxed the rest of that summer, reveling in the knowledge that Paige was making a positive impact for the Indians. Instead, he aggressively pursued other players for the team to consider. Saperstein traveled to New York to scout a pitcher in the Negro Leagues, but he listened carefully when this hurler raved about a teammate named Minnie Miñoso. Saperstein urged Cleveland to sign Miñoso, and team officials did so. However, the Indians later traded the Cuban-born Miñoso to the Chicago White Sox, where he blossomed into a solid hitter and produced a Hall of Fame career.[48]

As for Paige, he finished the 1948 season with a 6-1 record. Every one of those six wins mattered because the Indians ended the regular season tied with the Boston Red Sox. In a one-game playoff, Cleveland prevailed and went on to capture the World Series in six games.

Two years earlier, when Major League rosters remained all-white, a reporter asked Cleveland's Bob Feller whether he'd seen any Black players with the talent to play in Major League Baseball. "Haven't seen one—not one," he replied. "Maybe Paige when he was young. When you name him you're done."[49] However, the performances of the "aged" Paige and the talented Doby had a lot to do with the World Series ring that Feller won in 1948. And Veeck appreciated the man who had championed Paige. "Abe really delivered for me at that time," Veeck said. "If he hadn't come through with Satchel Paige when he did, I doubt we would have won."[50]

Black sportswriters were divided on Saperstein's role in desegregating Major League Baseball. Two months before the Paige tryout that Saperstein facilitated, sportswriter Doc Young lamented that Saperstein was "the door through which our players must step" to reach the major leagues.[51] That same week, Fay Young (no relation) wrote a *Chicago Defender* column praising Veeck's decision to lean on Saperstein's advice for choosing additional Black players for his club. "Veeck named the right man. No one else could or would give the time or energy," he wrote, adding: "If Abe can't do it, we don't know who can."[52]

Yet Doc Young complained that Saperstein should have done more while Satchel Paige was in his prime to get him into Major League Baseball. This criticism seems unfair. Owners of MLB teams stubbornly resisted integration, and even four straight last-place finishes by the Phillies couldn't persuade their owner to give Roy Campanella—a future Hall of Famer—the tryout that the Black catcher requested in 1942.[53]

Saperstein couldn't get Paige into Major League Baseball before 1948, but he did help the pitcher attain an affluent lifestyle through barnstorming games and temporary contracts that supplemented his Negro Leagues salary. By the early 1940s, Paige was earning about $40,000 a season. This was probably higher than any MLB pitcher and more than triple the average salary paid to players on the pennant-winning New York Yankees in 1942. In addition, if Veeck's Phillies scheme had come to fruition, Paige's name was surely high on the list Saperstein had prepared of players who could comprise an all-Black team for Philadelphia.[54]

Years later, Saperstein was concerned about his legacy as a groundbreaker who spurred integration. A sportswriter who talked with him in 1952 said that Saperstein felt Rickey deserved his share of credit but added that Saperstein "says some day he will tell the whole [backstory] of Negro players. He thinks he did much more than Rickey to make it possible for colored players to reach the majors."[55]

9

THE PEOPLE PERSON

*Saperstein charmed the press, befriended some players,
and was a family man from far away*

A be Saperstein was in the people-pleasing business, determined to lavish attention on the millions of fans who saw his teams perform as well as his players, his traveling staff, his office staff, local promoters, concession-aires, sportswriters, and anyone else he met in the course of business.

Tending to his family was at least as challenging, since he was often half a world away. He eagerly hired family members to staff his operation, and his wife and children sometimes traveled with him. But phone calls, letters, postcards, and air-mailed gifts often took the place of face-to-face contact. It wasn't the ideal situation, but it was the life that Saperstein chose, and he tried to make the best of it.

One group that was always well tended by Saperstein was sportswriters. There were no Excel spreadsheets or media management software to simplify his task. Instead he simply showed up in their newsrooms, offered them peppermints, and chatted with them for hours. He sent them news clippings, press releases, and personal notes. And he gave them fruit.

"Thanx to Abe Saperstein for that box of choice apples from Wenatchee, Washington," wrote sports columnist Chester Washington in the *Pittsburgh Courier*.[1]

Globetrotters players threaten Saperstein with a dunking in the River Jordan during a 1965 tour.

Sportswriter John O'Donnell of the *Davenport (Iowa) Democrat and Leader* got his own Saperstein package from Wenatchee, but not apples. They were "cherries as big as apples—crab apples anyway, if you want to get technical," O'Donnell wrote. And he seemed genuinely touched: "A guy never knows when somebody is having a kind thought about him somewhere."[2]

Saperstein often targeted sportswriters from small and midsized news outlets, figuring they would be more likely to respond to his attention than the big-city scribes. Joe Sephus of the *Cumberland (Maryland) Times* gushed at length about the "attractive pen and desk set" that the Globetrotters gave him. "It isn't often that traveling teams, especially one of the importance of the Globetrotters, bother to leave behind any evidence of their appreciation of publicity."[3]

Oh, Saperstein appreciated the publicity, alright. For years he threw a lavish luncheon for football writers gathered in Chicago for the annual exhibition between the National Football League champions and college all-stars, even though Saperstein had almost nothing to do with football. He knew, however, that fine food and drink would make sportswriters think fondly of him and his Globetrotters. The luncheons included such entertainment as Kentucky Governor Happy Chandler singing "My Old Kentucky Home" in 1956 and a comic doing a John F. Kennedy impersonation just a few months before JFK's assassination in 1963.[4]

Sports columnist Sec Taylor of the *Des Moines Register* disclosed in his column that Saperstein had presented him with a Swiss watch and gave plaques to other sportswriters at the 1952 luncheon. "However," Taylor wrote, "I want to assure everyone that they are not bribes. The foregoing column was written because I thought it would interest many readers."[5]

Beyond the freebies, it was clear why Saperstein was a favorite of the press. They had news holes to fill every day, and Saperstein supplied the anecdotes, rumors, and predictions that helped them do it. Saperstein's playfulness worked well with the press. A 1957 Associated Press story shared the tongue-in-cheek news that he was bringing a basketball-playing kangaroo named Jumping Jupiter back from Australia to join the Globetrotters.[6]

Saperstein's energy and reporters' laziness also played a role. Many of the Globetrotters' news releases went straight into newspapers' pages with little or no editing. Saperstein's staff wrote them for that very purpose. And Saperstein created his own echo chamber by sending newspapers' clippings to other newspapers. That compelled a sportswriter at the *Ogden (Utah) Standard Examiner* to turn the words of eleven other sportswriters into a column headlined "Newspapermen Praise Globetrotters."[7]

Saperstein endeared himself to plenty of other people who had no newspaper pages to fill. There are scores of stories about his contributions to charities ranging from the Olympic Fund to the March of Dimes. This was both good business and just plain good works. And in many cases Saperstein's generosity was quiet, with no attempt at publicity.

For example, in 1944, Saperstein presented a $525 check to the Service Athletic Fund during a Globetrotters game in San Francisco. But he later added $601 in cash privately, a fact revealed to the press by the fund's treasurer, not the donor. The US Olympic team was a special focus of Saperstein's charity, reflecting his interest in promoting America's place in the world. For a Globetrotters benefit in 1952 before a Seattle crowd of twelve thousand, the team wouldn't even accept reimbursement for rail fares, hotels, and meals. "That will be my own personal contribution," Saperstein said.[8]

A *Spokane (Washington) Spokesman-Review* story with an unfortunate headline, "Black Magic to Cure Polio," detailed a Globetrotters benefit appearance and quoted famed sportswriter Grantland Rice as saying the Trotters had "given themselves to more games staged for worthwhile causes than any team in sports."[9]

Saperstein's brother Morry, not an objective observer but a close one, declared: "I know he's given away fortunes to help old players, friends, acquaintances, charities. He never seeks anything in return. I try to tell him it would be nice to stash away a pile or two for a rainy day, but he looks at me with hurt feelings and says, 'The purpose of money is essentially to make people happy. Let's keep it that way!'"[10]

Of course, Saperstein and his players didn't always get along, and he eventually broke with some of his biggest stars, such as Goose Tatum and Marques Haynes. But those disagreements were often more professional than personal. Saperstein sued Globetrotters star Babe Pressley for breach of contract in 1945, yet three years later Pressley was Saperstein's trusted player-coach when the Trotters defeated the Minneapolis Lakers at Chicago Stadium.[11]

Saperstein sued Haynes and was countersued by him, but the star dribbler attended Saperstein's funeral anyway. "I wanted to make sure he didn't jump out of the casket," Haynes joked, but then added, "OK, I did it out of respect."[12]

Saperstein tried to foster a paternalistic but affectionate relationship with the players, calling them "the boys" and preferring that they call him "Skip." He paid careful attention to team dynamics. According to "clown prince" Meadowlark Lemon, Saperstein "kept players from forming cliques by changing roommates whenever he felt it necessary."[13]

Life on the road was demanding for all athletes and especially for those working for the hard-driving Saperstein. The pay was high compared to the other limited options offered to Black men, but it wasn't a bonanza. Salaries for professional athletes, both Black and white, were a tiny fraction of what they are today.

"What he paid us was in many cases better than what the [National Basketball Association] teams were making back in those days," said Mannie Jackson, a Globetrotter in the early 1960s, but "we worked a lot harder for our money than the NBA. We played every night."[14]

One of the Globetrotters who thought he was underpaid and otherwise mistreated by Saperstein was Andy Johnson, whose son Mark wrote a book about his father's career titled *Basketball Slave.*

"Abe tested [Andy] on occasion," Mark Johnson wrote. "One time on a European tour, Abe threatened Andy by saying that all he knew was basketball and he wouldn't be able to do anything else with his life. In true Andy Johnson fashion, Dad came back with a quip that, ironically, Abe probably remembers, even in the afterlife. Andy said, 'I will go back home and be a gravedigger, Abe, and I will definitely keep in touch.'"[15]

On the positive side, Mark Johnson noted in his book that Saperstein's son, Jerry, helped him secure his father's NBA pension when the league put up resistance.

Plenty of other players remembered Saperstein fondly.

"He believed in human rights," said Globetrotters veteran Hallie Bryant. "We were someplace . . . we couldn't stay in a certain hotel, so Abe decided he would cancel the game. That said a lot about him. He decided we would not even play and we would move on to the next city."[16]

Even in his later years when he was a businessman with far-flung interests, Saperstein tried to stay friendly with his Globetrotters players. "Abe was close to the players, knew us all, was on the court all the time," Mannie Jackson said, adding that Saperstein "was kind of a bridge between the white community and those of us who were on the other side of the fence."[17]

One way he stayed close was through card games with players. "We played a game called conquian," said Bobby Hunter, the last Globetrotter recruited by Saperstein. "It was a game from the Negro Baseball League. It's like gin and you take out the eights, nines, and tens. I used to beat his ass."[18]

Saperstein's card games with Hunter occurred during the recruiting process, and "I think he used the cards to enter into my mind. . . . He was pretty good because he could talk and play," Hunter said.

Saperstein was known for coming to the rescue when athletes struggled. He had helped Major League Baseball's Cleveland Indians acquire Black slugger Luke Easter. But in 1951, Easter was in a batting slump. The Indians asked Saperstein to travel to Cleveland, meet with Easter, and offer a pep talk. Saperstein brought something for Easter's ailing knee—an ointment Saperstein called "Colorado clay." Perhaps it was Saperstein's reassuring words or perhaps it was luck. Easter's bat suddenly got hot, and he went ten for twenty-nine over the next seven games. But then Easter's sore knee forced him to leave the Cleveland lineup. Saperstein's words couldn't heal a knee. Neither could Colorado clay.[19]

Among the athletes praising Saperstein's generosity was Bernie Price, a Globetrotter from 1936 to 1948. "I never went to college," Price said. "As a result, I couldn't find a job during the summer. Whenever I needed money, Abe gave it to me."[20]

Many other players had conflicting feelings about Saperstein, who gave them opportunities but left no doubt who was boss. "I felt like I had to treat him as a father figure, a Santa Claus, to get anything out of him," Meadowlark Lemon said. "None of us really liked him, but for some reason we loved him."[21]

The Globetrotter closest to Saperstein was Inman Jackson, of course. Saperstein's last will and testament left 4 percent of his estate to him. "Jackson was more like a brother to Abe than an employee," said Gloria Klotz, whose husband, Red, owned the Globetrotters' longtime opponent, the Washington Generals.[22]

Jackson was close enough to Saperstein that he could get away with playing practical jokes on him. At a crowded Kansas diner one day, Saperstein and Jackson had to sit apart at the counter. Saperstein was well known for wanting his food well done, and would tell waitresses his eggs should be "scorched." But this time the eggs came back only lightly cooked. When Saperstein and Jackson got back into the car, Jackson couldn't stop laughing, and Saperstein insisted he explain. Jackson told him he'd informed the waitress that Saperstein was a mental patient in Jackson's care, and that the waitress should ignore whatever he said about how the food was cooked.[23]

Like other friends, they would sometimes get on each other's nerves. They generally roomed together on the road, but after one fight they gave each other the silent treatment for three weeks even though they were stay-ing in the same room and sometimes sharing the same bed.[24]

Even when not on tour, they spent time together, frequently as fishing partners. "Inman Jackson was a big fisherman," Saperstein's cousin Gerald Saperstein recalled. "Abe used to take him for a week or two up to Interna-tional Falls, Minnesota, fishing. Abe didn't know anything about fishing but Inman Jackson knew about it."[25]

Saperstein eventually learned, though, and fishing became a part of many tours. He landed marlin off Hawaii, flounder in New Zealand's Auckland Harbor, walleye in Ontario, wahoo off Bermuda, and three-foot sharks in the North Sea.[26]

The private Saperstein was quite different from the version projected by his brassy quotes and his beaming public smile. He was not the life of the party. Family friend Burt Tucker recalled Saperstein as "a soft-spoken guy with a lovely smile. Never talked business. We didn't even talk politics. Just talked about things in general. He had a great knowledge of everything. He was a different person [in private]. Like he shut it off. He was soft; he was casual."[27]

Saperstein's relatives saved hundreds of postcards he sent from all cor-ners of the world. His wife, Sylvia, got various cards with sexual jokes, including a postcard from Mozambique of a bare-breasted woman that Saperstein called "the Jayne Mansfield of black Africa." He specialized in tortured puns, sending a postcard to his daughter Eloise from Barcelona, Spain, that included the phrase "con mucho goose toe." A card from the Netherlands to his sister-in-law Bernice Franklin said, "Wooden shoe know I would get in 'Dutch' over 'Two Lips.'" But Saperstein could be serious, too, with a postcard to Bernice from the Mediterranean Sea city of Tiberias that said simply, "A spiritual uplift—that's Israel."[28]

The obvious conflict between Saperstein's jet-setting and his desire to stay close to his family was demonstrated by a 1946 anecdote recalled by his nephew Roy Raemer.

"Our family was invited to his home for New Year's Eve along with a lot of other people, relatives and others, business associates, whatever," Raemer said. "So it was a big crowd in his home for New Year's Eve. Half-way through the party, maybe nine o'clock or so, he leaves. 'Where are you going?' 'I'm going to California for the Rose Bowl game.' Some people picked him up, his friends. They must've chartered a plane. They went to the airport and they went to the Rose Bowl game."[29]

In those rare times when he was home, Saperstein would take family members to the Tally-Ho restaurant in north suburban Evanston in his fire engine red Cadillac or treat them to his favorite musical, "South Pacific." Saperstein showed a special interest in the young people in his family. "He loved being my uncle," said nephew Guy Saperstein. "He was very attentive to me. He almost treated me like one of his kids. If I ever happened to mention anything I'd like or I wanted, a week later it would show up on my front doorstep."[30]

Abe's niece Joyce Leviton recalled his genuine interest. "When I went to college at the University of Arizona," she said, "he would call me at school at all different times and talk to me about how I was doing in school, what I was studying, to make sure I was doing the right thing."[31]

Like others, Leviton recalled his grueling travel schedule. In fact, "the only time I remember him canceling a trip" was when his daughter Eloise's child Lonni Berkley had roseola as an infant. "He and I walked her in her stroller all night," Leviton said.[32]

Lonni, who was six years old when Saperstein died, remembered him as "a big teddy bear."[33]

"He traveled with the team, and he was gone . . . probably three hundred days of the year would not be an exaggeration," Lonni said. "But there was not a day of my life when my Papa Abe was not there because I got a postcard, I'd get dolls from every country that he visited."

Lonni spent so much time at her grandparents' house down the block that her mother, Eloise, upbraided her for assuming she could visit anytime. When Abe overheard that, he called the top executive of the phone company at home at night and arranged for a hotline to be installed the next day between the two homes, allowing Lonni to call and invite herself over whenever she wanted.[34]

Lonni treasures a photo showing her as a young girl joining singer and bandleader Cab Calloway as he performs at halftime during a Globetrotters game. She's wearing a black velvet sequined skirt that Saperstein brought back from Mexico.

Saperstein lavished attention on his daughter. "His favorite was Eloise," said her friend Burt Tucker, recalling that she would recount stories of her trips with her father, including a car ride around Paris with boxer Sugar Ray Robinson. When they were apart, Abe was warm in his correspondence, ending letters with phrases such as "a whole barrel of kisses."[35]

Saperstein was less tender with his son, Jerry, and annoyed that he seemed to show more interest in spending money than making money.

Jerry's cousin Guy Saperstein recalled visiting Chicago from California when he was fifteen and being shown around town by Jerry, who was a few years older. "Jerry picked me up in a brand new Cadillac El Dorado convertible," Guy said. "He's got two Playboy Bunnies in the car. And we drive to the Playboy Mansion. . . . We'd go shopping and Jerry would pull out a wad, you know, $100 bills. No credit cards for him. If he liked a shirt, he would say, 'Give me a dozen of those.' I've never seen anybody spend money like that."[36]

Jerry's son Lanier Saperstein never met his grandfather Abe, but he heard a lot from his father. Lanier said he believed his grandfather loved Jerry and he knew Jerry respected his father, though Jerry held "a degree of anger and resentment" toward him.[37]

"Abe, from what I understand, did not trust Jerry because he viewed Jerry as a playboy," Lanier said. "I always got the impression that Abe would've liked to have Jerry take over the team, but he didn't trust him enough to take over the team."

Saperstein's relationship with his wife, Sylvia, was loving but was challenged by his long absences.

"My grandma let him travel around," said Abra Berkley, who was born two years after her grandfather Abe's death but was close with Sylvia. "That was his passion. They were together when he had already started traveling with the Globetrotters. She grew this with him. She knew that this was his dream. She would have liked for him to be around and help raise the kids. . . . She would go on the road with him every now and then. I mean, she had two little kids, so she wasn't traveling with him all that much. . . . I think it was hard, and she didn't complain. It was never that she didn't love him. He was just really big, so big of life, so large. And her life was here."[38]

Saperstein tried to let his wife know he was thinking of her. As their daughter Eloise recalled, "My father traveled a lot, but he made sure to arrange that my mother would receive a greeting card and a bouquet of flowers from him every Thursday."[39]

Sylvia didn't have much to do with the sports business. But in one case she contributed. Eloise said that when Saperstein was home, he kept a legal pad by his bedside and would brainstorm new plays for the Globetrotters. "One night, my mother, who knew nothing about basketball, was trying to get him to go to bed, so she came up with an idea," Eloise said. "She said, 'Why don't you put one player on top of another player's shoulders and have him dunk the ball?' My father liked the idea so much he used the play from then on to end all his games."[40]

People who knew Sylvia described her warmth and kindness. "Sylvia was a very bright woman . . . a lovely, lovely woman. A very caring person," said Burt Tucker.[41] But Sylvia referred to herself as a "typical, old-fashioned Jewish wife."[42]

Interviewed a few months after Saperstein's death, she described him this way: "Abe was a guy who liked to give more than receive. We lived in Chicago and one night after a show we were on the way home. Abe turned to me and said, 'Mom, you know how much I gave away tonight? You'd never believe it.' That was Abe, always giving money away to ex-fighters and guys down and out."[43]

Saperstein gave presents to her, too, but was oddly uncomfortable with her gratitude.

"Returning from a trip he would bring gifts," Sylvia said. "Well, he didn't like it when I got sentimental and thanked him. So I would write him a letter of thanks and send it to his office. Then he would cable an acknowledgement back to me."[44]

10

THE TEAM PLAYER

*Saperstein helped the NBA survive hard times, but
his relations with the league grew bitter*

The National Basketball Association is a slick, popular product today,
with franchises in thirty cities. But when Abe Saperstein started in
the basketball business, the NBA didn't even exist, and when Saperstein's
Globetrotters emerged as an unqualified success during the postwar years,
the NBA was a sloppy mess, with teams like the Anderson (Indiana) Packers and the Waterloo (Iowa) Hawks struggling to survive and often failing.

The NBA began as the Basketball Association of America for the 1946–
1947 season, founded by hockey team owners looking for additional uses
for their arenas. The league took its current name three years later, when
it merged with the National Basketball League. But it wasn't exactly big
time, despite the hockey moguls' venues like Madison Square Garden and
Boston Garden. Other teams performed in primitive conditions. The Syracuse (New York) Nationals, for example, played in the State Fair Coliseum,
where guy wires for the baskets went into the stands and could be yanked
by hometown fans to shake the basket when visitors shot free throws.[1] The
NBA started with seventeen teams, but five years later it had dwindled to
eight.

"For some unexplainable reason, professional basketball has never
reached the financial heights that its promoters hoped it would," sportswriter

Wilt Chamberlain was a Globetrotter for a year before he was eligible to join the National Basketball Association, and he also went on the Trotters' foreign tours in later years. The seven-foot-one star played point guard.

Wendell Smith wrote in 1950. "There are numerous leagues scattered around the country and all of them are operating in the red. The largest and most pretentious is the National Basketball Association. It stretches from Boston all the way to Denver. Some of the wealthiest promoters in the country have money invested in this basketball octopus and practically all are fighting off the wolf."[2]

The exception to pro basketball's tale of woe was an independent team, the Harlem Globetrotters. In a packed Chicago Stadium in 1948, the Trotters had defeated the Minneapolis Lakers, who were on their way to becoming the NBA's first great team. Saperstein recalled a conversation with Lakers star George Mikan after the game.

"You're the best center in basketball," Saperstein told Mikan.

"No, I'm not. Sweetwater Clifton is," Mikan responded.

"Sweetwater Clifton? Hmm. Is he a colored boy?"

"Yes."

"Thanks for reminding me, George. We'll have to have Sweetwater on our team."[3]

Always looking to improve, Saperstein indeed signed Nathaniel Clifton, a six-foot-six above-the-rim force who was given the nickname "Sweetwater" in his youth because of his fondness for soda pop.[4]

Clifton was in the Trotters lineup when they faced the Lakers in 1949 in an attempt to prove their last-second victory the previous year was no fluke. And prove it they did, winning so easily that they went into their comedy routine with six minutes left, let the Lakers score the last nine points and still won, 49–45. Clifton guarded Mikan effectively, and when the clowning began, Goose Tatum hid the ball under his jersey, toying with Mikan. The humiliation was accentuated because Movietone News was there to film a newsreel of the game to share with the nation's theater audiences.[5]

The Lakers' hometown paper, the *Minneapolis Tribune*, was disgusted. "After seeing the Harlems humiliate the tired Lakers with a twenty-three-point splurge in the third quarter, the majority of the thousands in the stands went home convinced that the real world champions of professional basketball are Saperstein's independent tourists," the *Tribune* wrote.[6]

The next six times the Globetrotters faced the Lakers, the Lakers won. But the Lakers put an end to the rivalry in 1958, prompting Saperstein to accuse them of committing a "breach of our agreement" under pressure from NBA President Maurice Podoloff. The Lakers apparently thought their six-game winning streak had established their superiority, but it couldn't erase the two times the supposedly greatest basketball team on Earth was toppled by a team of clowns called the Globetrotters.[7]

In fact, that team of clowns kept the whole NBA circus going in the late 1940s and early 1950s. To boost attendance for the struggling league, NBA teams scheduled doubleheaders in which the Globetrotters played another traveling team in the first game and then two NBA teams met in the "feature" contest afterward. There was a problem, though: so many fans left after the Trotters game that, as time went on, the NBA teams often switched up the order and played the league game first.[8]

Because the NBA relied on the Globetrotters to boost the gate, its owners were cautious about angering Saperstein by competing with him for Black players.

Pro basketball's color line wasn't as long-lasting and institutionalized as Major League Baseball's, but the NBA started out as an all-white league. The National Basketball League had Black players, but when it merged with the all-white Basketball Association of America to form the NBA, the surviving NBL teams' rosters had no Black players nor did the BAA teams add any.[9] Even baseball had started desegregating by this point, so the NBA's all-white status was a glaring statement of discrimination.

Red Auerbach, the new Boston Celtics coach at the time, said NBA owners "thought that if [Saperstein] wanted a player, nobody would stand up to him because he wouldn't play in their building. Everybody needed the extra income."[10]

It's unclear whether the threat of a Saperstein boycott was stated explicitly by Saperstein himself or was just something the NBA owners didn't want to test. Either way, Ned Irish, a Madison Square Garden executive who ran the New York Knicks, wasn't having it anymore. At a 1949 meeting of the NBA's board of governors, he asked for a vote on the issue and the board went against him—in effect making the color line official, if confidential. Irish asked for a revote six months later, saying he wanted to sign Sweetwater Clifton and might pull his Knicks out of the league if the policy wasn't rescinded.

Carl Bennett, general manager of the Fort Wayne (Indiana) Pistons and a member of the board at the time, told author Ron Thomas that Philadelphia Warriors general manager and coach Eddie Gottlieb, a close friend of Saperstein, was against letting Black players into the league and warned that "your players will be 75 percent Black in five years and you're not going to draw people." Nonetheless, the board voted to end the color barrier. According to Bennett, Gottlieb told him as they left the meeting: "You dumb SOB. You've ruined professional basketball."[11]

The dam broke at the closed-door NBA draft in Chicago on April 25, 1950.

"Boston takes Charles Cooper of Duquesne," announced Boston Celtics owner Walter Brown.[12]

Another owner asked him, "Walter, don't you know he's a colored boy?"

"I don't give a damn if he's striped or plaid or polka-dot," Brown said. "Boston takes Charles Cooper of Duquesne!"

Two more Black players were drafted by the Washington Capitols in later rounds. And the Knicks were free to bid for the rights to Sweetwater Clifton from the Globetrotters.

By proving that Black players could compete, the Globetrotters had created irresistible pressure on the NBA to eliminate its color line. "Probably those two wins over the Lakers in '48 and '49 were the final wedge for the NBA to integrate," Globetrotters expert Ben Green said. "When your best team gets beat two years in a row by the Harlem Globetrotters—who many people just considered clowns, a show team—it's time to integrate."[13]

But there's a common historical notion that Saperstein, infuriated that he no longer had a lock on Black players, retaliated by refusing to bring the Trotters to Boston and Washington to help the local NBA teams sell tickets. That account was stated as a fact in the *Boston Globe*—but with no indication that the reporter had even tried to talk to Saperstein. The source apparently was Celtics owner Brown, who said of Saperstein: "He is out of the Boston Garden now, as far as I'm concerned!"[14]

If Saperstein was angry, it may have had nothing to do with the color barrier. Saperstein had recruited Chuck Cooper out of college and put him in the Globetrotters lineup in a series of games just before the draft, but he didn't expect Cooper to stay with the Trotters. A week before the draft, he told reporters he had no contract claim to Cooper and thought the Duquesne star could succeed in the NBA because of his outstanding rebounding. Even so, Saperstein apparently wanted some sort of consideration from the Celtics—financial or otherwise—that he didn't get. A week and a half after the draft, the issue was smoothed over when Saperstein met with Brown and the NBA's Podoloff and "turned over the rights" to Cooper, according to a news report. What those rights were is unclear, but Saperstein had his satisfaction. As if to confirm that Saperstein held no grudge against the Celtics, he praised coach Red Auerbach's development of Cooper later that year, saying Auerbach was "bringing him along just right."[15]

Despite reports of a Globetrotters boycott of Boston and Washington to retaliate for their drafting of Black players, the facts tell a different story. The Trotters played a doubleheader with the Celtics at Boston Garden the next March. The supposed boycott of the Washington Capitols went untested because the Caps dropped out of the NBA a few months into the next season. But the Trotters went back to Washington's Uline Arena, owned by the Capitols' founder, the next March. Saperstein continued supporting the NBA with doubleheaders for several years afterward as the league desegregated and slowly built greater financial stability.[16]

The year of that memorable NBA draft, 1950, was Saperstein's breakout year. The Globetrotters made their first trip to Europe. Hollywood started filming a movie about him and his Globetrotters. The team adopted its signature red, white, and blue uniforms, patterned after the outfits worn by its college all-star opponents a decade earlier.[17]

That same year, the Globetrotters boosted their profile in New York by finally playing in Madison Square Garden and opening an office in the Empire State Building, staffed by Saperstein's youngest sister, Fay. The main Chicago office had moved a block east to 127 North Dearborn, to the fifth floor of a Loop building where the Rotary Club was founded decades earlier. Abe Saperstein Sports Enterprises had a plush five-room suite that impressed visitors, but it could have used better security. Burglars who were part of what the *Chicago Tribune* called a "fire-escape gang" broke into nearly a dozen of the building's offices over a weekend, including Saperstein's. The Trotters owner was the first tenant to discover the burglary because, in his usual workaholic manner, he showed up at the office on a Sunday morning. He reported losing at least $400.[18]

Of course, Saperstein was becoming so successful that he hardly missed it. Another highlight of 1950 was the launch of a competition against a new set of college all-stars, a national tour that may have been the single greatest boost to the team's growing fame.[19]

College basketball was still bigger than the pro sport during this era. Saperstein remembered the spectacular success of the Globetrotters' single-game face-off with college all-stars in 1940, as well as a less grand version in 1949, when the Trotters played a team of Midwestern college stars at Chicago Stadium. Saperstein thought a coast-to-coast tour by airplane, featuring the Trotters and a group of college all-stars, seemed like a sure hit, and he was right. With his typical bluster, he called it the World Series of Basketball. It began with eighteen games in 1950 and became an annual nationwide tour that sometimes overshadowed the NBA finals. On April 18, 1951, for example, the Globetrotters game against the College All-Stars in Milwaukee drew 11,275 fans. That same evening, the New York Knicks and the Rochester (New York) Royals drew only 4,500 for Game 6 of their NBA championship series in New York—a city with twelve times the population of Milwaukee. That same year, 31,648 saw the Trotters and All-Stars play in the Rose Bowl Parade in Pasadena, setting a world attendance record for a basketball game that would be surpassed by the Trotters later that year, with about 50,000 spectators in Rio de Janeiro, Brazil, and 75,000 in Berlin, West Germany.[20]

DePaul coach Ray Meyer was head coach of the All-Stars, a team of seniors whose college eligibility had expired. Basketball fans were thrilled to see so much talent in one place, but critics complained that it took student athletes away from their books at a crucial time and threatened their ability to graduate on time. Accusing Saperstein of "sordid commercialism," *Minneapolis Tribune* columnist Dick Cullum wrote: "The colleges are not going to stand, in the long run, for being mere feeders to the anything-for-a-quick-buck people." Considering how modern college basketball has become a quick route to the NBA well before graduation, it's safe to declare that Cullum's prediction was wrong, very wrong.[21]

The College All-Stars were well compensated. After four or five games on the first tour, Saperstein called the All-Stars into his hotel room and said he would double what he was paying them. That brought their pay for the full tour to about $2,500, plus meal money and various gifts such as wristwatches and radios.[22]

"I never had a contract with Abe Saperstein," Meyer said, "but he always was good to me. He would pay me two, three times what I expected. With the help of money I made from those trips, I was able to buy my home. I made $3,000 or $4,000 every year from that tour."[23]

Saperstein's Globetrotters were paid the same monthly salaries they got on any tour, which was about $300 a month for rookies and slightly more for most veterans. The Trotters were none too pleased by the pay disparity with the predominantly white college kids they were facing. That was one reason Sweetwater Clifton wanted to leave the Trotters, and he told Saperstein he wasn't coming back in 1950–1951, even though he was contracted for that season. Saperstein dealt Clifton to the Knicks during a lunch meeting at an Empire State Building restaurant just nine days after the NBA draft that took down the color line.[24]

But even that deal caused rancor. The Knicks paid Saperstein $12,500 for the rights to Clifton, and he gave $2,500 of that to Clifton. Later, Clifton claimed that Saperstein had promised to give him half of what the Knicks paid, when in fact he gave him only one-fifth. Saperstein's version of this incident is unknown, but it should be noted that he was under no obligation to give Clifton anything. Saperstein held the rights to Clifton, and he sold them.[25] Eventually Clifton and Saperstein reconciled enough that Sweetwater played for Saperstein's Chicago Majors in the American Basketball League at the end of his career.

Saperstein made several attempts to become a major part of the NBA but experienced bitter frustration. In 1950, the Chicago Stags franchise was in such trouble that other NBA owners were keeping it afloat, and the NBA's Podoloff flew all the way to Paris to try to sell the team to Saperstein, who was on the Globetrotters' European tour. Saperstein agreed, at a price of about $40,000, and planned to call the team the Chicago Bruins. The deal fell apart three months later, with Saperstein blaming the NBA's "total failure" to complete the sale and ensure that he had players to start the 1950–1951 season. He also accused the NBA's Minneapolis Lakers of trying to lure Marques Haynes away from his Trotters just as he was trying to join the league. Rather than battle with Saperstein in the press, Podoloff accepted his decision to bow out. Chicago wouldn't have an NBA team for the next decade.[26]

The NBA continued to annoy Saperstein in other ways. A year after the Clifton deal, New York Knicks coach Joe Lapchick said the Trotters had failed to teach Sweetwater the fundamentals: "His jump from the Trotters to the Knicks was comparable to a sandlot baseball player moving directly to the majors." Saperstein responded: "If Lapchick and his Knicks don't think we're big leaguers, why don't they play us? We'll play 'em anytime, anywhere." The Knicks never took up the challenge.[27]

Saperstein's irritation with the NBA might have been eased by the fact that he was doing so much better at the box office: "Right now Abe Saperstein's Harlem Globe Trotters are the only pro team making big money," the *Lincoln (Nebraska) Journal Star* declared.[28]

In 1952, Saperstein addressed one of the Globetrotters' growing needs: finding an opponent good enough to put on a competitive game but not good enough to show up the Trotters. Saperstein approached Louis "Red" Klotz, a former sharpshooting guard for the Baltimore Bullets of the BAA, and persuaded him to create the Washington Generals as a traveling team to tour with the Trotters. The Generals were named in honor of General Dwight Eisenhower, who was elected president that November. Klotz made sure his team was stocked with players who were talented but knew their place as straight men in the show and didn't mind losing. A five-foot-seven overachiever in basketball who was the son of Jewish immigrants, Klotz had a lot in common with Saperstein, and they became close friends. It probably was no coincidence that 1952–1953 was the team's first "regular season"— not including the College All-Star tours—in which the Globetrotters went undefeated.[29]

Saperstein finally bought a piece of an NBA team in 1952, co-owning the Philadelphia Warriors with his pal Eddie Gottlieb, also known as "Gotty" or "the Mogul." Like both Saperstein and Klotz, Gottlieb came from a Jewish immigrant family. Also like Saperstein, he had interests in Black baseball. Gottlieb was big in Philadelphia basketball, cofounding the city's first great team, the Sphas. It wasn't clear how much of the Warriors Saperstein owned—some news reports said 51 percent—but Saperstein left Gottlieb free to serve as the face of the NBA team. It was a close friendship and business alliance for a time, with "Gotty" joining Saperstein on his European travels.

Although he remained extremely busy with the Globetrotters, Saperstein stayed involved with baseball. In 1951, he and other investors helped his good friend Bill Veeck purchase the St. Louis Browns of the American League. Saperstein lent additional support to Veeck by identifying players to assign to the Browns minor league system.[30] By that time, Major League Baseball's integration had left the Negro Leagues in dire straits, and Saperstein's involvement there waned. But he did serve as a close adviser to former Birmingham Black Barons manager Winfield Welch when a syndicate headed by Welch bought the Negro American League's Chicago American Giants.[31]

While globetrotting to spread the gospel of basketball, Saperstein was also boosting baseball. Traveling in Japan in 1952, he sent an urgent cable to Veeck, offering to negotiate "an excellent working arrangement" between the Browns and a ballclub in Japan's Nippon Professional Baseball league. "Can I do it?" he implored Veeck. Although Veeck was unsure if the agreement would violate MLB rules, he gave Saperstein the go-ahead, telling a sportswriter the move might lead to "a real world series some day."[32] In the end, nothing came of that idea, but Saperstein's cross-Pacific diplomacy did bear fruit when he arranged for the Browns to lend the Hankyu Braves two Black players—infielder John Britton Jr. and pitcher James Newberry. It marked the first time that an MLB team lent players to a non-US club.[33]

Saperstein had become such a major sports mogul that his name often came up in speculation when a team was for sale. In 1954, it was rumored that he had MLB ambitions and was talking with the owners of the Philadelphia Athletics about buying their team. A columnist speculated that Saperstein was inquiring on behalf of someone else. Why? Because "it is questionable whether he would have time to operate a baseball franchise."[34] But that was an unlikely theory, considering that time was something Saperstein always seemed to find. The A's rumor never became reality, but Saperstein came far closer to acquiring a National Football League team. In 1953, Saperstein headed an investment group that had an opportunity to buy the San Francisco 49ers for $300,000, but he decided against it. Saperstein later said it was one of the biggest mistakes of his career, a view borne out by the facts: by the mid-1960s, the 49ers were making about $1 million a year from television revenue alone.[35]

Despite that misstep, Saperstein started the 1953–1954 season with a full head of steam in his number one sport, basketball. He had outbid the New York Knicks for their top draft pick, six-foot-eleven Walter Dukes, and made the most of the $25,000 deal by holding a signing ceremony for the press featuring a shiny prop: three thousand silver dollars in a wheelbarrow.

Although the Trotters had become a major draw in big cities, Saperstein was determined not to forget the smaller stops where the team had first established itself. "We owe a lot to the so-called 'sticks,'" he said. "We built ourselves on that solid foundation of one-night stands in the smaller cities and we don't intend to run out on our old friends."[36] In order to meet the demand, Saperstein fielded three separate Globetrotters units in 1953–1954, plus the Kansas City Stars, which functioned as a Trotters farm club.[37]

Weeks into that season, however, Saperstein suffered yet another unpleasant exit by a star player—this time, Marques Haynes. The split was a long time coming for Haynes, who wanted a more evenhanded player-owner relationship than was common at the time. Once when Saperstein came through the locker room and awarded him a $20 bonus for playing a good game, he handed it back, saying, "No, Abe, just put it on my salary." Haynes was particularly rankled by a private comment he said Saperstein made to him. "Abe said Negroes didn't need as much money as the white man needed," Haynes said.[38]

Haynes reportedly asked to be traded to an NBA team but Saperstein refused. So Haynes quit, and when that happened, Saperstein finally announced he was trading Haynes to the NBA, alright—to his own Philadelphia Warriors. Haynes refused to report and started his own barnstorming team, the Marques Haynes All-Stars.[39] Saperstein sued Haynes, complaining that his team's uniforms were too similar to the Trotters', and he won a court order prohibiting Haynes from mentioning the words "Harlem Globetrotters" in his advertising.[40]

A year and a half later, the Trotters' biggest star, Goose Tatum, was gone too. Tatum, considered by some to be the greatest Globetrotter, was a free spirit and a tortured soul. He sometimes seemed to consider the Trotters schedule to be only a suggestion of where and when he should show up. In late March 1948, he boarded a train with the team in Chicago bound for Omaha, Nebraska, got off in Clinton, Iowa, without telling anyone, and was missing for the next ten days. Saperstein fined him $200 and suspended him for the rest of the season, including a trip to Hawaii. This type of thing happened over and over, with suspensions to follow. Goose once explained: "I just used to get a notion I wanted to go some place, so I went."[41]

But when Tatum did show up, which was most of the time, his on-court brilliance and drawing power were so great that he earned the team's top salary, $3,500 a month. By this time the Globetrotters were playing nearly year-round, so Tatum likely made more than $40,000, the highest salary of any basketball player in the world. It wasn't quite up to baseball standards—Ted Williams led the majors with a $67,000 salary in 1955—but Tatum's pay was the equivalent of about $470,000 in today's dollars.[42]

Tatum got into run-ins with Saperstein's brother Rocky, who was the team's road manager, and he slapped or punched Rocky at least twice. But those incidents didn't seem to wreck Abe Saperstein's relationship with Tatum. Even today, the breaking point of their lucrative collaboration is unknown. In March 1955, the Globetrotters played a game that was a huge publicity coup, a benefit for the US Olympic Fund at Great Lakes Naval Training Center north of Chicago. CBS TV's cameras were there, delivering the contest live into twenty-six million homes in eighty-three cities. It was the first complete Trotters game ever broadcast nationwide. Tatum was terrific, pulling all his tricks and scoring thirty-four points. And then, when the cameras were turned off, he was gone. Saperstein suspended him after he missed three games, but he didn't return—ever. The next season he and Marques Haynes formed a team called the Harlem Magicians, which toured for the next two years.[43]

Saperstein did what he always did in such circumstances: find a replacement and tell the press how great the new guy was. As Saperstein bluntly put it: "I made Goose. And I'll make someone else."[44]

Even before he gave up hope that Tatum would return, Saperstein told the press he had four replacement candidates. "All four are good comics," he said, "but Lemon is a natural."[45]

"Lemon" was Meadowlark Lemon, who had dreamed of becoming a Globetrotter since he saw the team in a newsreel as a child. Though not the athlete that Tatum was, Lemon had a big comic personality, and his emergence was an indication that comedy had overtaken sports skill in the Trotters' success formula. Lemon's birth name was believed to be George Meadow Lemon III. "Meadowlark" was a tweak made after he joined the Trotters, and a smart one from a marketing standpoint. Lemon would serve as the team's "clown prince of basketball" for the rest of Saperstein's life and a dozen years thereafter.[46]

The team kept drawing big crowds through the 1950s, with Saperstein demanding and getting increasingly larger cuts of the gate, from 55 percent to 65 percent to even 70 percent. That suggested the overall product was bigger than the cast of characters, and it meant Saperstein held all the cards with his players. In addition, Saperstein controlled a whole suite of barnstorming basketball teams beyond the Globetrotters. In 1950, he boasted in a pitch letter that his office was "handling virtually all the outstanding novelty basketball attractions in the United States." He owned several of those teams: the Kansas City Stars, the Chicago Brown Bombers, and the New York Renaissance. Among other teams promoted and scheduled by Saperstein's office were the Hawaiian Surfriders, reorganized versions of the New York Celtics and Boston Whirlwinds, and the Indiana Clark Twins, a team featuring three sets of twins.[47]

Saperstein kept the Globetrotters busy well beyond the traditional basketball season with overseas touring and outdoor summer games at major US sports stadiums, including Philadelphia's Connie Mack Stadium, New York's Polo Grounds, and Boston's Fenway Park. In 1954, the House of David supplied lights for a night doubleheader featuring the Trotters at Chicago's Wrigley Field—the first time a sporting event took place under lights there. (Baseball's Chicago Cubs wouldn't follow suit until thirty-four years later.)[48]

While the Globetrotters were becoming a global sensation with their comedy and the NBA was gaining credibility for its athletic skill, they continued to compete for the same players.

When Bill Russell of the University of San Francisco emerged as a huge talent, *San Francisco Examiner* columnist Curley Grieve wrote that it was "generally assumed" that Russell would join the Globetrotters upon graduation. But the six-foot-ten Russell wasn't so sure, unless Saperstein offered a deal too huge to reject. "I don't want to be a basketball clown," Russell said. "I like to laugh. But not on the court."[49]

Despite comments like that, Saperstein courted Russell with determination. When Russell's college team was in Chicago for the DePaul Invitational Tournament in December 1955, Saperstein met with him privately and, according to Russell, tried to sell him on the "social advantages" of being a Globetrotter. Russell later wrote that he was put off by the approach but did agree to a second meeting that included Russell's coach, at Saperstein's suggestion, "to keep everything on the up and up." Russell said Saperstein annoyed him further at that second meeting by discussing his money offer only with his coach, without including Russell. To Russell, the message was: "As one Great White Father to another Great White Father this is what we'll do for this poor dumb Negro boy."[50]

But the courtship continued. In a misguided attempt to improve his negotiating position, Saperstein disparaged Russell's ability publicly. "Russell is a fine rebounder," Saperstein told a sportswriter. "But he can't shoot. He is a lousy shot."[51] In April 1956, Russell's father, Charley, expressed outrage at Saperstein's "cutting remarks" and said his son had rejected the Globetrotters' "bag of peanuts"—a $17,500 offer.[52] In the end, Russell was drafted by the Boston Celtics and became one of the most respected figures in NBA history, leading the Celtics to eleven NBA championships.

The Globetrotters did manage to land a future Hall of Famer for the 1957–1958 season, but he was a Hall of Famer in another sport. Creighton University's Bob Gibson was a two-sport star who preferred basketball to baseball, but he got no offers from the NBA. He gained Saperstein's attention by leading the College All-Stars to a victory over the Globetrotters, and Saperstein signed him as a Trotters regular, with a spot in the pregame Magic Circle. Gibson's run with the Trotters lasted just a single season before the team that held the rights to his baseball career, the St. Louis Cardinals, asked him to concentrate on pitching, and he agreed. One of the most brilliant careers in baseball history followed.[53]

Months after Gibson left, Saperstein landed his biggest prize, seven-foot-one Wilt Chamberlain. The man the press liked to call "Wilt the Stilt" was a star at the University of Kansas and led them to the 1957 NCAA championship game, with Saperstein and Gottlieb in attendance. Their NBA team, the Philadelphia Warriors, would ultimately have the right to claim Chamberlain under the league's territorial draft rule then in effect. That rule, intended to build local fan bases, meant that any team could surrender its first-round pick and instead claim a player from within fifty miles of its home arena before the draft began. Chamberlain grew up in Philadelphia, so the Warriors had rights to him. But another NBA rule prohibited signing a college player until his class had graduated, and Chamberlain wanted to skip his senior year at Kansas. Enter the Harlem Globetrotters. This time, Saperstein wasn't going to lowball a player he wanted. He offered Chamberlain a gargantuan contract worth $65,000, intended as a one-year deal until Chamberlain could join the Warriors. Just to show he was serious, Abe handed Chamberlain a wad of bills—$10,000—to seal the deal.[54]

The biggest contract yet for a college basketball player was major news, and Saperstein made the most of it. He didn't bring three thousand silver dollars in a wheelbarrow as he had with Walter Dukes, but he did dress Chamberlain in a Globetrotters warm-up suit, and he stood on a chair next to Chamberlain holding a tape measure to show how tall "Stilt" was. In another photo op, Abe posed with a ten-foot-long mattress especially made for Chamberlain.[55]

Because Meadowlark Lemon was established as the team's center and chief showman, Chamberlain took on a different role, point guard, which would have been inconceivable except for Wilt's athleticism. Saperstein was thrilled with the results. "I never thought I'd see the day when one player would mean as much to the gate as Chamberlain," Saperstein said.[56]

Not everyone approved, though. Joe Bostic of the Black newspaper *New York Age* viewed the Trotters as a demeaning minstrel show—no place for the brilliant Chamberlain. It was a mistake, Bostic wrote, "to sully the gloss of that brilliance by smearing him literally with the burnt cork and asking him to give with the hey-boss-I'm-a-shonuff-clown routine."[57]

Saperstein's business was increasingly pulled into the struggle for equal rights for Black people. Saperstein's brother Rocky claimed the Globetrotters turned down offers to play separate white-only and Black-only games in the South. But in 1957, separate games were arranged in Memphis—Black-only in the afternoon, white-only in the evening—and the segregation policy was scrapped only after Black protests. "It is perhaps unfair to assume that Abe Saperstein proposed the Jim Crow conditions, but it can be assumed that he yielded to them," columnist Marion E. Jackson wrote in the Black newspaper *Alabama Tribune*. And Saperstein did conform with Jim Crow rules in some places that banned Black athletes from playing in the same games as white athletes. In those cases, Saperstein's all-Black Chicago Brown Bombers served as the Trotters' opponents.[58]

Chamberlain's year with the Globetrotters went so well for both him and the Trotters that Saperstein tried to get him to stay with the team indefinitely. Chamberlain ultimately decided to join the Warriors, but Saperstein's attempt to keep him was understandably annoying to Gottlieb. It got even more tense the next year when Chamberlain became fed up with the NBA's "roughhouse tactics" and announced he was quitting the league. "I get it from all angles," Chamberlain said. "Some grab my shorts and hold me down."[59] Saperstein offered to take Chamberlain back with a pay raise—to $125,000. Chamberlain turned down Saperstein and decided to return to the Warriors but did join the Globetrotters for their summer tours of Europe throughout Saperstein's lifetime. Chamberlain later said the most fun he ever had in sports was playing for the Globetrotters.[60]

Saperstein's continued courtship of Chamberlain helped ruin his friendship with Gottlieb, and Saperstein sold off his shares in the Warriors. After Saperstein's death, when his family asked Marie Linehan for any correspondence between him and Gotty, she responded: "It will be remembered that after a violent quarrel, Abe did not speak to Eddie for a good many years before he died."[61]

Saperstein tried and failed to persuade another great player, Oscar Robertson, to choose the Globetrotters over the NBA in 1960. Saperstein seemed to realize the odds of luring the University of Cincinnati star were remote, and he became annoyed when his brother Morry raised the stakes by calling Robertson the Trotters' "number one project." "I called my brother about those remarks," Abe said. "He's the bookkeeper of the organization. He has no concept of what I have in mind."[62]

Saperstein's relationship with the NBA continued to deteriorate. He wanted a team that was all his own in the league, and until he got one, he seemed intent on serving as the league's loudest critic. He wasn't always wrong. For example, in 1956 Saperstein called for the NBA's expansion to the West Coast. "Everything is set up for the move," he said. "University of San Francisco Dons played to 15,000 regularly at the San Francisco Cow Palace. Ground has been broken for a new arena seating 20,000 next to the Los Angeles Coliseum."[63]

He called on the NBA to get there before Major League Baseball did. But the NBA didn't.

Three years later, Saperstein tried simultaneously to get new NBA franchises in Los Angeles and Chicago. He wouldn't have been allowed to hold both, so he seems to have been hoping he'd get one or the other. In the eight years since the Stags folded, the NBA had failed to place a team in Chicago, then the nation's second-largest city. But Saperstein was optimistic. "The interest is here," he said. "The Stags stopped because they didn't have any men with promotional ability in the organization."[64]

A few weeks after those comments, the NBA's Podoloff said he was talking with potential investors in a Chicago team but would not identify them, except to say they didn't include Saperstein.[65] It's not hard to see why Podoloff might have been wary of the Globetrotters boss. After all, Saperstein publicly slammed the NBA's leadership as "mossbacks" and said Podoloff was "like the president of France used to be: no authority, no voice."[66]

Saperstein told the press he was working on an NBA franchise for Los Angeles with a group that included oilman Ed Pauley, co-owner of the National Football League's Los Angeles Rams; Rams stadium announcer Frank Bull; and Paul Schissler, who founded the NFL's Pro Bowl. In announcing the Los Angeles effort, Saperstein decided to make new enemies, calling for the NBA to dump two current teams, the Cincinnati Royals and Detroit Pistons. "They're putting their money on a dead horse in Cincinnati and Detroit and leaving potentially great cities like San Francisco, Los Angeles, and Seattle [to] go to waste," he said.[67]

The NBA blocked both of Saperstein's shots. The league finally went into Los Angeles for the 1960–1961 season, but decided to let the Minneapolis Lakers move there instead of approving a new franchise. The next season, the NBA left Saperstein out of its Chicago plans, too, when it approved a new team called the Packers, which was renamed the Zephyrs a year later. The name change didn't help much, and the team soon left Chicago to become the Baltimore Bullets and ultimately today's Washington Wizards.

If NBA bosses thought they were done with Saperstein, they were wrong. If anything, his rhetoric got more stinging. He slammed the NBA for poor fundamentals and declared: "Pro basketball is sick, sick, sick." Then, with an insult particularly biting because it came from the king of basketball comedy, he added: "They play like a bunch of clowns."[68]

11

THE SHOWMAN

*Saperstein tried to broaden his entertainment empire
beyond sports, but it didn't always go well*

Abe Saperstein was a twentieth-century version of P. T. Barnum, the audacious American promoter who went to bizarre lengths to draw audiences. Saperstein never claimed he had a mermaid in his act, as Barnum did, but the Globetrotters owner's boasts certainly stretched the bounds of credibility. And like Barnum, Saperstein aggressively dispatched "advance men" to get the press to write about his circus before it arrived. In modern public relations, this type of publicity is known as "earned media." Saperstein called it "ballyhoo," and liked to say: "Everyone can buy media space—the real promoter gets space for zero."[1]

Saperstein and Barnum had similar rationales for their bluster. Barnum claimed it was alright to use hoaxes or "humbugs" to bring in crowds as long as the customers ended up pleased with his legitimate attractions. Saperstein said that no matter how much anticipation he created, his goal was to outdeliver when the show began. "You got to give the people more than they expect," he said.[2]

Saperstein knew his duty was to provide fans with a brief escape from the everyday. He argued that Major League Baseball's slow pace was frustrating to fans because "some guy in the upper left-field stands has had time to figure out how much he owes the bank, how mad his wife is at him, how much

The 1954 film Go, Man, Go! about the Globetrotters described Saperstein as "one of those fellows with a stubborn idea, who never knows when he's licked—a combination hard to stop."

work he's got tomorrow, how much the gas station is going to charge for his banged-up fender, and then he wonders why the action hasn't started."[3]

During his tours, Saperstein met plenty of entertainers outside the sports world. He hired some of them to perform at Globetrotters games. He managed some of their careers. He tried to make friends with them and become part of their celebrity circuit. And he created his own traveling variety shows. Along with some successes, he managed a number of flops.

Saperstein realized that, to set his Globetrotters apart, they had to be showmen. That's why they made court trickery a major part of their brand. Saperstein also knew it would help to bolster his Globetrotters games with other attractions—"pulls," he called them—to bring in potential customers who weren't big sports fans. The extra entertainment also served as a hedge if the main act was having an off night. A Saperstein advance man, Tom Walsh, once dismissed the idea that the Globetrotters required such help: "The Trotters need a bunch of vaudeville acts with them about as much as the late John Dillinger needs another hole in his head. The only way I can figure it out is that the boss just did it out of the goodness of his heart." J. Michael Kenyon, the Seattle sportswriter who was an expert on Globetrotters history, saw it another way: "I remain convinced that what [financially] saved Abe more than anything was his addition of the halftime vaudeville shows."[4]

One of the first entertainers who toured with the team was basketball adjacent. Harold "Bunny" Levitt, a Chicagoan who shot underhanded free throws with amazing accuracy, gained fame by hitting 499 straight in a 1935 Chicago exhibition before his 500th shot rolled around the rim and fell out. The Globetrotters hired him to put on a halftime routine in which he shot fifty free throws along with a fan. If the fan hit more—which never happened in his nearly five years with the Trotters—the fan would have collected a $1,000 prize. Levitt also played with the Trotters during games on rare occasions.[5]

As the years passed, Saperstein broadened into halftime entertainment that had nothing to do with sports. "I try everything," he once said. He hired jugglers, unicyclists, clowns, Wild West lasso artists, tightrope walkers, trampolinists, hand balancers, singers, a cancan dancer, an accordionist, and even a one-legged tap dancer named Clayton "Peg Leg" Bates.[6]

Bates, a Black son of a sharecropper who lost a leg in a cotton mill accident at age twelve, used his artificial leg to help propel his acrobatic dance moves, becoming a favorite at Harlem clubs and on Broadway. His signature move was the "jet plane," in which he leapt into the air, landed on his peg leg, and then jumped backward on the false leg over and over, with a trumpet blast from the band accompanying each leap. One time at the Paradise Club in Atlantic City, Bates's peg leg broke through a knothole in the wooden dance floor, and it took a half hour to get him unstuck.[7]

Sex appeal was welcome in the acts, as evidenced by the Bouncing Collegians, a trampoline team described by a Utah newspaper as an "athlete and his well-rounded girl partner." It is doubtful that "well-rounded" referred to the young lady's interests.[8]

Occasionally, Saperstein's guest stars were too sexy. When the Globetrotters toured with the Hawaiian All-Stars and brought along hula dancers in 1948, Creighton University in Omaha, Nebraska, banned the young women from performing. "Our gymnasium was rented to Abe Saperstein for basketball, not a carnival," athletic director Frank Hagan said. But Hagan tried to show he was reasonable by adding, "Hawaiian singing is permissible."[9]

Saperstein's halftime and pregame entertainment also promoted sports other than basketball. He featured world championship table tennis players such as Richard Bergmann and Norikazu "Cannonball" Fujii. And in 1959 he grabbed headlines by signing Black tennis champion Althea Gibson to a $100,000 contract to tour with the Globetrotters—surely the largest amount paid to a Black female athlete up until that time. Gibson's white opponent on the tour, Karol Fageros, got $30,000. Fageros was a talented player, ranked as high as fifth in the world at one point, but she had another attraction for a promoter like Saperstein: a year earlier, Fageros had created a sensation by wearing gold lame underpants in the French Open, prompting Wimbledon officials to ban her until she agreed to cover them with white lace.[10] One columnist wrote: "Miss Gibson is the renowned U.S. and Wimbledon champion. . . . Miss Fageros is 36-24-36½."[11]

Gibson won 114 of the 118 matches, prompting sportswriters to grumble about the uncompetitive "fiasco."[12] Gibson had a different complaint about the tour: separate sections for Black and white fans at the City Arena in Norfolk, Virginia, as required by state law at the time. "This is a sport, an international thing," she said, "and yet you have some people sitting here and some people sitting there. I don't like it. I didn't know this sort of thing still existed."[13]

Saperstein understood star power and arranged for celebrities to appear at his games even when they weren't doing much of anything except signing autographs. Satchel Paige, fellow baseball star Ernie Banks, and boxer Sugar Ray Robinson greeted fans at Trotters games. But perhaps the highest-profile sports celebrity to tour with the team was Olympic hero Jesse Owens.

Owens's relationship with Saperstein has been subject to severe criticism in recent years, but they considered themselves friends and allies.

In a situation inconceivable in modern times, Owens's financial situation was extremely poor in the years after he won four gold medals in the 1936 Berlin Olympics and dismantled Adolf Hitler's myth of Aryan supremacy. After the Games, Owens refused to join other Olympic stars at a meet in Sweden and instead headed home, where he hoped to earn endorsement money. The Amateur Athletic Union responded by revoking Owens's amateur status, in effect ending his track-and-field career. When Owens arrived in New York City, he quickly realized that his hero status could not outrun racism. Hotels refused to give a room to him and his wife, but finally the Hotel Pennsylvania agreed, as long as they used the service entrance.[14]

During the years after the Olympics, Owens worked as a playground janitor, a gas station attendant, and co-owner of a dry cleaner.

When Saperstein offered work to Owens about eight years after the Olympics, he didn't have to fight his way through a crowd. But Saperstein understood Owens still had star power and thought they could help each other, which they did. Many of the duties Saperstein hired Owens to perform were aboveboard, such as serving as traveling secretary and giving short halftime speeches about character building. But Saperstein also arranged for Owens to participate in a demeaning series of stunts.

Some of the stunts might have seemed fairly innocuous, such as when Owens raced against basketball players at halftime, jumping hurdles while his competitors had a clear path. But during Owens's tours with the Globetrotters baseball team, Saperstein also had him race a man on a motorcycle and even run against horses. In Ogden, Utah, in 1945, he lost to a thoroughbred named Flash in the hundred-yard dash, and the Associated Press reported, "Owens for a brief spurt held a lead over the horse, but was overhauled and passed at the halfway mark. 'Flash' finished with room to spare."[15]

At a time when Black people were struggling for respect and being treated in some quarters as subhuman, plenty of people thought races against horses were a humiliating spectacle. But Saperstein also had his defenders. Haskell Cohen, a syndicated sports columnist for Jewish newspapers, wrote:

> Abe takes advantage of Owens' fine condition. He has him running exhibitions against horses, and humans are given distance handicaps. Jesse tells us he still runs the hundred-yard dash in 9.7. Not bad for a man approaching the 40-year mark. A New York sport columnist took offense at Saperstein racing Owens against a horse. Thought it was undignified. Saperstein says he doesn't know what the columnist makes a year, but Jesse has realized over $20,000 in one year, and rarely goes under $10,000 under the Jewish promoter's aegis.[16]

Owens considered himself to be a "public relations man," explaining at the time, "The public seems to like my exhibition performances. And remember, it keeps my name alive."

Later in his life, Owens justified the stunts as necessary for his family's well-being: "People say it was degrading for an Olympic champion to run against a horse, but what was I supposed to do? I had four gold medals, but you can't eat four gold medals."[17]

The horse-racing stunts were only one aspect of the complex Saperstein–Owens relationship. Saperstein also partnered with Owens in founding the West Coast Negro Baseball Association, which lasted for only three months but raised Owens's profile at a time when it was fading. Also, as a later chapter explains, Saperstein played an integral role in a spectacular event in Berlin, Germany, that was among the most honorable and uplifting of both Saperstein's and Owens's careers.

Owens's daughter Marlene Rankin was asked in 2022 whether her father had positive or negative feelings about Saperstein. "Very positive," Rankin said. "It was because they worked together. My father was the kind of person who was always grateful when someone extended themselves to offer him something. Saperstein offered him this position [with the Globetrotters]. He was fond of him for not only that reason, but they got along very well."[18]

Rankin said her father considered Saperstein "a friend."

Given Saperstein's rising prominence and his fascination with show business, it seemed inevitable that he would explore the movies.

In 1951, Columbia Pictures released *The Harlem Globetrotters*, a fictional account of the Trotters on the road, featuring a made-up player named Billy Townsend and real Globetrotters portraying themselves. The cast included Goose Tatum, Pop Gates, Marques Haynes, Babe Pressley, Ermer Robinson, Ted Strong Jr., Frank Washington, Clarence Wilson, and Duke Cumberland. Inman Jackson played himself as a coach, but Saperstein was portrayed by Thomas Gomez, an actor best known for appearing with Humphrey Bogart in *Key Largo* and for an Oscar-nominated supporting role in *Ride the Pink Horse*. Gomez looked a lot like Saperstein, except that Gomez was of average height.[19]

Perhaps the most noteworthy cast member was Dorothy Dandridge, playing the supportive wife of Billy. Three years later, the gorgeous Dandridge would star in *Carmen Jones* and become the first Black woman nominated for an Academy Award for best actress. According to one report, Saperstein tried to persuade Chuck Cooper to stay with the Trotters instead of joining the NBA's Boston Celtics by offering to let Cooper play Dandridge's husband in the film.[20]

The movie generally steers clear of the race angle, but there is a scene in which some of the players scold Billy about his selfishness, which hurts the team. The actor playing Saperstein later tells him: "You don't understand how Tatum felt, do you? You don't know what Cumberland meant, do you? Well, after twenty-four years I think I know what they meant. I think they meant that in some way this team represents more than themselves. It represents your people."

"I don't go for that business, Abe," Billy responds, prompting the Trotters owner to pay him for the rest of the season and fire him.[21]

A higher-profile feature film about the Globetrotters arrived three years later when *Go, Man, Go!* opened in eleven thousand US theaters. The movie tells how the Trotters gained their fame. Players again portray themselves, with Sweetwater Clifton joining Tatum and Haynes as the team's stars. As with the 1951 film, a supporting actor is the most noteworthy: a young Sidney Poitier plays Inman Jackson.

While the film was being cast, a *Washington Star* gossip columnist reported that Marlon Brando would portray Saperstein, but that didn't come to pass.[22] The Trotters skipper was played by Dane Clark, who had dropped his birth name, Bernard Zanville, and adopted his stage name at the suggestion of Humphrey Bogart. Clark, who described his image as "Mr. Joe Average," bore less resemblance to Saperstein than Gomez had. Not only was Clark of average height, but he also lacked Saperstein's pudginess.[23]

This second Globetrotters film is more Saperstein-centric than the first, in both marketing and content. The movie's promotional poster features drawings of Saperstein with his family and even depicts his wife-to-be in a beauty contest. The film's opening crawl reads: "This is the story of a sports wonder of our time. More exactly, it's the story of the man who made it so—one of those fellows with a stubborn idea, who never knows when he's licked—a combination hard to stop."[24]

Like the first film, *Go, Man, Go!* deals with racism indirectly. A striking aspect of the movie is the ease with which white and Black characters collaborate as friends and colleagues in an atmosphere of mutual respect. It's almost as if widespread discrimination in American society didn't exist. The *New York Times*, however, considered racism to be a major offscreen character: "Strongly implied as the reason for non-recognition of the team is racial discrimination, and, although it is never mentioned in so many words, this well-understood social barrier provides the adversity in the film." The *Times* said Clark was "especially proud" of the film because he saw it as "a forerunner of others that decried racial discrimination and championed civil rights."[25]

Both the 1951 and 1954 films were written by Alfred Palca, a publicist for Twentieth Century Fox who saw a newsreel about the Globetrotters and thought the subject would play well on film. Between the release of the two movies, Palca got caught up in the Hollywood blacklisting of leftists, and he couldn't find a distributor for *Go, Man, Go!* until he removed his name as producer and screenwriter. Palca's brother-in-law became the producer, and Palca's cousin, a pediatrician, got the screenwriting credit. Palca denied being a communist, but because of the accusation, "my career was phhhttt," he recalled. Palca never made another movie. His screenwriting credit for *Go, Man, Go!* was restored in 1997, a year before his death.[26]

James Wong Howe, the director of *Go, Man, Go!*, also had an unusual backstory. Like Saperstein, Wong Howe immigrated to the United States as a child. Wong Howe was Chinese, which meant he couldn't become a US citizen until the repeal of the Chinese Exclusion Act in 1943. Because of

California's anti-miscegenation laws, he could not marry his longtime love, a white novelist named Sanora Babb, until 1949. Wong Howe's friendships with leftists and the supposed communist sympathies of Babb caused him to be "graylisted," meaning he was not banned from movie work altogether but was shunned by major studios for a time.[27]

In composing film shots, Wong Howe became known as a master of the shadow and worked his way into the first ranks of American cinematographers. *Go, Man, Go!* was his first directorial job and one of only two films he directed. He later won two Academy Awards for cinematography.

Go, Man, Go! didn't crack the top twenty at the box office in 1954 and it was not a big award winner. But it was influential to one of the greatest basketball players ever, Kareem Abdul-Jabbar. "In a scene that stayed with me," Abdul-Jabbar said, "Marques Haynes dribbles past Abe Saperstein in a narrow hotel corridor. After that, I worked at handling the ball. I didn't want to be just a good big man. I wanted to be a good little man too."[28]

Saperstein made inroads in other types of arts and entertainment, too. He sponsored an auto thrill show that toured Europe in the mid-1950s. He promoted the Ice Capades show on an international tour in the 1960s. He even promoted a French portrait painter, Raphael Pricert.[29]

He also made an impact in the recording industry when the Globetrotters adopted "Sweet Georgia Brown" as their theme song around 1950, twenty-five years after the tune was written. Like the Globetrotters, the song was a multiethnic collaboration, composed by a Jew, Ben Bernie, and a Black man, Maceo Pinkard.[30]

There are conflicting accounts regarding how "Sweet Georgia Brown" became associated with the team. According to Saperstein chief aide Marie Linehan, the Trotters were looking for a theme song and considered "Darktown Strutters Ball" but "it did not have the right sound or rhythm." It's unclear who first pitched "Sweet Georgia Brown" to Saperstein. By one account, it was a West Coast recording industry figure named Albert Van Court. But there are also stories about a member of the Globetrotters organization first hearing the tune in a store. "He bought it, brought it back, and put it on the PA one night as we went out on the court, without us knowing it," former Trotter Bobby Milton recalled. "You know what happened. We all started moving about and dancing with the music, and now it's as much a part of us as the name."[31]

The version adopted by the Globetrotters was a 1949 recording by Brother Bones and his Shadows that featured the whistling of bandleader Freeman Davis and the playing of "bones" (curved pieces of ebony and ivory). Brother Bones toured with the Globetrotters for several years, and the team sold the record as a souvenir. At one Trotters game in Albuquerque in 1953, fans bought five hundred copies.[32]

Saperstein's smashing success in the early 1950s may have led him to think that everything he touched would turn to gold, and his hiring of half-time entertainers may have convinced him that he was a gifted discoverer of show business talent. Thus he embarked on a few traveling variety shows that attempted to resurrect vaudeville but instead threw a few more handfuls of dirt on its grave.

In late 1954, Saperstein launched "Harlem Globetrotters Varieties of '55," a tour of the West and Midwest by a group of entertainers—but no Globetrotters. Saperstein was playing on the team's name recognition, but unless bandleader Earl "Fatha" Hines was going to do the hidden-ball trick, the name didn't make any sense. Other performers included King and Zerita, "America's outstanding mentalists"; Tony Ponce, a French opera singer; the Romano Brothers, Italian comedy acrobats; the Tong Brothers, Hong Kong hand balancers; and Mason & Anderson, New Orleans dancers.[33]

Saperstein admitted that the show was an "experiment," and an expensive one, too, with a weekly payroll of $15,000. "If successful on the road, Abe plans to spend a bundle to dress up the show and move on to Broadway," the *Toledo Times* reported.[34]

By the time the tour ended, the press coverage didn't have the word "Broadway" in it.

"Abe Saperstein apparently is not as successful with stage shows as with his Harlem Globetrotters basketball team," the *Ottumwa (Iowa) Courier* reported. "His 'Varieties of '55' were seen by fewer than 200 people in the Coliseum this week, despite the fact that it was one of the best shows of its kind ever given here. The same story is heard from other communities across the country, which means that the venture lost heavily on its tour, which ended this week."[35]

In 1961, Saperstein tried it again with a "World of Music" tour, featuring British singer Lester Ferguson, American singer-actress Olga James, Norwegian accordionist Toralf Tollefsen, and Spanish flamenco dancer Rosalita

Martinez. But the *Sacramento Bee* reported that attendance was "nothing short of appalling. There could not have been more than 125 or so in the audience—counting the ticket takers, usher, usherettes, and the man who manipulates the spotlight in the first balcony."[36]

If Saperstein couldn't bring his road shows to Broadway, he did manage to bring Broadway to his road shows. A truncated version of the musical *Hellzapoppin'* was presented to Globetrotters fans at halftime in 1960. But even then, it drew negative attention. A *Lincoln (Nebraska) Journal* columnist thought it was a sign that "Abe Saperstein's Harlem Globetrotters may be losing some of their appeal."[37]

Saperstein constantly tried to build his connections with celebrities, hanging out with movie star Bob Hope at baseball's spring training, spending time with singer Eddie Fisher in Tokyo, dining with luminaries such as bandleader Xavier Cugat, and doing favors for baseball star Joe DiMaggio and boxer Rocky Marciano.[38]

DiMaggio called Saperstein to get a ticket to a Globetrotters game for his son Joe Jr., and Saperstein told him: "I'll do better than that—I'll have him on the bench with me." And then Saperstein made sure reporters heard about it.[39]

A sports columnist reported in 1955 that Saperstein, known for his public relations mastery, had accepted the task of "supplying the halo" for Marciano. Just a day later, Saperstein called a different columnist and told a story about the boxer asking Saperstein to arrange a Globetrotters appearance in Marciano's hometown, Brockton, Massachusetts. "And that," Abe told the gullible columnist, "is the kind of apple Marciano is. He's champion of the world here, but it matters more to him to please the hometown people in other ways."[40]

Saperstein was friends with Danny Thomas, star of the popular television show *Make Room for Daddy*. Thomas broke his ankle in 1956, supposedly while demonstrating the Trotters' tricks to young fans. Saperstein sent him a cable from Paris: "If you just had to play basketball, what was wrong with the Harlem Globetrotters?"[41]

Saperstein managed and promoted the careers of several musicians and movie stars.

In the 1940s, there was Black bandleader Sir Oliver Bibb, whose sidemen wore eighteenth-century French costumes, including wigs and lace sleeves. Bibb's biggest claim to fame was hiring experimental jazz icon Sun Ra. Saperstein said he spent $3,000 on Bibb but gave up because the bandleader—as one newspaper put it—"had one weakness, an eye for women."[42]

Saperstein had better luck with Hadda Brooks and Olga James, two Black singers who put together solid careers.

James, who graduated from the Juilliard School of Music in New York City, was signed by Saperstein after he heard her sing in the Beige Room on Chicago's South Side. With Saperstein's help, she got a huge break, playing the role of Cindy Lou opposite Harry Belafonte in the film *Carmen Jones*. The next year she performed at halftime during the nationally televised game that turned out to be Goose Tatum's last with the Globetrotters. A year after that, she costarred on Broadway with Sammy Davis Jr. in *Mr. Wonderful*, a show that Saperstein claimed he invested in. In the 1960s, James married famed jazz saxophonist Cannonball Adderley.[43]

Hadda Brooks was known as the "Queen of the Boogie." In the early 1940s, she was married to a Globetrotter named Shug Morrison, who died of pneumonia at the age of twenty-one. A decade later, Saperstein signed her to a personal management deal, and she performed with the Globetrotters during their 1952 European tour. Brooks's obituary in the *San Francisco Chronicle* offered this rich detail: "Ms. Brooks frequented the blues clubs on Central Avenue and met Billie Holiday in a bathroom when Holiday opened the door of Ms. Brooks' stall and offered her a hit on her marijuana cigarette. The two became fast friends."[44]

As improbable as it might seem, multiple sources said Saperstein had the opportunity to represent the Beatles on their first US tour but turned it down. Avi Berkley, Saperstein's grandson, said he heard the story from his father, Saperstein's son-in-law, Irwin Berkley.

"He told me that my grandfather was offered that tour when they were coming over to the United States, or a little bit before that," Avi said. "He was born in England, so there was some kind of a connection there. And my dad was with my grandfather and there were a couple of his friends. . . . It was almost like a joke: 'Aw, these young kids. They're not going to go anywhere.' You know, kind of like that talk. That's how my dad remembered it."[45]

Former Globetrotter Bobby Hunter recalls talking to Saperstein about it and telling the promoter he should have arranged for the Beatles to "do some concert events with the Globetrotters." According to Hunter, Saperstein said he had been offered the chance to represent the Fab Four but declined because he hadn't expected them to become a musical sensation.[46]

Terry Moore, who was nominated for an Academy Award for best supporting actress for the 1952 film *Come Back, Little Sheba*, was frequently claimed by Saperstein as a client. Moore had a colorful private life, married to and divorced from Heisman Trophy-winning football star Glenn Davis and later claiming to be secretly married to one of the wealthiest Americans, Howard Hughes—a claim credible enough that Hughes's estate gave her a settlement.[47]

Ed Sullivan, who hosted a popular television variety show, wrote in his syndicated *New York Daily News* column in 1953 that Saperstein was "Terry Moore's personal manager, his only show business client." Moore may have been Saperstein's only *white* show business client, but Hadda Brooks had signed with Saperstein about half a year earlier.[48]

In 1955, Moore tossed the first jump ball for Globetrotters games in London and Paris. An article that same year in the *Des Moines Tribune* said, "Abe became her agent six years ago." It told a story about Moore wearing an ermine bathing suit to entertain troops in Korea during the Korean War and then giving the suit to Saperstein, who sent it to his eighteen-year-old daughter Eloise, a student at the University of Wisconsin.[49]

Yet, despite Saperstein's claims about Moore, his longtime assistant Marie Linehan insisted that he never represented her professionally. After Saperstein's death, when his family asked Linehan to turn over correspondence from famous people, she wrote about Moore: "There is no file. At Sylvia's personal request to 'get rid' of all that type of file, this was disposed of. It is, however, an absolute fabrication that Abe was her personal representative for pictures or anything else. The subject herself will attest to that."[50]

While researching this book, the authors sought out Moore to see if she would so attest. In her nineties and living in California, Moore did not respond to multiple requests for an interview.

Saperstein's associations with show business figures and his frequent travels led to various rumors of extramarital affairs. Saperstein's brother Harry, interviewed by author Ben Green at the age of ninety-one in the early 2000s, said, "Abe didn't drink or smoke. His only vice was women—lots of them! He had women stashed all over the world."[51]

One alleged affair with an entertainer who performed with the Globetrotters became public eighteen years after Saperstein's death—and was revealed in a most unusual way.

Gertrude Kapiolani "Kapi" Miller, a Hawaiian woman, began touring with the Globetrotters and performing hula dances at halftime as early as January 1953, when she was twenty.[52] The next year, she won the Miss Hawaii pageant. The hazel-eyed beauty was a particularly popular choice for the honor because she was a member of a Hawaiian royal family and her maternal grandfather was Robert Wilcox, Hawaii's first delegate to the US Congress.[53]

"Six ancestries are blended in Miss Miller—Hawaiian, Swedish, German, Polish, French, and English," reported the *Honolulu Star-Bulletin*.

Miller didn't finish in the top five in the Miss America Pageant, but she won a special talent award of $1,000 for her hula dancing.[54] She soon returned to tour with the Globetrotters, and she served as Miss Outdoor America at the Chicago Sports and Outdoor Show in early 1955.[55]

Miller made less positive news in early 1957 when she, Saperstein, and the Globetrotters were in Hawaii. Newspapers revealed that Miller had been secretly married to dance instructor Victor Yankoff since 1955 and that she and Yankoff had separately filed in court for an annulment. Yankoff said Miller owed him $7,000 as her agent, and he tried to garnish the money from Saperstein. But Miller and Saperstein both ducked process servers. "Mr. Saperstein, manager of the Harlem Globetrotters, reportedly boarded an early flight yesterday and left the Territory for parts unknown," the *Honolulu Advertiser* reported.[56]

Miller got her annulment and performed with the team in the States in 1958 and in Hong Kong in early 1959.[57] In October 1959, Miller gave birth to a daughter, Celine, and stopped appearing with the team. She stayed in touch with Saperstein, though. A 1961 *Honolulu Star-Bulletin* gossip column item said simply: "Abe Saperstein (Harlem Globetrotters) and Kapiolani Miller enjoying the eatery and bistro circuit."[58]

Kapi Miller also enjoyed the company of Robert Toledo, owner of Hawaii's largest dairy, and she eventually married him, becoming Kapi Toledo. Their unhappy marriage ended about two decades later when she shot him to death in their home. Prosecutors charged her with murder despite her claim that Toledo had come at her with a knife and she was acting in self-defense.[59]

Abe Saperstein had been dead eighteen years when the trial took place in 1984, but his name came up in court. Lenore Walker, a psychologist who was an expert on spousal abuse, testified that Mrs. Toledo had told her she had an affair with Saperstein, that her daughter Celine was Saperstein's child, and that Saperstein had bought them a home in the Kahala neighborhood of Honolulu. Saperstein came up in Walker's testimony because she cited a story about him as an example of Robert Toledo's "pathological jealousy." Walker said Mrs. Toledo told her about a visit Saperstein had made to see her and their daughter at their home in late 1962 or early 1963 and how Robert Toledo had been violent afterward, slapping and choking her.[60]

This trial testimony was reported in both major Honolulu newspapers. But in the pre-internet news era, it never made it to Chicago, at least not to Chicago's newspapers. Kapi Toledo was acquitted of the murder and died in 2006.[61]

Her daughter, Celine Kapi'olani, was living in Florida when contacted by the authors in 2022. She wrote in a series of emails that her mother and at least five other people had told her that Saperstein was her father. Those people included "Abe Saperstein's secretary (so long ago, I think her name was Marie)."[62]

Asked if she remembered Saperstein visiting her as a child, Celine said: "Yes, besides at the games we also went & saw him at his hotel."

Celine described her mother's relationship with Saperstein: "They were very close, he sent her postcards & such when he was abroad, and we went to see him every time he was in Hawaii."

Celine said she had not taken a DNA test nor had she ever reached out to Saperstein's family in the Chicago area. Saperstein's grandchildren in Chicago's northern suburbs said they had not heard of the alleged relationship before being asked about it by the authors in 2022.

12

THE FREQUENT FLYER

Saperstein served as a worldwide evangelist for basketball,
taking his Globetrotters to six continents

During their first two decades, the Harlem Globetrotters traveled from coast to coast, earning the team's owner a reputation as "the boy who will travel the length of the country to make an honest dollar," as one journalist put it.¹ The Trotters had also been to Canada, Mexico, Cuba, and the US territory of Hawaii.

But Abe Saperstein was determined to go farther—to truly put the "globe" in Globetrotters. And in doing so, he made his team an international sensation, the most famous basketball team in the world. Today's global popularity of the American-born sport is attributable in no small part to the journeys of Saperstein and his Globetrotters.

During the winter of 1947–1948, Saperstein tried to arrange a tour of Japan so his team could perform for US soldiers stationed there. For unknown reasons, General Douglas MacArthur vetoed the visit, but Saperstein kept looking overseas. His interest in taking his team to Europe was piqued by correspondence with an old acquaintance: Tommy Brookins, who had formed the first Chicago-based basketball team using the name "Globe Trotters." Brookins left the sport to build a career as a nightclub performer, working in Europe and staying in touch with Saperstein. "Tommy's letters got me charged up," said Saperstein.²

Expert traveler Abe Saperstein packed so meticulously that "he can walk in his hotel room in the dark and find any article he looks for," a newspaper columnist wrote.

Abe's brother Rocky traveled to Europe in 1949 to work out arrangements for a tour the next year. Abe himself took a flight across the Atlantic
during the winter of 1949–1950 to observe the quality of basketball and
fans' reception of it. He watched a game between French and Yugoslav
teams and was unimpressed with the caliber of play, concluding that "if they
like this trash, we'll kill them with our showmanship."[3]

In 1950, the year of the Trotters' first major tour abroad, more Americans traveled by train than by plane. Civilian jet aircraft weren't available yet,
so travelers relied on propeller-driven planes that required regular refueling
stops. This prompted a popular saying, "Time to spare, go by air." What's
more, air travel was much less safe than it is today. During 1949, a civilian
airline flight crashed on average every nineteen days in the United States.
But Saperstein was undeterred.[4]

Careful planning and logistics were essential to stage a basketball tour on
a continent where the sport wasn't widely played. Before he and his team
departed by plane in early May 1950 for Lisbon—their first stop—Saperstein
shipped a special bus for his team and other equipment to Portugal on a
freighter. Saperstein tried but failed to acquire a portable basketball floor
that could be transported abroad. However, he did ship regulation-sized
baskets and glass backboards for use in the games.[5]

Saperstein couldn't have hoped for a better reception in Portugal. Enthusiastic crowds watched the team play in three cities. The Globetrotters
"delighted the audience with their marvels and their incredible juggling
skills," a Portuguese newspaper reported.[6] In one city, the Trotters went to
a gymnasium for a practice, hours before their evening game. They arrived
to see five thousand fans who had already gathered in the gym, awaiting the
evening game.[7]

Although Saperstein's team beat their Portuguese foes by about ten
points in each of the first two games, local sportswriters were not ready to
praise the Globetrotters' talent. Saperstein said their interpreter told him
that "we'd have to win by a big score or they'd think we were bums. 'But we
don't want to beat 'em bad,' I told him. He just shrugged. 'In Portugal, you
must,' he said."[8]

The Globetrotters confronted a big cultural hurdle in the United Kingdom. Basketball was rarely played there; its closest cousin was a game the
British called "netball"—mostly played by schoolgirls. Given the public's

perception of the sport, the manager of London's Wembley Stadium initially discouraged Saperstein from playing there. "It won't go," he told Saperstein.[9]

Saperstein was so concerned about the British public's perceptions that he hired an announcer to provide a detailed explanation of the Trotters game in progress. However, his fears proved unwarranted. The Globetrotters' performance at Wembley Stadium was a huge hit and changed the Brits' perspective. The game, a local reporter wrote, "wasn't anything like the netball you played at your girls' school, Aunt Agatha. It wasn't like *anything* we have *ever* seen."[10] A British columnist praised the "magic in those Harlem fingers" after watching Saperstein's players spin, pass, and shoot the basketball.[11]

The first game in London was televised, so positive impressions reached far across Britain. A media critic at the *Guardian* called it the best TV program of the week that wasn't produced by the British Broadcasting Company. Ticket sales were so strong that stadium officials agreed to add an extra Globetrotters game to their six-day London series. British basketball enthusiasts capitalized on the Trotters' presence. A newspaper in one London borough announced that people "whose interest has recently been aroused by the visit of the 'Globe-trotters' and the 'All Stars' to this country will soon have the opportunity of seeing a local team in action."[12]

Unfortunately, the Globetrotters encountered a racist barrier in London that they did not face in other European cities—discrimination in accommodations, which forced the players to settle into hotel rooms on the outskirts of London.[13]

Several of the Globetrotters games on this tour were played outdoors. In one of them, rain fell during the second half in Grenoble, France, leaving nine thousand fans soggy yet happy. The next day, a heavy downpour greeted the Trotters as they arrived in the French city of Nancy. After several hours of rain, Saperstein assumed local organizers would call off the game. The entourage packed up and prepared to leave for Nice, the next city on the team's itinerary. When a local organizer in Nancy asked him why the Globetrotters had not arrived at the outdoor court, Saperstein replied, "But it's raining cats and dogs." The Frenchman quipped, "Does it not rain in your country?" So the Trotters jogged onto the soaked surface and did their best to dazzle thousands of wet spectators. Marques Haynes made the most

of the opportunity by dribbling a basketball with his right hand while holding an umbrella with his left.[14]

In Antwerp, twenty-five thousand Belgians watched the Globetrotters.
Impressive crowds showed up in Milan and Bologna, Italy. The only disappointing crowds were in Switzerland.[15]

In Germany, the Globetrotters were shocked to see the lingering wartime
devastation in Berlin and Munich. Ellie Hasan, who worked the tour as a
referee, said the team's performance "made Berlin laugh for the first time in
a generation."[16]

The Holocaust, just a few years in the past, sometimes loomed over
Saperstein on his European tours. The only venue he disliked in Europe
was the Palais des Sports in Paris, where thirty thousand detainees had
been held during the war, awaiting shipment to Nazi camps. "When you get
down in those dark, gloomy dressing rooms, there's a ghost around every
corner," he said.[17]

Saperstein's descendants tell a story about anti-Semitism from that first
European tour. Abe's daughter Eloise accompanied her father in Germany.
While he gave a news conference at a hotel, the thirteen-year-old went to the
lobby and asked a naive question.[18]

"Mom went down to the bellman or the concierge," said Eloise's daughter Abra Berkley. "She had a taste for Jewish food, is how she [remembered
it]. So she wanted to go find a Jewish area. Papa Abe was upstairs on the top
floor having a press conference. And she went and asked, 'Can you tell me
where the Jewish neighborhood is?'"

Berkley said the hotel worker spit in Eloise's face and told her, "Hitler
should have gotten rid of all of you."

"She was horrified," Berkley said. "She ran into the elevator, went up to
the penthouse floor, just crying hysterically, and she burst open the door,
like both doors, how she explained it, with all these newspeople around."
With spit still dripping from her face, she told her father what had happened. He cut short the news conference, demanded the hotel worker's
firing, and went next door to a jeweler and ordered a pendant made in the
shape of the Star of David for his daughter to wear proudly.

"She never took it off," Berkley said. "She wore it all the time. This meant
everything for her." Decades later, Eloise made copies of the pendant as gifts
for both of her daughters when they turned sixteen.

When the Globetrotters finally were allowed behind the Iron Curtain after years of trying, Saperstein was able to pay his respects at the Auschwitz death camp in Poland. "It has been a week since the Auschwitz death scenes were before me," he wrote. "Food has not tasted the same."[19]

Although the 1950 tour concentrated on Europe, the Globetrotters detoured south to play in Morocco and Algeria. In Casablanca, the main drama occurred off the basketball court when Goose Tatum disappeared—twice. The first time Tatum vanished, Saperstein and his players combed the city's twisting alleys looking for Goose. No luck. At four o'clock in the morning, they were ready to give up the search when Tatum appeared. He was safe, sober, and happy, having commandeered a horse-drawn taxi. After Tatum disappeared again a few days later in Algiers, Saperstein suspended him for two weeks and assigned him to one of the Trotters farm clubs.[20]

The Globetrotters capped their 1950 tour by returning to Europe and drawing sixty thousand fans in Paris over five nights. The $75,000 in revenue from the Parisian games was more than Saperstein had expected to net for the entire tour.[21]

During this tour, the Globetrotters were accompanied by the Stars of America, a team that served as the Trotters' opponent when no local team was available. No pushover, the Stars were led by Tony Lavelli, who became the all-time leading scorer in college basketball in 1949, and Bob Hahn, a six-foot-ten center who had played for North Carolina State University.[22]

Lavelli wore two hats—one as an athlete and a second as an accordion player who performed during the intermissions within games. During one such break in England, Lavelli played "The Charge of the Light Brigade" and was followed by a Globetrotter player who juggled flaming torches with the overhead lights turned down.[23]

In Rome, Paris, and other cities, Saperstein and his players devoted a little time to sightseeing and fun. A journalist reported that Saperstein "had a tough time prying the boys loose from a couple of harmless house games" in the casinos of Monte Carlo.[24]

The Globetrotters left Europe in late July, returning home on the cruise liner *Caronia*. Saperstein must have plopped himself in a deck chair and smiled. Despite a few stressful nights in North Africa, the trip had been a smashing success. *The Sporting News* called it "a triumphant tour from every standpoint."[25] Much to Saperstein's delight, Europeans and North Africans had embraced basketball. "They didn't care much for the game until we went over there," he said. "Now they're mad about it."[26] And as their ship sailed to New York, Saperstein had already booked more than 130 games to be played abroad the following year.[27]

So many overseas games had been scheduled for 1951 that it required two Globetrotters teams to fulfill the itinerary. Saperstein assigned the Trotters west unit to play fifty-six games in South America. The team's east unit traveled to Europe and North Africa, playing fifty-seven games. Each Trotters unit was accompanied by a team of college stars who served as their opponents when a local squad wasn't available.[28]

The 1951 tour in South America included games in Argentina, Brazil, Chile, Colombia, Ecuador, Panama, Peru, Uruguay, and Venezuela. The first stop was Lima, Peru, where the Globetrotters played in a bullring, entering the playing area from the tunnels normally used by bulls. In Rio de Janeiro, the Globetrotters drew nearly 150,000 fans over four games. One of those games attracted about 50,000 spectators, setting the world record for highest attendance at a basketball game.[29]

There was one hiccup in Venezuela. A Trotters game there was canceled by rain, so the players prepared to head to Panama. But Venezuelan authorities wouldn't issue exit visas until the team made up the game. They did so the next morning and then departed.[30]

Before his team arrived in Argentina, Saperstein had been warned by the US embassy about civil unrest there surrounding President Juan Perón. But the Globetrotters' visit was not marred by political strife. The president welcomed Saperstein and the players to his palace and told them to enjoy themselves and "if anyone gives you any trouble, you come back to this office and I will deal with it."[31] Perón and his wife, Eva, gave each player a sword-shaped letter opener engraved with the president's signature. And Eva declared that "Sweet Georgia Brown" would be played at all international basketball games in her country. The Argentines proved to be much fonder of basketball than of Perón, who was toppled from power four years later.[32]

The 1951 tour of Europe was equally successful. Most of the destinations were a repeat of the Globetrotters' first trip to the continent, but Greece, Luxembourg, and Spain were included this time around, and Tunisia was added to the itinerary for North Africa.

In Spain, the starting time for Globetrotters games was midnight because Spaniards didn't finish dinner until late in the evening. A local official told Saperstein that "one cannot expect people to rush through their dinners."[33] To salute the players' agility, French journalists began calling the team *les danseurs* (the dancers) rather than the Globetrotters. That August, the team set a global record by drawing seventy-five thousand fans for a game in West Germany.[34]

While in Italy, the Globetrotters visited the Vatican with a larger group of tourists but never expected to catch a glimpse of Pope Pius XII. However, the Catholic Church patriarch instructed a Vatican official to invite the Trotters to the pope's summer residence, Castel Gandolfo. During this visit, the pontiff marveled at Goose Tatum's hands. "The Pope said he had shaken a lot of hands, but mine was the biggest," said Tatum.[35] Saperstein missed the visit with the pope, having briefly traveled back home to help his friend Bill Veeck buy the St. Louis Browns. "When I got back [to Europe]," said Saperstein, "all the guys could talk about was how much the Pope knew about basketball."[36]

The following summer, the Globetrotters visited the pope again—this time with Saperstein. Although the players were dressed in street clothes, they performed their Magic Circle routine. When the Trotters finished, Saperstein asked the pope if the team could do anything else. The pontiff requested an encore of what he had just seen, and the Globetrotters obliged. Saperstein, ever the perfectionist, said afterward: "If we had known the Pope had wanted us to put on a show, we would have brought along another ball without the shine on it. That new ball was tricky to handle."[37]

Besides the Peróns and the pope, many famous people mingled with Saperstein and his crew. While visiting Athens, the Globetrotters gave an autographed basketball to a teenager who, twelve years later, became Greece's final monarch: King Constantine II. In India, Prime Minister Jawaharlal Nehru tossed the jump ball to start a Trotters game. On the island of Trinidad, Saperstein and his squad crossed paths with actors Robert Mitchum and Rita Hayworth. The two flipped a coin to decide who would toss the jump ball to start the Trotters game; Hayworth won.[38]

Queen Narriman of Egypt attended a game in Italy and sent an emissary to request that all of the Globetrotters autograph a program for her. Saperstein got all of the players to sign it during the game's time-outs. Then he walked up to the Queen's box to hand-deliver the autographed program.

Attendants refused to let him pass.

"All I want to do is hand this over to her," he implored.

The attendants stood their ground.

Saperstein tossed the program to an ordinary fan and angrily told the queen's sentinels to inform her that "the next time she wants an autographed program, she can come and get it herself."[39]

The next year, the queen and her husband, King Farouk, were deposed in a bloodless coup, and Saperstein ran across Farouk in exile on the island of Capri off the Italian coast. The king came over to Saperstein's table to chat. After Farouk said he was looking for a job, Saperstein sent a joking cable to an American friend suggesting that he hire the unemployed king as a wrestler.[40]

A year after that, Saperstein visited Egypt and paid his respects to one of the men who had overthrown Farouk, General Mohammed Naguib, the nation's first president. Saperstein was so proud of a photo of him with Naguib that he used it on a custom-made case of playing cards that he gave away to friends, relatives, and business associates for Christmas. The decision to feature the photo was especially noteworthy because Naguib had commanded Egyptian forces against the new nation of Israel in 1948, and Saperstein was a proud supporter of the Jewish state. Perhaps the playing cards were Saperstein's way of showing that sports could transcend politics. Or perhaps he just wanted people to know he had hobnobbed with a world leader.[41]

Beyond getting face time with the foreign glitterati, Saperstein and the Globetrotters burnished their reputations by drawing the interest of major European companies. In an era when corporate sponsorship of sporting events was less common, Saperstein signed an agreement with Dubonnet, a French producer of a wine-based aperitif. The 1951 games played by the Trotters in France were promoted as *la coupe Dubonnet*. That same year, the Lavazza coffee company in Italy distributed a card—smaller than a base-ball card—featuring the Globetrotters.[42]

Language barriers presented Saperstein and his players with unwelcome surprises. In a West German city, Goose Tatum noticed several youngsters seated in the aisles of the arena. During a time-out, he motioned for them to come down and sit between the front row of seats and the court's sideline. But his invitation was misinterpreted. The children happily strolled onto the basketball court, and it took several minutes to clear them all from the court.[43]

In 1952, Saperstein said he would limit his team's future trips abroad. Although the duration of the Trotters tours was shorter during the next few years, the team spent more time abroad in 1957 than ever before.[44]

In their initial trips overseas, the Globetrotters found that the quality of playing surfaces varied widely. By the summer of 1952, the Trotters' traveling units had a portable basketball floor they could access—two floors stored in Europe and a third in Japan. Later, a fourth floor was tucked away in Hong Kong. Each floor weighed eight tons and was made of one-hundred and fifty interlocking pieces. A crew of eight people could assemble one of these floors in two hours—and take it apart in thirty minutes.[45]

The Globetrotters' portable court simplified their lives abroad, except when the floor failed to show up. In Australia, the team was forced to make do when the portable court arrived three weeks late. In a game in Naples, Italy, the score was tied at thirty when a player on the opposing team drove in for a layup and suddenly fell through the portable floor. The accident occurred because that part of the court, laid above an orchestra pit, was unsupported. The crowd laughed, assuming the mishap had been planned.[46]

It was sometimes difficult to find large, flat indoor playing surfaces. Five of the team's thirty European games in '53 were played outdoors. To minimize the impact of rain, Saperstein paid to have a special skid-proof coating—first developed for the US Navy—painted onto each piece of the Globetrotters' portable floor. George Mikan, who coached a team that traveled with the Trotters, said the coating provided players with even better footing than a typical indoor court.[47]

The special coating made rainy weather less problematic for outdoor games, but Saperstein could do nothing about the temperatures. The Globetrotters did their best to dazzle fans in thirty-five-degree weather in Lille, France, during the 1953 tour. And they endured sizzling heat in Asia. "It was so hot at Taipei, our players had to wear water-soaked towels, wrapped turban-style around their heads," Saperstein recalled.[48]

Each year, Saperstein tried to add new destinations to the Globetrotters' overseas tours. In 1955, for example, the team made first-time visits to Iran,

Iraq, Israel, Syria, and Yugoslavia. The trip to Yugoslavia was the first time the Trotters breached the Iron Curtain, and their visit was well received.[49]

In 1956, the Globetrotters were prepared for political turmoil when they arrived in Central and South America. Harry Hannin, a Saperstein associate, contacted American embassies to get updates on any unrest. In the end, everything worked out. It helped that student protesters in Honduras called off a strike long enough for the Trotters to play their game and exit the country. A local newspaper suggested the team be asked to stay longer to ease tensions in the capital city. "The offer was refused, with thanks," said Hannin. "Our schedule didn't permit it. Anyway, that's what I told them."[50]

By that autumn, Saperstein said he had traveled more than three million miles to arrange or attend the Globetrotters games abroad.[51] And there were a lot of events to organize.

By January 1957, Saperstein had three Globetrotters units simultaneously playing on different continents. One unit was traveling in Europe, a second unit was in Australia, and a third was performing in Wichita, Kansas. At one point, the Globetrotters opened an office in Rio de Janeiro to coordinate planning for their South American tours.[52]

Year after year, Saperstein's team had been well-received in Western Europe. But the Globetrotters' trip to Yugoslavia had whetted his appetite to explore more of Eastern Europe—in particular, the Soviet Union. The Trotters finally played there in 1959, as is detailed in the next chapter.

Saperstein also set his sights farther east—to another large communist country. "I don't know why we couldn't . . . or wouldn't . . . play in Red China," he told a reporter in 1960.[53] But although the Globetrotters made several visits to Hong Kong, the team never played a game in the People's Republic of China during Saperstein's lifetime.

Meanwhile, the Trotters found their way to plenty of other Asian countries.

Spectators in the Philippines expected serious basketball, so fans in Manila booed when the Globetrotters displayed their hijinks. "They wanted straight basketball," said Saperstein. "And we had to give it to 'em." The Trotters owner left the country with great respect for its basketball knowledge and talent. "I'd say the [Philippines] have some fine players," Saperstein said. "They have teams capable of beating many clubs in this country."[54]

During the Trotters' first appearance in Hong Kong, they heard hisses, not boos. "It was a load off our minds when someone got 'round to telling us that hissing indicated that the Chinese liked us," Saperstein said.[55]

A friend cautioned Saperstein not to include Japan on his basketball team's Asian tours. "That is baseball territory," he said. But Saperstein ignored the advice, and his team was welcomed by good crowds in Japan.[56]

There were many strange and awkward moments during the Globetrotters far-flung tours.

One evening in London, a Globetrotters player mistakenly went to the wrong arena, expecting to find his teammates there. A basketball game was about to start, but it was not the Trotters event. Once the teams realized they had a Globetrotter in their midst, they persuaded him to participate in their game. Saperstein forgave the mistake, a sportswriter reported, because the player's error "turned into a good piece of public relations work."[57]

In Morocco, a local official offered to arrange for a visit by the Globetrotters to a harem. But when members of the team arrived there, they were informed that the women were gone—staying at a summer palace many miles away. Saperstein shared this story with a reporter and chuckled that his team was disappointed to find "the cupboard was bare." A Trotter player chimed in: "Yes, but he didn't tell you the most disappointed of all was Saperstein."[58]

The Trotters owner had a close call during a 1962 visit to the Netherlands to plan tour dates. A Dutch booking agent bought him a first-class rail ticket, waved goodbye, and Saperstein prepared to board a train leaving Rotterdam. A gate attendant told Saperstein he could take an earlier train if he jogged quickly down the platform. The Globetrotters owner did so. Later that morning, the original train booked for Saperstein left the station, headed toward Amsterdam. Nearly thirty miles into its route, the train was struck by another locomotive whose engineer blew through a red signal in heavy fog. Meanwhile, Saperstein reached Amsterdam, checked into his hotel, and phoned the Dutch agent. "I thought you were dead!" the agent exclaimed.[59] By catching the earlier train, Saperstein had avoided adding to the death toll of ninety-three in the deadliest railway accident in the Netherlands' history.

In 1964, Saperstein and the Trotters made their first tour of sub-Saharan Africa. Their itinerary included Angola, Mozambique, and Northern and

Southern Rhodesia. Saperstein was surprised that the initial game's crowd was mostly white, but he quickly realized that most Black Africans could not afford tickets. He decided to give two hundred free tickets to Black people at each subsequent game.

Saperstein was unable to book games in two other African countries. Civil unrest in the Democratic Republic of the Congo caused him to abandon plans to play there. "I'm not taking a million dollars' worth of Globetrotter talent over there," he said, "unless I am assured by both sides that we will be safe and welcome."[60] And Saperstein could not reach a deal with officials in South Africa. He received a visa permitting the Trotters to stop in Johannesburg for only one night—but not allowing them to play a game. At the time, Nelson Mandela was living underground as an enemy of the white Apartheid regime.[61]

Not all of the Globetrotters' games were scheduled well in advance. Soon after the Trotters arrived in the Philippines, a wealthy owner of sugar plantations asked Saperstein if his team would play in a city that was a two-hour flight from Manila. Saperstein feared he would lose money because of the cost of transporting, housing, and feeding his entourage—twenty-seven basketball players, four entertainers, and two referees. But the plantation owner offered to pay those expenses and disclosed two promising details. First, he had built a solid mahogany court on his estate. Second, tickets could be pitched to the eighty-one thousand people who worked on his eight plantations. The revenue for this game was the highest of any contest played during the '52 tour.[62]

By the autumn of 1965, the Globetrotters had played in eighty-seven countries on six continents. And Saperstein couldn't hide his competitive nature when discussing his travels. "In November, I'll pass the five-million-mile mark in air flights," he said. "I doubt that anyone can match that."[63]

Although the Globetrotters players logged plenty of miles themselves, Saperstein traveled at a more grueling pace. Sometimes, he journeyed ahead to the next city to confirm that everything was ready for his team. Other times, he detoured to meet with staff or clients in his Paris office. Saperstein occasionally returned home to negotiate deals or tend to other business. Once, he left Turkey right after a Trotters game to catch a series of flights to Chicago, where he hosted his annual luncheon of football writers. Within a couple days, he was on his way to Singapore to rejoin his team.[64]

Managing the logistics of tours across the globe required more than buying airline tickets and booking hotels. Saperstein also had important financial tasks to handle. One chore was paying taxes on the income that the team earned abroad. Another task was deciding how to take the Globetrotters' revenue out of countries, as many of them restricted the amount of local currency that could leave their borders. This was a particular challenge in 1959, when Saperstein and his players had to spend their Russian earnings on local merchandise or leave it behind in a Soviet bank account. Saperstein purchased a suitcase full of Russian commemorative postage stamps and spent the rest of his money on furs, including a sable coat for his wife. Then he asked his players to lend a hand. A reporter for the *New York Herald Tribune* described how "each of the towering basketball players boarded a plane for Vienna bearing an armful of sables and presenting a strange sight indeed."[65] But some of the furs had to be shipped to the United States.

Bringing home the furs turned into a project that tried Saperstein's patience. Unconvinced that the fur shipment was aboveboard, a US customs office shipped them back to Russia. Seven weeks later, the furs were delivered to a customs office in Portugal, where the team was playing. But local officials required Saperstein to buy an importer's license to take possession of the furs—and then purchase an exporter's license to leave the country. By that time, a Saperstein associate recalled, most of the furs "had gone bad."[66]

As for the Russian stamps, Saperstein brought home eighty thousand of them. He spent months trying to sell the stamps, running ads in multiple newspapers. "Prefer disposing in whole or half sheet quantities," his ad stated.[67] "I'm losing money on the deal," Saperstein chortled, "but I'm meeting a lot of stamp dealers!"[68]

Saperstein's jet-setting lifestyle earned him a platform to dish out travel advice. US tourists lacked patience when traveling abroad, he told a reporter. "Most Americans are in a rush and too many of them have a chip on their shoulder," he asserted. "If they'd take it easy, they'd have no trouble."[69]

A fashion columnist for the *Chicago Tribune* shared Saperstein's "secret to traveling light." His packing method was so systematic, the columnist noted, "that he can walk in his hotel room in the dark and find any article he looks for."[70]

All his life, Saperstein was a planner. Both big and small tasks were scheduled—even as he marched around the globe. He once sent a cable from

Singapore to his Chicago barber, making a haircut appointment for the following week when he would be home.[71]

Saperstein used a personal "air log" form to record details about his international flights. Each form provided lines for Saperstein to write the flight number, departure time, arrival time, and weight of his baggage. The form also provided room for Saperstein's comments. On one form, he criticized Austrian Airlines' "silly rules" forbidding him from stepping off the plane to make a phone call.[72]

Some of his travel commentary was shared with the media. In a postcard to gossip columnist Hedda Hopper, he complained that France's tourist products were overpriced. But Hopper was having none of it. In her column, she answered, "Come now, Abe, with the money your Harlem Globetrotters make, you can afford it."[73]

During his trips abroad, Saperstein received more than enough francs, lira, or yen to pay for meals and other personal expenses. So he went long periods without writing personal checks. Unfortunately, this led his Chicago bank to decline to honor the check Saperstein had mailed to a hospital for his 1957 hernia operation. Bank officials explained that because it had been so long since they'd seen his signature on a check, they suspected it had been forged.[74]

Like his signature, Saperstein himself had become less familiar—at least to a neighbor's dog. Returning home from Mexico, he expected little more than a bark from the animal, but the dog bit him. "Guess he thought I was a prowler, or maybe he was just a lonesome chihuahua," he said.[75]

Throughout his overseas tours, Saperstein charmed the press. At a news conference in London, a reporter complimented Saperstein on his necktie—a red, white, and blue cravat with a Globetrotter figure woven into the design. "You like it? Here, take it," Saperstein replied, untying his tie and handing it over to the reporter. Always thinking like a promoter, he added: "Just be sure to wear it whenever you report one of our games."[76]

Despite the occasional frustrations that came with being a frequent flyer, Saperstein appreciated his life in the clouds. In the late 1950s, he told a reporter, "The old days were good days, but I'll settle for the present and these trips around the globe in chartered airliners."[77]

The international travel that marked the last third of Saperstein's life reflected his love of adventure and discovery. When he gathered at home with his family for the winter holidays, "he would always bring something very interesting that would keep us so mesmerized," said his niece Joyce Leviton. "I remember one year he brought a record. They were still large records that you played on a phonograph, and it was of African chants, and he talked to us about what each one meant. Another year he brought us wooden toys that were made in Germany."[78]

Saperstein urged—and even badgered—his players to soak up the cultural experience while on foreign tours.

"We had time to do other stuff," player Hallie Bryant recalled a half century later. "He encouraged the players, since it was a once-in-a-lifetime [opportunity] to get to see these places. He used to make comments about me. He said, 'Some of you are not very sharp. You ought to watch Hallie Bryant, because he goes out to those places and makes notes, etc.' He paid me a nice compliment. I'll never forget that."[79]

But although Saperstein liked many types of sightseeing, the sight he most liked to see was a packed stadium cheering his team. As an expert at counting spectators, he couldn't resist comparing the Globetrotters' appeal at home and abroad.

"We get good crowds here in this country," he told a US reporter, "but overseas it's fantastic."[80]

13

THE DIPLOMAT

*During the Cold War, Saperstein and the Globetrotters sought
to win games, hearts, and minds around the world*

When Abe Saperstein launched the Globetrotters' first tour outside
of North America in 1950, he was confident that he could conquer
overseas markets. The US government, on the other hand, gazed at the
globe with worry. The United States and the Soviet Union, the world's two
superpowers, had entered the Cold War. And there was growing concern in
America that the Russians were winning this ideological clash. A front-page
headline in a Virginia newspaper declared: "U.S. Propaganda Effort Called
Feeble Compared to Russians'."[1]

Soviet propaganda was capitalizing on the racial discrimination widespread in US schools, housing, public services, and employment.

When Supreme Court Justice William O. Douglas visited India in 1950,
the first question at his initial press conference was: "Why does America
tolerate the lynching of Negroes?" Secretary of State Dean Acheson called
racial discrimination "a source of constant embarrassment to this Government" that jeopardized America's moral leadership role.[2]

A few months before he was elected president in 1952, Dwight Eisenhower called for America to spread its ideals with "friendly contacts through
travel and correspondence and sports." Using sports in this way especially
appealed to the diplomatic corps. According to scholar Damion L. Thomas,

One day on a Moscow street, Abe Saperstein ran into Soviet leader Nikita Khrushchev (right). It was not an accident.

the "absence of overt political meaning" in sporting events made many countries—even those hostile to US foreign policy—receptive to tours by American athletes.[3]

That same year, 1952, the Globetrotters circled the globe, playing on five of the seven continents. Acheson cited their "value as ambassadors of goodwill, particularly in countries that are critical of U.S. treatment of Negroes." He saw "unlimited possibilities" to leverage athletes such as the Trotters to "provide an effective answer to Communist charges of racial prejudice in the U.S.A." The State Department circulated the itinerary for the Globetrotters' 1952 global tour to diplomats abroad, requesting that "all appropriate courtesies and assistance be extended" to the team.[4]

Saperstein was pleased to cooperate with the State Department. "All the Communists talk about is the way the American Negro is abused here," he said. "If they see colored kids playing with white kids and living together at high-class hotels, it's got to do us some good."[5]

Of all the team's appearances abroad during the Cold War, none is more memorable than the day in 1951 when the Trotters—accompanied by Olympic star Jesse Owens—appeared in West Berlin. Years later, Saperstein called it the greatest thrill of his sports career.[6]

Germany's capital was a politically divided city then, even though the Berlin Wall wouldn't be constructed for another decade. The Soviets controlled East Berlin, and authorities there were busy that June preparing for a two-week youth festival that would attract two million young people.

That same month, West Berlin hosted a middleweight boxing bout between Sugar Ray Robinson, a Black man, and Germany's Gerhard Hecht. The referee disqualified Robinson for knocking out Hecht with a kidney punch, a blow that was banned in Germany but not illegal in all US states. (The fight was later declared a "no contest," meaning there was no winner or loser.) Enraged spectators threw bottles at Robinson, forcing police to escort him out of the arena. Robinson insisted the low punch was inadvertent, but newspapers in both East and West Berlin assailed him as an "unclean" fighter who tried to "butcher his victim for money."[7]

It seemed like a bad time for Saperstein to bring Black athletes to Berlin. Acheson instructed US diplomats in Germany that the Trotters should not be scheduled there. But three weeks later, Acheson reversed himself after US officials grew concerned that the East Berlin youth festival would be a Communist propaganda triumph. According to the US embassy, West Berlin officials believed a Trotters game would "bring East Youth into West Berlin" and serve as an "antidote to unfavorable reactions [to the] recent Robinson-Hecht fight."[8]

Saperstein agreed reluctantly. "I was just sick with worry over what might happen," he said.[9] His concerns also extended to the former Olympic champ. "Jesse Owens was traveling with us and I didn't want to take him back to the scene of his Olympic triumphs and have him booed," Saperstein said.[10]

A record crowd of seventy-five thousand fans gathered at West Berlin's Olympic Stadium as a nervous Saperstein arrived with his players. The Globetrotters won their game, 58–46. But the most memorable performance of that day was delivered during halftime by Owens, who had won four gold medals in that stadium fifteen years earlier.

The Olympic hero's entrance was theatrical. An Air Force helicopter circled the stadium three times before landing and out stepped Owens, waving to fans and wearing a light-colored suit. The crowd gave him a five-minute standing ovation. The Trotters players formed a ring around him, and Owens removed his suit and stepped out of the circle to reveal himself dressed in his Olympic track uniform.

In his remarks, Owens recalled competing against Germany's Luz Long in 1936 and becoming friends with the silver medalist, who died seven years later in World War II:

> Hitler stood way up there in the box. But I believe the real spirit of Germany, a great nation, was exemplified down here on the field by athletes like Long. I want to say to the young people here to be like those athletes. I want to say to all of you to stand fast with us and let us all work together to stay free and God Almighty will help us in our struggle. That is what the United States stands for and I know you are with us. God bless you all.

The crowd roared. Then Walter Schreiber, the acting mayor of West Berlin, walked to the microphone. "Hitler wouldn't shake your hand. I give you both hands," said Schreiber.[11]

Fans urged Owens to take a ceremonial run around the track where he had achieved fame. Earlier that summer, Owens had strained a tendon in his left ankle during an exhibition run in Barcelona. Doctors had advised him to stop running so the ankle could heal. Owens shared both of these details when he addressed the Berlin crowd, but the translator did not pass along his physicians' instructions.[12]

Moments later, Owens gave in to the spectators and started jogging around the track. "I just got a glimpse of him as he jogged away," said Saperstein. "I couldn't see through the tears in my eyes."[13]

Owens made it two-thirds of the way around the Olympic Stadium track before stopping at a point that was adjacent to where Hitler's box had been located. "With the crowd's cheers ringing in his ears, he made a sudden leap and sank in pain as he landed on his injured ankle," a United Press reporter wrote. Owens walked slowly off the track, in pain but also in triumph.[14]

The excitement inside the stadium was unforgettable. "Those kids, including the ones from East Berlin, went absolutely crazy when he jogged around the track," Saperstein recalled.[15] Marlene Rankin, Owens's daughter, said her father occasionally talked about his 1951 appearance in Berlin. "He was very moved and touched by that," she said.[16]

The US embassy in Berlin declared the Globetrotters–Owens event to be a major victory, informing the State Department that it was "even more successful than anticipated."[17]

As the Trotters traversed the globe, journalists and politicians back home lavished praise on Saperstein and his players. Columnists called the team "diplomats in short pants."[18] An Indiana congressman told Saperstein that the US government should consider erecting "a big monument to you because of the good-will you have spread all over the world."[19]

Saperstein reveled in these accolades. "A general in Berlin told us we do more good than all the statesmen we send over there," he said.[20] To hear journalists tell it, the Trotters were winning hearts and minds around the globe. "Indonesia's role as one of the 'Uncommitted Nations' of Asia has been severely shaken by, of all people, the Harlem Globetrotters," wrote a reporter.[21]

Saperstein's stock was rising—so much that during the election year of 1952, a correspondent for the International News Service pondered whether Saperstein had a future in politics. "He denies that he has presidential aspirations, but if it came to a showdown with others in the race he'd get his share," wrote journalist Bob Considine. "And if they let the people overseas vote, Abe might be a favorite."[22]

His players also felt the love abroad. "When we'd play down in the [American] South, there were times when there were some racial slurs—people yelling out things to us," said ex-Globetrotter Connie Hawkins. "And then, when we got over to Europe, it was just the opposite. People loved us over there."[23]

During a trip to South America, Saperstein said his team was well-received despite widespread anti-American attitudes. "It's pretty hard to get mad at somebody you're laughing at or with," Saperstein said.[24] Although the team was usually welcomed warmly during these tours, there were a few anxious moments. During a stop in Syria, anti-American protesters hurled stones at the Trotters' bus. Fortunately, the main things that Saperstein and his crew had to dodge were propaganda ploys. In 1951, Saperstein innocently accepted an invitation to attend a rally in Lyon, France. But he skipped the event after the city's mayor tipped him off—the rally was sponsored by communists and would criticize the Globetrotters tour.[25]

Yet there were certain communists whom Saperstein was eager to meet: the Russians. During the early 1950s, Saperstein repeatedly tried but failed to arrange a Globetrotters tour of the Soviet Union. It speaks to the Globetrotters' fame that important people were aware that Saperstein wanted to go there. In 1955, several years before he became US attorney general, Robert F. Kennedy told a newspaper that America should restrict exports to the Soviet Union but support athletic and cultural exchanges. "In fact, I favor sending the Globetrotters to Russia," said Kennedy. "They're extremely interested in basketball in Russia. But I don't think they'd let the team come, as that would benefit the United States."[26]

But Saperstein kept pushing. "They turned me down again this year," he said in 1956. Later that year, he said the Russians seemed interested, but the State Department was opposed. Saperstein later said that "playing behind the Iron Curtain had become as important to me as anything I've ever done—and as time went on I began to give up hope."[27]

By 1959, two important things changed. First, instead of working through Soviet embassies, Saperstein reached out to Vasily Napastnikov, director of Lenin Central Stadium in Moscow. Saperstein and Napastnikov soon reached agreement on the dates and conditions of a visit. Second, the State Department withdrew its opposition.

It isn't clear what changed the State Department's position. The relationships that Saperstein built with editors and reporters might have helped persuade the department. At least one sports editor, the *Honolulu Advertiser*'s Red McQueen, traveled to Washington, DC, to encourage diplomatic approval for the Soviet tour. McQueen wrote, "If Abe feels this played a role in making the historic jaunt eventually materialize, I am deeply honored."[28]

Syndicated columnist Drew Pearson hailed news of the Soviet tour and said the trip would provide "visual proof that Negro athletes hold a high place in this country."[29]

In July 1959, the Globetrotters arrived in the Soviet Union, accompanied by seven variety acts, including jugglers and acrobats. Because Russian fans expected high-quality play and no shenanigans, the Globetrotters' comedy was met with stony silence during the first game in Moscow. Although Soviet state media praised the team's ball-handling skills, it criticized the Trotters' style of play: "This is not basketball; it is too full of tricks."[30]

Saperstein adjusted quickly, working with Walter Kennedy, the team's public relations director, to write an announcement to be made before each subsequent game. The message informed Soviet fans that the Globetrotters' performances combined both basketball skill and entertainment. The announcement helped. "The crowds understood," Kennedy said. "In the remaining eight games, the Trotters got the same big laughs they had received all over the world."[31]

Another insight emerged from the first game. Russian fans had gasped when a Globetrotter deliberately tossed a basketball at a referee's head, so Saperstein dropped this gag from their remaining games. Dave Zinkoff, Saperstein's traveling secretary, said the team learned a lesson: "In Russia you don't do such things to an overseer or supervisor."[32]

These hiccups were overshadowed by a pleasant, surprise greeting that the Trotters received while strolling near the Kremlin. Saperstein was ready to return to the team's hotel when Soviet guides insisted that the team see a collection of czarist armor. A black limousine suddenly pulled to a stop nearby. Out stepped a smiling Nikita Khrushchev. "Harlem Globetrotters?" asked the Soviet leader in a thick accent. Khrushchev shook hands with the players and Saperstein. Then the Soviet premier turned to one of his aides, gestured as if he were bouncing a basketball and uttered something in Russian. Khrushchev laughed exuberantly, and a nearby crowd of Russian pedestrians laughed with him.[33]

By this time, a sea of photographers had arrived. Khrushchev stood with the team while camera shutters clicked. Then it dawned on Saperstein—the guides had deliberately delayed the team until Khrushchev arrived. "The whole thing was planned," said the Trotters owner. "The [Associated Press] bureau chief told me he never saw pictures pass the censor so fast."[34]

The team was prepared for Soviet propaganda schemes, such as the time Russian officials asked some Globetrotters to appear on a radio show that was being transmitted to South Africa. Clarence "Cave" Wilson, one of the players, objected. "We're Americans. We don't know anything about Africa and its problems, and we resent your trying to use us because of a similarity in the color of skin," Wilson said.[35]

But Wilson enjoyed a humorous diversion in Russia early one morning when he and Saperstein decided to test whether their hotel was bugged. "[Clarence] called me at 3 a.m. and said he was deathly ill, would I come right down," Saperstein recalled. "I opened his door a few minutes later, and a doctor and nurse were already there! 'I think the boy's had a nightmare,' said the doctor without batting an eye. 'He seems to be perfectly well.' When they left, Clarence rolled on the floor with laughter."[36]

All nine games at Lenin Central Stadium were sellouts, drawing a total of 135,000 fans. In a country that claimed to reject capitalism, ten-ruble tickets were scalped for ten times their face value. The Soviets provided the Globetrotters with free air and ground transportation, hotel accommodations, and meals, as well as a performance fee of $28,000 for the trip.[37]

Despite a few logistical headaches, Saperstein felt great about the Soviet trip. The man who was born on the Fourth of July had led his team into the backyard of America's archenemy, where they entertained many thousands of Russians and put a smile on Khrushchev's face. The media back home fawned. Perhaps the recipe for easing world tension, wrote one columnist, was more basketball players and fewer diplomats.[38]

The Globetrotters were among many Black athletes for whom the State Department facilitated overseas tours. In 1956, the department funded a tour by the University of San Francisco Dons basketball team. The Dons were spearheaded by their Black center, Bill Russell. The team's head coach, Phil Woolpert, actively recruited Black players, and this had prompted hate mail, including a note from someone who addressed him as "Saperstein"—intended as a derogatory reference.[39]

State Department officials disclosed few details about how they supported the Globetrotters' tours. During a Congressional hearing in 1956, one official was asked specifically about the Trotters. "We work with them and help them," he replied, "but only once have we given them financial assistance." The official reported a one-time payment of $1,000 in July 1955.[40]

However, the government's definition of "financial assistance" omitted a number of ways in which the State Department aided the Globetrotters. To encourage the Trotters to add a game in Rome one year, the US embassy promised that it would "meet all expenses" for the team's subsequent travel to Florence. To facilitate the team's 1951 game in Berlin, the Air Force provided three C-119 cargo planes to transport Owens, the Trotters, their opposing team, equipment, and a portable playing court. State Department officials also helped with advance publicity in several countries.[41]

In 1961, the State Department paid the Globetrotters $80,000 as part of a reimbursement deal. Saperstein had negotiated a fee of $4,000 per game for the Trotters to play twenty games in Eastern Europe, but he was being paid in foreign currency—money that couldn't be taken out of these countries. So Saperstein turned over the foreign currency to the US embassy in each country, and the State Department in Washington, DC, paid back the Trotters in US dollars.[42]

Department officials significantly influenced Saperstein's decisions on tour destinations, and Saperstein was candid about this. In 1952, he told a reporter that the Globetrotters had scheduled a game in Thailand "at the request of the State Department."[43] Years later, a Trotters press advisory reported on the team's recent tour of Eastern Europe where it "performed a mission for the United States State Department and came through with colors flying."[44]

In 1954, Saperstein wrote a letter to Mary Stewart French, a department official, naming several nations he wished to include in upcoming tours. French or a colleague scribbled a note at the top of the letter—probably a suggestion for Saperstein: "Be sure to tour Arab countries first."[45] The next year, French informed Saperstein that the US embassy in Amman, Jordan, was seeking information on local arenas where the Globetrotters could play.[46]

On the surface, the Trotters' 1957 trip to North Africa appeared to be organized by Saperstein and columnist Drew Pearson to entertain soldiers at US military bases. But documents from the National Archives reveal that the State Department was deeply involved in the planning and execution of this tour—and for a particular reason. In his diary, Pearson wrote that the United States Information Agency (USIA) saw the trip "as a means of putting the quietus" on the negative media coverage generated by the recent school integration crisis in Little Rock, Arkansas.[47]

A USIA cable encouraged the US embassy in Tripoli, Libya, to ask the Globetrotters to offer free admission to their game for civilians. According to the cable, the USIA "would have to finance facility (for the Trotters game) unless you can make other arrangements locally."[48] State Department staff in Casablanca, Morocco, printed invitations and tickets for the local Globetrotters' game and helped to promote press coverage.[49]

Pearson tried to persuade Saperstein to waive or lower the $2,500 fee he wanted for each Trotters game for civilian audiences. A USIA official in Washington, DC, informed the embassies in Tripoli and Rabat, Morocco, of the "slight possibility Pearson might be able [to] get Trotters to forget or cut fee" for playing in front of civilians.[50] Twelve days later, the USIA sent an update. The initial draft of that cable read: "For your information Trotters fees prepaid by Pearson." But a revised version that was actually sent to the embassies read: "For your confidential information Trotters fees prepaid by outside group here."

Perhaps an outside group paid the fees, or maybe this term was used to conceal Pearson's role as a financial go-between passing on State Department funds. In his diary, Pearson wrote: "We are to announce that [Saperstein] is getting his regular fee. . . . Later he will return the check to the government. I suppose I will end up giving him the check. I hope I get it back."[51]

These shadowy financial arrangements must have satisfied the three parties because Pearson and the Globetrotters teamed up on another trip the following year—again with the State Department's support.

Pearson got more out of the 1957 trip than a rush of patriotic pride. A US embassy in Morocco informed the USIA: "Audience for Pearson arranged with king this morning, first for any American newspaperman after [king's] return from U.S., resulting red carpet treatment and good story."[52] The story was a Pearson column, which pleased the State Department by portraying the Moroccan king favorably.

Saperstein felt proud of the impact his players made abroad. "We have helped dissipate the illusion that the American Negro is downtrodden and misused," he told a columnist. "Our boys dress well, live well, and behave themselves like gentlemen."[53] His comments echoed a common notion among white Americans in that era—that Black people could overcome racial barriers if they were well attired and behaved.

Though Saperstein was well aware of racial injustices at home, he chose his words carefully to align with the role the Globetrotters were playing abroad. "Now we all realize that everything isn't exactly as it should be here in the United States, but it's not nearly as bad as the Communists are making out," he said.[54]

After the Globetrotters' 1964 visit to sub-Saharan Africa, Saperstein criticized the reluctance of white people there to address longstanding injustices.

"The whites have to realize the world is changing, and that their first consideration immediately should be to raise the standard of living and to educate the masses of people," he said, adding that "a man making 75 to 85 cents a day should be given a living wage."[55]

The State Department–supported tours generated headlines and stories that were at odds with the reality of America's racial problems. An Indiana newspaper published a story headlined "Globe Trotters Abroad Prove Non-Exploitation of Negroes."[56] A Utah columnist wrote that the team's tours "served to dispel the rumor that the American Negro is a downtrodden person in the U.S."[57]

Did tours by the Globetrotters and other Black athletes help to counter communist propaganda abroad? It's a tough question to answer.

On one hand, the nation's foreign policy leaders believed these trips blunted the impact of communist messages that portrayed the United States as hypocritical on human rights. The USIA director told a Senate committee that sports exchanges abroad were "the most effective thing we're doing in the Orient."[58] Black historian Timuel Black said the Trotters helped America's image overseas because the team's presence proved "that there [were] possibilities of change, and all was not evil in the United States."[59]

On the other hand, Soviet propaganda could not be fully neutralized until America's leaders seriously addressed discriminatory laws and practices. Overseas visits by Black athletes could not prevent the world from learning about the turmoil created by racist policies. As the Black-owned *Pittsburgh Courier* pointed out, when the Russians assert that Black people face widespread discrimination, "they are telling the gospel truth, and the whole world knows it."[60]

The ugly resistance to school integration in Little Rock, Arkansas, in 1957 created fallout that lingered for years. On a trip to Latin America in 1958, Vice President Richard Nixon was greeted by protesters who chanted: "Little Rock! Little Rock!"[61] Late that year, the US ambassador to Ireland asked Saperstein to bring the Globetrotters there to help offset "the total lack of understanding of our racial problem, accentuated by occurrences in Little Rock and elsewhere."[62] During the Trotters' visit to southern Africa in 1964—seven years after the Little Rock crisis—Saperstein said he learned that "about all the Africans know about the United States are the stories of Birmingham, Little Rock, et cetera."[63]

In some instances, the Trotters may have aided US diplomacy without necessarily changing perceptions of race relations. In 1951, before the team arrived in Argentina, an embassy official told them that relations were poor between the US government and Argentine leader Juan Perón. But Perón and his wife attended the Globetrotters' game, and Frank Washington—one of the Trotters players—said the Peróns "ate it up." Afterward, Washington said the official told the team: "Whatever you fellows have done, it's a miracle. We are now talking to the Argentinian people."[64]

Basketball was not the only sport that Saperstein sought to showcase abroad—with State Department support—to promote American values. In early 1952, he planned a tour in which the Brooklyn Dodgers and Cleveland Indians would play a series of twenty-two baseball games in Hawaii, Japan, India, Egypt, Australia, and North Africa.[65]

The Dodgers and Indians had been the first racially integrated teams in their respective leagues. Secretary of State Acheson cited the race dynamic as a significant reason why the US government would support the baseball tour. Because both teams had players "of every nationality, creed, and color," he wrote, the trip would attest to America's democratic values.[66]

State Department officials felt the Dodgers–Indians tour was so relevant to US foreign policy that they briefed Joseph Feeney, a close aide to President Harry Truman. The officials told him the baseball tour could give foreign nations a positive impression, similar to the one created by the Globetrotters.[67]

Although MLB Commissioner Ford Frick voiced support for the trip, the Dodgers–Indians tour never happened. The teams' owners wanted the trip to pay for itself, but that seemed impossible. In addition, several Indians players did not want to participate.[68]

State Department leaders appreciated Saperstein's willingness to cooperate with them in proposing or carrying out sports tours. However, they were probably annoyed by the disparaging comments he made about US diplomats and leaders.

The same year in which the State Department instructed its global representatives to offer the Trotters "all appropriate courtesies and assistance," Saperstein complained that diplomats rarely greeted his team. "It takes a movie cutie or big shot to bring those diplomats out," he remarked.[69]

After student protesters in Venezuela hurled rocks and debris at Vice President Nixon in 1958, Saperstein offered no sympathy. "Nixon goes into a foreign country with a big entourage, a lot of bodyguards, and so on," he told the *Chicago Daily News*. "What does he know about the man on the street?" The newspaper summed up Saperstein's advice: "if the U.S. really wants to build 'good-will,' it might keep Vice President Nixon at home and send some sports figures—or sports teams—instead." And Saperstein delivered a broader punch: "Somewhere our diplomats or front men are doing a helluva lousy job."[70]

At the heart of Saperstein's criticism was his view that local diplomats were not giving him and his team the respect they deserved. "The complacent attitude of the State Department slays me," he said in 1963. While in West Berlin, Saperstein noticed US diplomats "making all kinds of preparations" for a visit by President John F. Kennedy. By contrast, his team received little attention from diplomats when they last played in the city, Saperstein said. "I don't resent this as the owner of the Globetrotters," he declared. "I resent it as an American."[71]

Beyond the meet and greet, it isn't clear what forms of attention Saperstein wanted but wasn't receiving from diplomats. Many of these officials personally thanked Saperstein for the Globetrotters' efforts. After an appearance in Iran, a US embassy official told Saperstein he would "take pleasure in informing the State Department of the [game's] impact on Iran–American relations."[72] The US ambassador to Iraq sent Saperstein a gift of stamps for his son, Jerry, and included a letter praising "the very fine entertainment" that his team had recently provided in Baghdad.[73]

Saperstein's criticisms went beyond the diplomatic corps and the vice president. "I don't think any congressman or senator can show me much advantage to the way we're presently spending foreign aid millions," he told a reporter.[74]

Saperstein knew his team's diplomatic role built the Globetrotters' brand as both entertainers and patriots. And this image paid dividends at the box office when the team played in America. Nonetheless, Saperstein's patriotism was heartfelt.

During a European tour in 1963, he and his team arrived at the airport in East Berlin—the communist sector—and boarded a bus to head west. The Globetrotters' bus faced a long delay to cross Checkpoint Charlie, prompting the players to step off the vehicle briefly. "The boys got out and walked around," said Saperstein, "and from all the surrounding apartment houses, the people looked down wistfully at them." He felt sad that "we were moving on to freedom, leaving all these people behind."[75]

14

THE COMMISSIONER

*In his rivalry with the NBA, Saperstein founded a
fiasco called the American Basketball League*

A be Saperstein and Maurice Podoloff had a lot to talk about.
Saperstein, frustrated with the National Basketball Association's
refusal to give him a franchise in either Los Angeles or Chicago, had decided
to create an American Basketball League to compete with the NBA. Podoloff, the head of the NBA, was intent on limiting the damage that Saperstein's
new upstart ABL might cause.

The two basketball bigwigs met in the NBA chief's apartment on New
York's Park Avenue on July 2, 1961, in a summit arranged by a mutually
trusted person, sports editor Max Kase of the *New York Journal-American*.
Podoloff was alarmed that the San Francisco Saints, in Saperstein's upcoming league, had poached forward Kenny Sears, a two-time scoring leader for
the New York Knicks who was the first basketball player to appear on the
cover of *Sports Illustrated*. The nightmare scenario, from Podoloff's standpoint, was an all-out bidding war between the leagues.[1]

As Saperstein described the three-hour meeting to his ABL colleagues,
"A lot of 'conversation' was indulged in, a lot of it meaningless in the final
analysis. However, for the record, I made what might be called a 'peace'
overture to them."

Abe Saperstein drew a map designating areas where his American Basketball League teams had draft rights.

Saperstein had demands. First, he insisted the NBA reverse plans to put a team in Chicago to compete with the ABL's new Chicago team. Second, he wanted the NBA to extract the Lakers from Los Angeles, where they had just relocated from Minneapolis the previous season, and relocate the team to Texas so it wouldn't compete with the ABL's new Los Angeles Jets. Barring that, Saperstein said, if the Lakers wanted to stay in Los Angeles, they would have to reach a "mutual benefit pact" with the Jets like baseball's Dodgers and Angels had done.[2]

It's difficult to understand why Saperstein would suggest something as absurd as the Lakers leaving Los Angeles just a year after they'd arrived. Maybe it was a negotiating tactic, or perhaps Saperstein's antipathy toward the NBA got the better of him. In any case, "Podoloff turned these suggestions down categorically, making no compromise suggestions," Saperstein said.

The launch of Saperstein's league was just months away. He was so determined to outperform the NBA that he considered calling his circuit "the Major League of Basketball" before settling on the less braggadocious "American Basketball League."[3] But some of Saperstein's friends were more realistic, urging him to back away and avoid what they saw as a costly mistake. In remarks to the press, Podoloff tried to play to Saperstein's ego and feed his insecurity about whether his ABL partners were up to the challenge. "Abe is reluctant to have his image destroyed," Podoloff said, "but there are some in the organization who may not be so inclined."[4]

Amid rising tensions, Podoloff and Saperstein held a secret second summit. This second meeting was revealed only after Saperstein's death, in a column by the *New York Journal-American*'s Kase, who set up both get-togethers. Kase didn't say when the meeting took place, but considering its tone, it almost certainly came after the first summit.

Kase wrote that Saperstein was his "devoted friend, but he could be stubborn and vengeful when he thought he had been imposed on." This was one of those times. Kase said the NBA's refusal to give Saperstein a Los Angeles franchise not only soured his feelings toward the league but also toward Warriors owner Eddie Gottlieb, because Saperstein thought Gotty "had failed to stand up for him in his L.A. application." Saperstein's Los Angeles bid occurred simultaneously with his maneuvering to grab Wilt Chamberlain from the Warriors, so both actions were probably factors in the torching of his friendship with Gottlieb.[5]

Podoloff asked Kase to set up this second meeting with Saperstein, who went grudgingly. They met at a neutral location, the Town House Restaurant near both Podoloff's Park Avenue apartment and Saperstein's Empire State Building office. Podoloff was "conciliatory" while Saperstein was "glowering," Kase wrote. "Abe quickly stated his position. He wanted nothing to do with the NBA, berated the league as ungrateful but, because of his promise to me, would listen to Podoloff."

Then Podoloff threw his Hail Mary pass, an attempt to make the whole problem go away.

"After some preliminary warming up," Kase wrote, "Podoloff offered Saperstein the San Francisco franchise, gratis, with special draft concessions if he would forgo plans for a new league. This was offering Abe $250,000 on a platter. That's what NBA franchises were bringing at the time."

Saperstein "said he'd consider it if several of his American League members were brought into the NBA and some weak sisters of the NBA were scratched," Kase wrote. "This infuriated the generally urbane Podoloff. 'We make you a generous offer and you have the audacity to make demands. Who do you think you are?' he shouted. The dove of peace curled up and died."

Saperstein told Podoloff, "I don't want anything from the NBA," and asked the waiter for the check.

Podoloff responded, "I asked you here as my guest," and he insisted that the waiter give *him* the check.

Kase said the two argued awhile over who would pay for dinner until "a compromise was reached. 'Let Max take the check,' they both agreed. Which I did. Thirty-six bucks and change. Saperstein and Podoloff each tried to reimburse me but I refused. It was, to me, a fitting touch to a memorable evening."

Accepting a free NBA franchise in San Francisco would have made the wealthy and powerful Saperstein even more wealthy and powerful. So why did he say no? Was it irrational pride? Or was it admirable loyalty to his ABL colleagues? We'll never know. But Saperstein's messy and foolhardy attempt to start a new basketball league ensued.

There was a misconception about what Saperstein was doing, however. Many people thought he started the ABL out of spite because the NBA refused to give him a franchise in either Los Angeles or Chicago. But in fact, Saperstein had been talking about a new basketball league well before he lost out on those NBA franchises. The ABL wasn't revenge—it was his backup plan.[6]

He had talked about it publicly in May 1959—well before his NBA bids for Los Angeles and Chicago died—when he met in Los Angeles with interested parties from that city as well as San Francisco, Portland, Chicago, and Houston.[7]

"We do not intend to encroach on the NBA in any of their present cities," he said at the time but allowed that if the NBA made a quick move into Chicago without him, there might be a shootout there. In the early days of his ABL planning, Saperstein seemed to envision a regional split with the NBA in which his new league would take Chicago and points west, leaving the East to the NBA. But his talk in the press aroused interest east of Chicago, and when Saperstein announced the league's launch in April 1960, Cleveland and Washington, DC, were in the mix, along with Los Angeles, San Francisco, Chicago, and Kansas City. Two more cities would later be added: Pittsburgh and Honolulu.[8]

Saperstein stated unequivocally that Wilt Chamberlain—who was then deciding whether to return for a second season with the NBA's Warriors or defect to the Globetrotters—would not be a part of the ABL. That was probably a relief to the NBA, but Saperstein's plans forced the established league to scramble and finally do what it had long delayed: bringing a team to Los Angeles. Saperstein wanted to get his league going for the 1960–1961 season, but there wasn't enough time to pull that off, and the delay allowed the Lakers to get into Los Angeles a season ahead of the ABL.

Saperstein's league launched in 1961–1962, the same season that the NBA's new Packers franchise started in Chicago. Saperstein initially owned the San Francisco Saints, but before the first season started, he switched his ownership to the Chicago Majors because of shakiness in the original Chicago investor group. Saperstein was not only a team owner but also the ABL's unpaid commissioner—an obvious conflict of interest that was accepted by owners such as Washington Tapers President Harry Lynn, who said, "It's a tribute to Saperstein's integrity and his know-how." Indeed, Saperstein's involvement was one of the few reasons that close observers thought the league might work. *Detroit Free Press* columnist Lyall Smith argued that Saperstein had "done more to popularize the sport than anybody," even more than basketball founder James Naismith. Noting a new postage stamp honoring Naismith, Smith wrote that "Dr. Naismith actually put basketball on a postage stamp. But Lil' Abe is the guy who made it stick."[9]

When Saperstein took over the Chicago Majors, he handed off the San Francisco Saints to George McKeon, a construction company executive known as the "fourplex king" for the four-family housing complexes he built.[10] The rest of the ABL teams featured other colorful characters.

The Pittsburgh Rens, whose nickname was a tribute to the New York Renaissance, were run by Lenny Litman, who had managed movie cowboy Hoot Gibson and once organized "donkey basketball" events, which were just what you might guess: five players on donkeys playing basketball against five opponents also on donkeys. Litman said the NBA's Podoloff offered to give him a Pittsburgh franchise, but he chose Saperstein's ABL instead. Lit-man's reason was surprisingly frank: he thought his team would be a weak sister in the NBA but "the ABL teams would be more balanced and equal in competition."[11]

The Washington entry was called the Tapers because it was owned by the Technical Tape Corporation, which had sponsored a team called the Tuck Tapers in the amateur National Industrial Basketball League (NIBL) the previous two years. Tapers General Manager Paul Cohen said undiplo-matically before the season, "If we don't win the championship, it will be the fault of the coaches. We have the talent."[12]

The Los Angeles Jets' investors included singer-actor Bing Crosby. The team's general manager and player-coach was Bill Sharman, a former NBA all-star who jumped from the Boston Celtics, prompting Celtics owner Walter Brown to call him a "quitter" and denounce the ABL as "a bunch of pirates" that "won't last until Christmas."[13]

The Cleveland Pipers were owned by George Steinbrenner, who later would become the controversial owner of baseball's New York Yankees. The Pipers were already an organized team playing in the NIBL. In Febru-ary 1961, Steinbrenner praised the NIBL as a "solid" league, and according to the *Cleveland Call and Post* indicated that he "never had any intentions" of joining the ABL. But a month later, he quit the NIBL, jumping to the ABL.[14]

Steinbrenner's coach was John McLendon. When the Pipers joined the ABL and went from amateur to pro, McLendon became the first Black person to serve as a head coach in a pro basketball league. (During that era, Saperstein struck another blow for inclusivity by employing a woman, Carol Ziegler, to referee a Globetrotters game in Iowa in 1959, saying he was "always on the lookout for something with a novel twist.")[15]

The Kansas City Steers were founded by St. Louis real estate executives Ken Krueger and Bud Hoeber, but Hoeber died of a heart attack a few months before the start of the season. A baseball great, Stan Musial, was a minority owner. The Steers' hiring of former NBA player Jack McMahon as coach set the Steers on a course to become one of the ABL's few bright spots.[16]

Perhaps Saperstein's most eyebrow-raising move was including a team from Hawaii. That created such severe travel challenges that the ABL's

Constitution required the Honolulu team to subsidize other teams' visits there. Team owner Art Kim wanted to call his team the Hawaii Aliis—a word for Hawaiian royalty. But some of the islands' royals complained that the term shouldn't be used for commoners such as basketball players, so the team name was changed to Chiefs.[17]

To coach the Chicago Majors, Saperstein chose an Illinois hero, Andy Phillip, who had led his Granite City team to the state championship and whose University of Illinois "Whiz Kids" had won the Big Ten. Saperstein's best friend, Inman Jackson, served as the Majors' equipment manager, and Ermer Robinson, the Globetrotter whose buzzer shot beat the Minneapolis Lakers in 1948, was the team's business manager.[18]

Saperstein promoted his league as more innovative and exciting than the NBA. Most notably, the ABL featured the three-point shot, a groundbreaking experiment that is examined in detail in the next chapter. In another move to limit the impact of very tall players, the ABL announced "a new rule increasing the [width of the] foul lane from twelve feet to eighteen, the Olympic Games size, which tends to keep the elongated cager further away from the basket." Also, there was a thirty-second shot clock (the NBA's was and still is twenty-four seconds), and the ABL allowed "more liberal use of hands in body contact."[19]

Article 3 of the ABL Constitution was six words: "The League shall have perpetual existence." But Saperstein's grand vision lasted just a season and a fraction, and it was ugly almost the entire time.[20]

An incident that encapsulated the ABL's frustrations occurred on January 3, 1962, when the hometown San Francisco Saints hit a basket with five seconds left for a 102–99 lead, the Kansas City Steers called a time-out, and a teenage fan grabbed the game ball, sprinted down a corridor, and fled the arena before anyone could stop him. The game was delayed while the refs found another ball. The Saints held on to win the exciting game, but the national ABL roundup by the Associated Press led with the dramatic steal by the teenager.[21]

Perhaps the most crushing setback for the ABL occurred in Los Angeles. The simple fact was that Saperstein was right about basketball's potential on the West Coast, but he got there too late. The NBA's Lakers had the best venue, the fifteen-thousand-seat Sports Arena, as well as stars Elgin Baylor and Jerry West. The Jets were mostly relegated to playing in the Olympic

Auditorium, described by a local sportswriter as an "old wolfpit." The Jets had talent: player-coach Sharman; seven-footer Bill Spivey, who had been acquitted in a point-shaving scandal but was blacklisted by the NBA anyway; and George Yardley, who had retired from the NBA's Syracuse Nationals after becoming the league's first player to score 2,000 points in a season. But Yardley was a part-timer: he agreed to come out of retirement under the condition he wouldn't play out-of-state games because that would disrupt his mechanical engineering equipment business.[22]

The Jets were the first ABL team to fold, lasting only until mid-January. But Los Angeles wasn't the first city to lose a team: the Washington Tapers had already moved to Long Island by then and would move a second time to Philadelphia. The Hawaii Chiefs paddled to Long Beach, California, for season 2. The San Francisco Saints shut down after the NBA's Philadelphia Warriors were sold by Eddie Gottlieb and brought their high-profile team featuring Wilt Chamberlain to the Bay Area for the 1962–1963 season. To maintain a toehold in that region, Saperstein set up the Oakland Oaks as an "orphan" team owned by the league and coached by Ermer Robinson.[23]

Saperstein, a master at grabbing the public's interest, encountered rare frustration on that score. His campaign to get CBS to offer the ABL a television contract met nothing but frustration. And although the Pittsburgh Rens boasted the league's best player, Connie Hawkins, they struggled financially. Owner Litman later admitted to lying about attendance. "In the second quarter, I'd look at the scoreboard, and if the score was 34–26, I'd tell the sportswriters the attendance was 3,426," he said.[24]

Then there was George Steinbrenner. The Cleveland Pipers owner made the league look bad by missing his players' payroll in January 1962. The next month, Steinbrenner further infuriated his fellow owners by selling his team without consulting them. Steinbrenner, who continued to run the Pipers after the sale, was also accused of refusing to play games out West and of failing to submit his team's statistics to the league. When ABL owners moved to kick the Pipers out of the league, Saperstein met with Steinbrenner for five hours and persuaded the owners to give him another chance. But the constant acrimony took its toll on Saperstein. He vented in a telegram to Steinbrenner that March: "I am sick and tired of innuendoes, needling of one and all, and going to back doors to achieve any and all efforts."[25]

The Pipers made it to the 1961–1962 finals, facing the Kansas City Steers. The best-of-five series should have been a great promotional event for Saperstein's ABL, but it turned into another opportunity for Steinbrenner to create chaos. The Steers won the first two games in Kansas City, and the Pipers took the next two in Cleveland. The league scheduled the rubber game for Kansas City, but Steinbrenner refused to play there, demanding that it take place at a neutral location such as St. Louis. Saperstein eventually persuaded the Pipers to accept game 5 in Kansas City after days of bad publicity, and Cleveland won the championship.[26]

Then Steinbrenner did something that might have helped Saperstein's league, but it turned sour too. He signed Ohio State star Jerry Lucas, considered the best player in college basketball, to a two-year contract with the Pipers worth $60,000. But then Steinbrenner started secret negotiations with the NBA to move his team.[27]

Saperstein was conducting secret negotiations of his own, though they didn't stay secret long. Asked about NBA–ABL merger talks, the NBA's Podoloff said, "'Negotiations' is too strong a word. Perhaps the best way to describe the situation is to say that two men who have been friends for many years have had some friendly conversations on the subject."[28]

Podoloff apparently had strange definitions for the words "friend" and "negotiations." By this time, he and Saperstein were not friendly, and they were most definitely negotiating a merger. Saperstein had given Podoloff a proposal to take to his board, suggesting that the NBA accept three ABL teams—Kansas City, Pittsburgh, and Cleveland. It's unclear whether Saperstein overlooked his own team out of unselfishness or because he was sick of the hassle. In any case, Saperstein submitted the proposal on his way to join the Globetrotters on their European tour, and while he was in Spain, news broke that Steinbrenner was taking the Pipers and Lucas to the NBA. Abe denounced the NBA's "piracy" but stayed overseas, leaving his fellow owners to cope with the crisis and assure the public that the ABL was still in business.[29]

After all that intrigue, there was a hitch in Steinbrenner's plans. He failed to come up with the money he'd promised the NBA, and league owners rejected his bid for membership. The Pipers were out of both the NBA and the ABL, and Lucas was freed from his deal with Steinbrenner. Saperstein made one last-ditch effort to get Lucas into the ABL with either the Pittsburgh Rens or his Chicago Majors. He did so in typical Saperstein style, showing up at Lucas's grandparents' home with a suitcase full of money. "He opened it and there were all these bills," Lucas said. "He took some of them out and was waving them around as he talked. He offered me $60,000."

Lucas opted instead to take $30,000 from a Cleveland group not to play anywhere and to be available if they got an NBA team the next season. That didn't happen, and Lucas joined the NBA's Cincinnati Royals after a year off.[30]

The other owners were becoming increasingly annoyed that Saperstein seemed to be out of the country whenever the ABL needed him the most. After the Pipers' attempted defection left owners wondering whether the league would make it to a second season, Saperstein went to South America for a Globetrotters tour. His top aide Marie Linehan explained that the political situation down there was "so volatile" that "Abe felt he would be less worried and concerned about the boys if he was on hand."[31]

It was rational for Saperstein to put the Globetrotters first. They were the main brand and were helping the secondary brand—the ABL—in a number of ways. The Trotters were the reason Abe's Chicago Majors got the best venue in town. Chicago Stadium owner Arthur Wirtz made money off Globetrotters games and didn't want to tick off Saperstein. And as they had with the NBA for years, the Globetrotters were playing doubleheaders with ABL teams to jack up attendance. Sportswriter Wendell Smith described the Globetrotters as "a team which has no organized affiliation carrying an entire league on its shoulders."[32]

It was remarkable that Saperstein dared try a second season, considering the unrelenting negativity, with headlines like "Saperstein Losing Touch," and sports stories about the ABL "puffing like an asthmatic locomotive." The owners were at least $1 million poorer after the first season, but Saperstein said, "I don't really look on it as a loss but rather an investment." In any case, he said, it was an "artistic success."[33]

Any artistic merit in season 2 was abstract, at best. But Saperstein stayed positive. En route to Rio de Janeiro, Brazil, he delivered a stirring message to his ABL partners via the league bulletin: "We have taken a mammoth step, marked on every hand with tough situations, danger, and an unscrupulous competitor . . . with the help of God and some banner box offices, we must succeed!"[34]

But in a later bulletin he sounded more desperate, begging his colleagues to come up with original ideas to build excitement: "Any new gimmick is worthy of a try!"[35]

One gimmick they tried was a new kind of doubleheader in which two teams played back-to-back thirty-minute games against each other with fifteen-minute halves, instead of the usual single forty-eight-minute game with four quarters. The teams wore home uniforms in one game and away uniforms in the other. The Majors and Tapers attempted this doubleheader arrangement just once, Saperstein wrote, "but it did not go over too well and for the moment we are forgetting it."[36]

The last game that Saperstein's Majors would ever play occurred on December 30, 1962, in Chicago Stadium. It was a grim scene. *Chicago Tribune* columnist David Condon described "an audience so sparse it wouldn't have crowded a hermit. . . . The press box was filled with the entire population of Antarctica and then some. . . . [It was] probably the first time a wake featured dancing girls."[37]

Yet, Condon noted, "From Abe's gait and smile, no one would guess that the future of his infant league was uncertain." And the visionary Saperstein was still looking far into the future: "All I can guarantee you is that someday—when pay television is the big thing—a fellow is going to make a million out of pro basketball."

The American Basketball League died the next day, after Saperstein had lost about $250,000 and his fellow owners were down about $1.5 million more.[38]

The titans of the sports business seemed amazed that Saperstein was willing to part with so much cash due to what they considered a grudge. "I can get mad too," said Arthur Wirtz. "But not that mad."[39]

Thinking back on the debacle a few years later, Saperstein found a bright side to his failed challenge of the NBA.

"Well," he said, "I had them worried."[40]

15

THE INNOVATOR

*Saperstein campaigned for oddball basketball rules but
pioneered a popular one: the three-point shot*

Out of Abe Saperstein's greatest failure, the American Basketball League, came his most significant innovation: the three-point shot.

It took a maverick like Saperstein to introduce such a rule change, which has transformed how basketball is played. Saperstein was unafraid to try things that others would see as gimmicks. His whole career, in fact, could be dismissed as a series of gimmicks, except that those gimmicks were often highly successful.

Saperstein was a tinkerer, and for decades before he pioneered the three-point shot, he had called for a variety of changes in how basketball was played. His theories about the sport's rules, shared at length with sportswriters, evolved along with the game.

When Springfield, Massachusetts, physical education teacher James Naismith came up with the original rules of basketball in 1891, they didn't include dribbling or backboards. The game was a work in progress. Early basketball advocates experimented with up to fifty players per team then put nine on each side before finally settling on the current five-on-five. Early baskets counted as one point, not two, and there was no such thing as a foul shot in the first few years.[1]

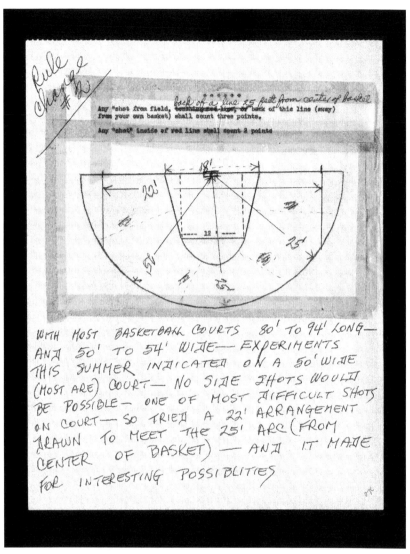

If the American Basketball League's three-point length had been twenty-five feet for the whole arc, shots on the sides would have been impossible. This rule change in Saperstein's handwriting created side lanes twenty-two feet from the basket.

When Saperstein started touring with the Globetrotters in the late 1920s, the rules still required a jump at center court after each field goal was made. This gave an advantage to teams with tall players, kept the game slow paced, and encouraged planned, half-court plays rather than free-form action.

In the 1930s, Saperstein and other basketball advocates pushed for an end to the jump ball after every basket, calling for a new rule letting the team that was scored upon take the ball inbounds. "I think the tipoff should be eliminated as it puts a premium on the big man, giving the little man very little chance," said Saperstein, who often stuck up for his fellow short people when discussing basketball rules.[2]

In 1938, the rule favored by Saperstein was approved, establishing the order of play that we see today. But oddly enough, Saperstein later changed his mind, urging a return to the center jump.

In his contrarian view, Saperstein saw the return of the center jump as a way for basketball to become more of a team sport, with a premium on passing, organized play, and defense. He became increasingly concerned that defense was being neglected as basketball became a contest for big men—or "flagpole freaks," as he called them—and also something of a track meet.[3] It's difficult to understand why Saperstein thought a return to the center jump would have cut down on the dominance of tall players. But indeed it would have been a boon to defense by allowing players to get set.

One of Saperstein's least convincing arguments for returning to the center jump was that it would slow down the game enough for fans to cheer each basket thoroughly. "The trouble is they have saturated the game with too many thrills," he said. "In every other sport spectators have a hesitation period. After a home run is hit, the player jogs around the bases. In football, after a touchdown run, there's a lull while the ball is lined [up] for the extra point."[4]

Saperstein's pleas for restoring the center jump were largely ignored. After all, fans were not complaining that the game was too fast paced to allow adequate cheering. But there were indeed concerns among basketball lovers that the dominance of tall players was ruining team play. University of Kansas coach Phog Allen called for raising the height of the basket from ten feet to twelve feet.[5] Saperstein had another idea: "Let the defensive men use their hands. . . . If you really want to see those tall men cut down to size, just let the average-sized player shove or push them to keep them off balance. Then they'll have to rely on their ability to play basketball, not just on their ability to grow."[6]

Although Saperstein wished to make defense a more critical component of the game, he called for shortening the length of the basketball court by about ten feet, a step that probably would have boosted offense. "In most courts, the ten feet or so of space in the center court is just dead space," he said. "Nothing happens there except running back and forth with the ball."

If the courts were shorter, he said, teams could start their plays sooner and players wouldn't get as tired. But no one paid much attention to that reform idea either.[7]

It's possible that Saperstein proposed so much rule tinkering in order to provide good copy for sportswriters and to establish himself as an outsider with big ideas. He even called for a rule that would have, in effect, banned the hook shot close to the basket. "Abe would have a cross-court restraining line drawn at the inner edge of the foul circle and would prohibit the pivot man from taking a shot with his back to the basket from any point inside the line," wrote a sportswriter who interviewed Saperstein in 1949.[8]

Saperstein even expressed interest in an experimental backboard that was curved so the ball would take odd bounces, making rebounds less predictable. This supposedly would have evened things up for shorter players. "They say this curved backboard will not allow the big man just to stand there and grab the ball," Saperstein explained in 1960. "We're going to try it out and see if it's workable."[9]

It wasn't.

The rule change that has stamped Saperstein's image on modern basketball—the three-point shot—went far beyond mere tinkering. In 1961, looking for a way to set his ABL apart from the National Basketball Association, Saperstein became a major booster of the idea of giving three points for long-distance field goals.

Saperstein's newfound emphasis on outside shooting was rather inconsistent, given that in an interview only a year earlier he denounced the NBA by saying: "They don't play it as a team game anymore. All they do is shoot, shoot, shoot. It's monotonous. It stinks. . . . They're pros? Phooie!"[10]

But Saperstein didn't feel an obligation to stick to his old beliefs. His obligation was to be entertaining.

Decades before Saperstein pioneered the three-point shot in pro basketball, people had been talking about it and even trying it out at the college level. In the 1940s, Howard Hobson, former basketball coach at the

University of Oregon, wrote a doctoral thesis at Columbia University that proposed a three-pointer from twenty-one feet and beyond. Columbia and Fordham University experimented with it in an exhibition game on February 7, 1945. The teams combined for twenty three-pointers. Columbia won 73–58 and would have won by the same fifteen-point margin if there had been no bonus point for longer shots.[11]

Showing the kind of elitism that Saperstein disdained, the *New York Times* deemed the Columbia–Fordham innovation a failure, reporting that coaches, referees, and sportswriters opposed it, even though spectators favored it by a vote of 148–105 in a postgame survey. The *Times'* Louis Effrat complained that the rule caused confusion: "At the outset, players were seen backing up to take pop shots from the bonus distance, often leading to whistle blowing, because of carrying the ball." Effrat predicted that the three-pointer would "be permitted to die a natural death."[12]

In 1958, two New York colleges, St. Francis and Siena, played a game with a twenty-three-foot arc for three-point shots. But according to a newspaper report, "Each team scored one three-pointer, then forgot all about it."[13]

No one in a position of responsibility wanted to make the three-pointer a regular part of the game. That is, except for Saperstein, who was looking for a way to set his ABL apart. "We must have a weapon," he said, "and this is ours."[14]

George Steinbrenner, owner of the ABL's Cleveland Pipers, recalled Saperstein pushing for the three-point shot. In typical Steinbrenner form, he gave himself a generous share of the credit. "The three-pointer was Abe's idea, but I pushed very strongly for it," he said. "It was going down to defeat before we championed the cause. We allied with Abe and that swung it."[15]

Two key advisers and friends who helped Saperstein work out the details of the shot were Ray Meyer, DePaul University's head coach, and Bill Sharman, the former Boston Celtics standout who served as a player-coach in the ABL. Meyer and Saperstein went to a Chicago basketball court in 1961 and figured out how long the three-point shot should be.

"You could draw the line damn near anywhere you wanted," said Jerry Saperstein, Saperstein's son, more than half a century later. "They just arbitrarily drew lines. There's really no scientific basis. Just two Hall of

Fame coaches getting together and saying: 'Where would we like to see the line?'"[16]

It's obvious that Ray Meyer had no idea of the impact the rule would have. In fact, Joey Meyer, who succeeded his father as DePaul's head basketball coach, said his father, who died in 2006, never talked to him about his role in developing the three-point shot. "I always compare him to people during the [war] who come back and don't want to talk about it," Joey Meyer said. "Coach was one of those."[17]

Saperstein and Ray Meyer settled on twenty-five feet, but it wasn't as simple as that. Sharman and Saperstein went to a gym so that Sharman, a strong outside scorer, could try to hit some shots from that distance.

"It's farther than it looks," Sharman said in an interview decades later, recalling that he persuaded Saperstein to draw the three-point line a bit closer—twenty-five feet from the *back* of the rim rather than twenty-five feet from the center of the basket or the front.[18]

Sharman said Saperstein "wanted to call it 'the twenty-five-foot home run.' He was such a great promoter. He said, 'When the fans see this, they'll think it's one of the best things in basketball.'"

Sharman tried to talk him out of the "home run" marketing. "I told him I didn't think the name was appropriate for basketball," he said.[19] Still, Sharman endorsed the three-pointer. "I thought it was great because I was an outside shooter," he said.[20]

One problem with the twenty-five-foot arc was that it left no room for shooting three-pointers from the sides. Saperstein solved that with a rule change that carved out alleys on both sides, making the distance twenty-two feet there.[21] Some ABL owners worried that their players wouldn't make enough shots from twenty-five feet. So while Saperstein was away on Globetrotters business, the other owners voted 4–3 to shorten the length to twenty-two feet for the entire arc. Showing where the true power rested in the league, commissioner Saperstein simply ignored their decision, and the length for the main part of the arc remained twenty-five feet.

The length remained a topic of concern, with Sharman once asking if he could shorten it to twenty-four feet on his own home court only. The answer was no. Minutes of an ABL meeting in February 1962 said owners agreed that "there should be discussion as to whether the twenty-five-foot line is right or not." But there's no indication that they revisited the issue in earnest.[22]

The three-pointer had the desired result of attracting media attention to the new league, and it did indeed excite the fans, who chanted "hit a home run" and "go, go, go for the long one" at games. The league urged teams to turn on a flashing red light or fire a gun with blanks whenever a three-point shot was made. The red lights, posted at each end of the court, became the preferred method. To jazz it up further, Saperstein purchased boxing bells, like those rung at the ends of rounds of a fight, for each team to sound for successful three-pointers.[23]

In the ABL's first regular season—its only complete season—teams attempted 4,349 three-pointers and made 1,303 of them, for 30 percent shooting efficiency. (For comparison, NBA players hit 36 percent of three-pointers in 2022–2023.) Tony Jackson, who played for Saperstein's Chicago Majors, led the 1961–1962 ABL with 141 of 383 for 37 percent and hit a record twelve three-point shots in one game.[24]

The wise men of basketball either loved or hated the three-pointer.

University of Maryland coach Bud Millikan said it was "strictly a gimmick for the pros."[25]

Jack McMahon, coach of the ABL's Kansas City Steers, disagreed: "It's no gimmick. I credit the innovation with stiffening defenses. With the outside shot worth a bonus, you can't afford to sag in the middle or gang up on the offense's best scorer."[26]

Joe Lapchick, coach at St. John's University, was thumbs down: "It won't bring the five-ten players back into pro ball. The ABL is playing five-tens because they don't have any six-threes."[27]

Saperstein, of course, disagreed, seeing the shot as a salvation for his favorite kind of basketball player: short but skilled. "Until now the small man has followed the path of the buffalo," he said. "He was becoming extinct in basketball."[28]

But like the buffalo, the three-pointer almost went extinct.

After the ABL collapsed on New Year's Eve 1962, there was no league using the shot. The Eastern Professional Basketball League, a regional association based in eastern Pennsylvania and New Jersey, began shooting three-pointers during its 1964–1965 season.[29] But no major basketball league was using the three-point shot when Saperstein died in March 1966.

Then came the American Basketball Association (ABA), which launched as a rival to the NBA in 1967 and was determined to set itself apart with a red, white, and blue basketball, a flashier style of play, and the three-point shot. The ABA's first commissioner was George Mikan, who exemplified the dominance of the big man but nurtured Saperstein's dream that the three-point shot would keep short players in the pro game.

The ABA closed down in 1976, when four ABA teams joined the NBA. The NBA still wasn't using the three-point shot, and the idea again seemed near death. But in 1979, the NBA was looking for an injection of excitement, and it introduced a three-point line twenty-three feet and nine inches from the front of the rim, about the same length as Saperstein's twenty-five feet from the back of the rim. One member of the NBA's Board of Governors was so opposed to the rule change that he resigned.[30]

The college game joined the three-point party in 1987, but with a shorter length: nineteen feet, nine inches. That was lengthened to twenty feet, nine inches in 2008 and then again to twenty-two feet, one and three-quarter inches in 2019.[31]

Joey Meyer said the innovation that his father and Saperstein helped develop has been nothing short of revolutionary:

> It's unbelievable. I mean, the game is a different game. . . . I don't even think you have to be a coach or a student of the game. If you follow the game just as a fan, you would recognize the difference in the game. Such simple things as a three-on-two fast break, where did you run? We ran to the rim. Now where do you run? You run to the three-point line. . . . Just the analytics of the game have proven that the three-point shot is obviously an extremely valuable weapon. I was coaching when it first came in college and we didn't use it that much because you just didn't know. You didn't really realize how valuable it was. [But now] you don't post up as much. Everything revolves around getting an open three-point shot. It's changed the game.

Bobby Hunter, who joined the Globetrotters under Saperstein, emphasized how the three-pointer affects play down low. "The three-point shot was huge not only because it enhanced the outside game, but it helped open up the lane to make it less congested—allowing more activity there," he said.[32]

"A strong three-point attack is the gateway to everything else good offenses do," wrote *Bleacher Report* sportswriter Stephen Babb. Along with opening up the lane, he wrote, it "forces defenders into difficult choices between remaining glued to their assignments and helping on the ball."[33]

And it sustains fan interest late in the contest. When a team is trailing by twelve points with only two minutes to go, it's not out of the game anymore.

Today's NBA would be unrecognizable without the three-point shot. Nearly 40 percent of the NBA's field goal attempts are three-pointers.[34] As sportswriter Babb put it, it's "the NBA's great equalizer."[35]

Yet Saperstein never saw the impact of his magnificent innovation. The legendary promoter wasn't one to dwell on his defeats, however, and less than a month after the ABL and its three-point shot ended in failure, Saperstein was pushing another audacious idea. He wanted to move the baskets fifteen feet from the end line into the court and remove the backboards altogether. This would allow players to shoot from behind the basket and give more players opportunities to get rebounds, he figured.

"Hockey has action behind the goal cage," he said. "My change would help the short, alert player. After all, less than 30 percent of Americans are taller than six feet."[36]

Saperstein pushed this idea for years, with no takers. Some people thought it was wacky. Kyle Given, a columnist for California's *Monrovia News-Post*, asked: "How you gonna hang the basket if you don't have a backboard to suspend it from? Levitation? Wires from the ceiling?"[37]

Actually, Saperstein had an answer for that: the basket could be "hooked at the end of a horizontal pole or suspended from the ceiling." But would either of those methods have worked? Who knows? After all, Saperstein was a visionary, not an engineer.[38]

16

THE PERPETUAL
MOTION MACHINE

Saperstein ran at only one speed, and he kept
going as long as nature allowed

rank Rose remembered his Uncle Abe's Coca-Cola machine.
"He had a Coke machine right behind his office desk," Rose said.
"He used to turn around about every fifteen minutes and drink a Coke. . . .
His secretary, Marie Linehan, used to get all over his case, but it didn't stop
him. He was really overweight from a number of years of drinking Coca-
Cola. He was not what you call advertising."[1]

Even so, Saperstein was incredibly energetic even into his sixties. Sportswriter Al Heim of the *Cincinnati Enquirer* recalled trying to find Saperstein
at the Cincinnati Gardens around 1965:

> Being the top executive of the Trotters you'd think he would be easily avail-
> able at a courtside box seat. But not this guy. When he came to town he was
> here to work. He was all over the place—up in the cheap seats chatting with
> the fans, out at the windows checking the gate, down at the dressing rooms
> seeing that things were running smoothly there. He rarely found time, at least
> when he was here, to sit down and enjoy his team.[2]

Although Saperstein remained hard driving and forward looking, American culture was catching up with him and even passing him.

Abe Saperstein, workaholic.

Athletes were demanding more say in their careers, and Saperstein thought they should simply trust him to look out for their best interests. The idea of negotiating with players' agents offended him. "He was a man of his time, and [agents were] something new and different," said Saperstein aide Wyonella Smith.[3] Though the Globetrotters players had taken note of the National Basketball Association recognizing its players union in 1957, they never unionized under Saperstein. But their growing demands would finally come to a head when they went on strike in 1971, five years after Saperstein's death.[4]

Saperstein was dealing mostly with college graduates now, unlike in the early days. They were more sophisticated, more questioning of authority, and more fond of their own personal styles. When two of his rookies showed up with beards in 1966, Saperstein ordered them to shave unless they wanted to be fired.[5]

As the civil rights movement gained steam, Saperstein found himself out of sync with it. Despite his image as a breaker of racial barriers, Saperstein clung to a go-slow approach in which white supremacists would be persuaded to change their ways instead of being forced to. A remarkable interview in 1963 with Leonard Lewin of the *New York Mirror* provided the most complete version of Saperstein's views on race. He called for winning over white people whose views of Black people were warped by a lack of direct contact:

> You have to educate people who have fears, just like I had to educate the Negro athletes that I was their friend. I didn't do anything special to gain their confidence. I just went about my business. It's only natural that they have resentments. Who wouldn't with what they had to go through? . . . I am a firm believer that you can't solve a problem like this by jamming it down throats. You may force people to do things your way but you're not going to cure the sickness. . . . I know people get impatient. I have had them say to me that they have waited 100 years and 'what are we supposed to do, wait another 100 years?' My answer is simple. I tell them that Negroes really don't know what discrimination really is. They have had the problem about 400 years, the Jews have had it for thousands.[6]

Obviously, it was a losing argument to tell Black Americans that four centuries of persecution constituted a short period of time and that they should be patient and hope for the best. But Saperstein was trying to find middle ground between Black people and their tormentors. During a time of angry rhetoric by leaders such as Malcolm X, Saperstein was dead set against confrontation:

> I don't think those who advocate belligerence and force appreciate the harm they're doing. The advances made in sports are tremendous. The Negroes were accepted without making people swallow bitterly. Did you ever hear of a place called Brownwood, Texas? Well, ten years ago with no fanfare, the Globetrotters moved into the best hotel in that town. The things we accomplished were unbelievable. It was done simply by getting the people to see the human side of the Negro, by educating them quietly to the fact that he is not an animal.[7]

Texas wasn't the best example of racial progress at the time. The Globetrotters may have been welcome at that Brownwood hotel, but Texas still had poll taxes that discouraged Black voting. And a columnist at the *Corpus Christi Times* shared an account in 1965 by an unnamed "observer" about the Trotters dropping the ball twice while performing their Magic Circle routine. "Kind Old Massa Abe Saperstein will probably reduce their ration of chitlins and bagels," the observer wrote, in a double shot of racism that a professional journalist somehow thought was worth sharing with his readers.[8]

Although Saperstein saw himself as a racial peacemaker, he couldn't resist the temptation to mock out-and-out racists such as Senator Theodore Bilbo of Mississippi, a member of the Ku Klux Klan who wrote the book *Take Your Choice: Separation or Mongrelization.* Saperstein relished the fact that Britain's Prince Philip had invited the Globetrotters to play in a charity fundraiser, commenting, "That's enough to make the late Senator Bilbo of Mississippi turn over in his cotton-pickin' grave, old boy."[9]

Very late in his career, Saperstein acknowledged that some aspects of past Globetrotters shows annoyed Black people. "We have eliminated things that were distasteful to the Negro," he told a sportswriter. "There is not an offensive moment in the show."[10]

Although some of Saperstein's players thought he was prejudiced, others believed his paternalistic style toward his players reflected his aggressive business approach, not his racial attitudes. Bobby Hunter, who was a leader of the players' unionization movement after Saperstein's death, said, "Abe was about six different kinds of asshole, but racist wasn't one of them."[11]

Saperstein stayed on good terms with many of the players by putting Black people in positions of authority—and by letting his friend Inman Jackson be the heavy instead of him. "He's the only person I know, including myself, who hasn't become so enchanted by our players that he succumbs to their charms," Saperstein said. "He'll whip them in line. . . . I need a coach like Jackson, a fellow who can frighten them with nothing more than a scowl, a wrinkled brow, a hard stare."[12]

Former Globetrotters player and owner Mannie Jackson said Inman Jackson "took no shit off anybody. . . . He was a serious professional. Very, very smart. Probably would've been an NBA coach if he were around today."[13]

As well as empowering Black people in his organization, Saperstein also earned points by looking out for aging athletes, as he had for Jesse Owens in past decades. In 1964, the Globetrotters hired Satchel Paige as an "assistant business manager" whose main duties were to travel with the team, meet fans, and add to the star power.[14]

And Saperstein didn't stop looking for opportunities to be a pioneer. According to Globetrotters player Bobby Milton, Saperstein considered an attempt to diversify one of the whitest sports, professional golf. "Abe Saperstein was quite enthusiastic about sponsoring me on the pro golf tour," Milton said. "So I spent two years really learning the game. Then, when I was really reaching my peak, Abe died."[15]

It would be wrong to think Saperstein had money to throw around on things like golf, however. The American Basketball League was a costly flop. The annual "World Series of Basketball" against college all-stars had been a great showcase for the Globetrotters, but it ended in 1962 because of a crackdown by the Amateur Athletic Union, a longtime Saperstein adversary. The AAU ruled that college seniors who played in the spring series would immediately lose their college scholarships—rather than losing them at the end of the school year—and would therefore have to pay a portion of the year's tuition and room and board.[16]

Saperstein's promotion of the Ice Capades tour in Hawaii, Australia, and Europe in the mid-'60s was a cultural delight but a business blight. He told a sportswriter in 1965 that "the Ice Capades wanted some dates outside the United States and they asked if I would book them. I got them into Hawaii a year ago and they were such a smash they thought they would like to try Australia." But Saperstein himself lost $24,000 on the Hawaii tour and $30,000 more when the skaters went to Australia and Europe.[17]

Amid the Ice Capades losses, Saperstein sent a telegram to advance man Joe Anzivino: "IF COUPLE ICE CUTIES MUST DO LADY GODIVA ACT TO STIMULATE LAGGING BOX OFFICE LET'S GET GOING." He was kidding, probably.[18]

Even the Globetrotters, who served as Saperstein's cash cow when other ventures were shaky, began to struggle. Saperstein called the 1963–1964 Globetrotters season "a most disastrous one," and he laid off staff, including an entire unit. Among the casualties was Ermer Robinson, the hero of the 1948 Lakers game who had stepped in to coach the Oakland Oaks as the ABL circled the drain. "I am terribly sorry," Saperstein told Robinson in a letter. "You will always be part of our Globetrotter family, but like so many who have been in the family, and who have gone their own ways and left the 'nest' . . . I hope with all my heart that you can go on to even bigger and better things."[19]

In some ways, Saperstein was making peace with the NBA. In other ways, he never would. During the 1964–1965 season, his Globetrotters resumed their role as an added attraction with NBA games after three years of shunning the league. Saperstein may have relented because of his own financial difficulties and also because his rival Maurice Podoloff was no longer the NBA boss. Succeeding Podoloff was a Saperstein ally, Walter Kennedy, former publicity director for the Globetrotters.[20]

But just because his Globetrotters were again doing doubleheaders with the NBA didn't mean Saperstein would get the league's respect. When he suggested a series of games between the NBA's reigning champion Boston Celtics and the Globetrotters, Boston coach Red Auerbach mocked the idea as "ridiculous" and said, "Why don't the Trotters get a reputation first and play some legitimate team before they challenge us?"[21]

Ironically, the NBA was developing a more crowd-pleasing style influenced by the Globetrotters' showmanship. "Over time, I began to notice that pro basketball stars like Bob Cousy started dribbling and moving the basketball in ways that were first done by Marques Haynes of the Globetrotters," said Don Shelby, a Minneapolis broadcast journalist and basketball writer. "The behind-the-back passes that Pete Maravich did also have their roots in the passes that the Globetrotters had started doing many years earlier. I think the no-look passes that Magic Johnson delivered to his teammates can also be traced back to the Globetrotters."[22]

Despite Saperstein's struggles, he enjoyed some glorious times in the '60s. One was the invitation from Prince Philip, which inspired Saperstein's swipe at racist Senator Bilbo. The Globetrotters made a special trip across the pond to answer the prince's call, playing a team assembled by the Lord's Taverners, a sports and social club that raised money for charity. The Trotters' opponents were British comedians and TV personalities, with Philip in reserve as the "twelfth man." With the Trotters up 20–0 at halftime, the husband of the queen donned a wine steward's jacket, rolled a refreshment cart onto the court, and served champagne to the Globetrotters. As was signaled beforehand, the Trotters let the Taverners catch up and win, with British comic Richard Hearne shimmying up the basket's support pole and dropping in half a dozen basketballs one after another. "They're a great bunch of guys and do a lot of good," Saperstein said. "How could we let them lose?"[23]

Saperstein relished his popularity in his native land, including a plaque installed at the site of his first home in London's East End. But when that plaque was unveiled by Britain's Amateur Basketball Association in 1963, Saperstein was ill and unable to attend.[24]

Although demand may have faded a bit for the Globetrotters' local appearances, they were gaining a wider audience through their performance in the first sports event at the 1964–1965 New York World's Fair and their increasing exposure on television.[25] It's unclear whether television appearances hurt the Globetrotters at the box office. Certainly sports teams of the era thought TV hurt their gate and applied broadcast blackouts when there wasn't a sellout. But one could also argue that television only raised the Trotters' image as American icons.

The Trotters were the perfect novelty act for television shows hosted by Jack Paar, Steve Allen, and Ed Sullivan. The team appeared five times on Sullivan when his program was a major Sunday night event. The Globetrotters' first color TV appearance was on Sullivan's show on Halloween night 1965, when they guested along with nineteen-year-old singer-actress Liza Minnelli and Barry McGuire, whose song "Eve of Destruction" was a big hit at the time. Celebrities liked appearing with Saperstein's team. Steve Allen formed a celebrity squad featuring actor Peter Lawford and baseball's Leo Durocher to play the Globetrotters on the air. *Hollywood Showcase* pitted the Trotters against a team composed of actor David Janssen, singer Vic Damone, and comedians Mel Brooks, Carl Reiner, and Tim Conway, with coach Saperstein also given a place on screen, sitting on the bench.[26]

But perhaps the best showcase for the Trotters was CBS's *Sports Spectacular*, which featured the team once a year from places such as Rome and Mexico City. By 1966, the Globetrotters were earning $150,000 a year from the CBS deal. In January of that year, they played the Washington Generals at Michigan State University, and *Sports Spectacular* devoted ninety minutes to it, including a halftime show by the Czechoslovakian Folk Dancers, a group that Saperstein had recruited on a European tour. The game's outcome was not in question—the Globetrotters were playing the Generals, after all—but the TV ratings demolished those of a more competitive contest on ABC at the same time: Bill Russell's Boston Celtics versus Wilt Chamberlain's Philadelphia 76ers. Perhaps the NBA game drew poorly because Chamberlain stayed on the bench, suffering from food poisoning. But maybe the truth was that the public still found the Globetrotters to be more entertaining. The Trotters defeated the NBA that day in the ratings game, 16.2 to 3.2.[27]

If the TV exposure was an investment in future success, the outlook for Saperstein's enterprises was encouraging. But on a personal level, the future of Saperstein's business didn't look so bright.

In a 1956 letter, Saperstein had told daughter Eloise: "One day, you will be running this deal, and I know that you will do a real good job."[28] But after Eloise got married three years later and started having children, that idea seemed to fade. Eloise's friend Burt Tucker said running the Globetrotters had been her dream. "We talked about that all the time," he said. "Eloise had the capability of doing that. I think it was the wrong time in terms of a woman coming in at that level. That's just my guess today."[29]

Some saw Eloise's brother Jerry as a more logical heir to the Globetrotters, especially after Abe made him quit graduate school in economics at the University of Arizona and join his father's operation full time. Jerry started at the bottom, touring small towns with a Globetrotters farm club. "He would jokingly say he was the lowest paid member of the Globetrotters organization, and that included the bus driver," said Jerry's son Lanier. "He said he was paid very badly. He also told me his father fired him multiple times. . . .

As tough as Abe might have been on his players and everyone else, I suspect he was even tougher on Jerry."[30]

An incident in December 1963, when Jerry was running a unit of the Globetrotters, raised questions about whether he had the right temperament to follow in his father's footsteps. A game in Ottumwa, Iowa, attracted only 221 fans during a heavy snowstorm, and Jerry decided that wasn't a big enough crowd, so he called off the show, disappointing those who had struggled to get there. "The Globetrotters were suited up and ready to play," the *Ottumwa Courier* reported, "but Jerry Saperstein, son of owner Abe Saperstein, said it would take $2,000 to put the Trotters on the floor." Instead, the local promoter gave refunds.[31]

People were thinking about a succession plan because Abe, once described as "the human vitamin capsule," seemed to be working himself to death.[32]

Saperstein's health had occasionally made news over the years, and his death was even announced in 1951 in an erroneous report in the *Cumberland (Maryland) News*. The paper had confused Abe with his brother Rocky, who had indeed died after suffering a heart attack at a Globetrotters game in Denver. Rocky, who was in poor health after contracting malaria in the Pacific during World War II, had worked for the Trotters since leaving the service.[33] His death at an early age, forty-six, was an exception for the Saperstein family, many of whom lived very long lives. Abe's father survived to age 70, his mother to age 84. Two of his siblings lived into their nineties, and another was 101 when she died. Abe's time on Earth would measure only 63 years, much less than most of his close relatives but surpassing the life expectancy of American men born in 1902, which was only 49.8 years.[34]

It is difficult to track Saperstein's illnesses for a number of reasons, including his organization's tendency to obscure the facts and the way that medical conditions were described during that era.

It's clear that Saperstein underwent surgery in May 1953 at Chicago's Michael Reese Hospital, but news reports simply called it an "operation" with no specifics.[35] Four years later, Saperstein flew home from Europe for hernia surgery at Chicago's Mount Sinai Hospital and almost died. "The hernia turned out to be a very, very serious one—very involved—and afterward Abe went into surgical shock and for a while nobody knew whether they were going to be able to bring him out of it," the *Honolulu Advertiser* reported.[36]

In 1963, just six weeks after the collapse of the ABL, Saperstein was admitted to Mount Sinai for treatment of what was described as pneumonia. According to a news story, "close associates said there was no cause for worry." Saperstein spent a week in the hospital, then recuperated in Florida and Jamaica for a few weeks before returning to work.[37]

It appears that Saperstein had a "mild" heart attack in the fall of 1964 and a more serious one in the summer of 1965. That second heart attack occurred near the end of a grueling four-month tour in which he met with promoters in Europe and Asia and checked on the Ice Capades tour in Australia.[38]

When Saperstein was nearly through the tour, he wrote a letter on Tokyo Hilton stationery to his friend Red Klotz, impressed by the new infrastructure in Japan. "One cannot help but marvel at man's ingenuity to improve his way of life . . . despite his desire to 'kill' off competition in any way possible," he observed.[39] After describing how exhausting his trip was, Saperstein added in Japanese: *"Watashi wa natsuno aida takusan shigoto arimasu,"* which translates to "I have a lot of work to do this summer."

His health broke in Australia in late July. In addition to the Ice Capades, the Globetrotters and their rival Washington Generals were also touring Australia, which meant Red Klotz was there to tend to his friend. "At one point, I brought him some soup up in his hotel room," Klotz said. "He looked terrible. All he would admit to was being tired, but I knew that he just wasn't right. He ate some of the soup. He was in bad shape. I knew he was dying, and Abe knew it too."[40]

Saperstein was diagnosed with a heart attack and hospitalized in Australia for seventeen days. When he got back to Chicago, he spent a week in Woodlawn Hospital but went right back to work, ignoring doctors' advice to take it easy.[41]

Family friend Burt Tucker, who had been a medical student in Chicago, recalled checking on Saperstein in the hospital. "I spent my afternoons stopping by to see how he was doing. . . . It was, 'How are you doing?' [He said] 'I'm OK. You don't have to do anything. I didn't have a heart attack' type thing. I said, 'You *did* have a heart attack. You've got to take care of yourself.' 'No, as soon as I'm out of the hospital I'm going on the road again.'"[42]

By the end of 1965, Saperstein was losing weight at an alarming rate, down 60 pounds to 160.[43] But he told Klotz, "Red, I'm too busy to die."[44]

In January and February 1966, Saperstein took a series of plane trips that seemed so ill advised that it's hard to see them as anything other than a farewell tour. First he flew from Chicago to Kansas City, then back to Chicago two days later, and on to Salt Lake City for three days. His next stop was San Francisco for four days, then down to Los Angeles for four days, back to San Francisco for two days, and on to Seattle for four days. Then he traveled up to Vancouver for a day, back to Los Angeles for a week, back to Portland, Oregon, for two days, and over to Honolulu for a week.[45]

Honolulu Advertiser columnist Eddie Sherman said later that when he saw Saperstein in Hawaii, he leaned over to Max Winter, Saperstein's old pal who had helped him set up the 1948 Globetrotters–Lakers game, and whispered, "Abe looks like he's dying."[46]

After his week in Hawaii, Saperstein returned to Los Angeles to be with his wife, Sylvia; daughter Eloise; and grandchildren Lonni and Avi, who were wintering in a Hollywood condo owned by television host Steve Allen. Southern California became a sort of second home base for the Saperstein family, especially at a time when the temperature in Chicago got as low as sixteen below zero.[47]

Saperstein's health further deteriorated in Los Angeles, and he was hospitalized for ten days. His daughter Eloise later remembered her father's persistent cough, which she described as a "heart cough." Doctors said he needed a prostate operation, and he flew back to Chicago to get it done, leaving his family in California.[48]

Saperstein's granddaughter Lonni, who was six at the time, recalled saying goodbye to him in California. "I just had this really compelling sense that if he left now, I'd never see him again," Lonni said. She begged him not to go, becoming so upset that she grabbed a pocket on his suit coat and ripped it off. "I was holding onto it," she said. "I wouldn't give it back to anyone."[49]

After the last plane trip he would ever take, United Airlines Flight 102 from Los Angeles to Chicago, Saperstein wrote in his personal travel log: "Nice ride over."[50]

Saperstein was accompanied on that last flight by his old friend Inman Jackson. "Abe loved Jack as much as he loved his brothers," said Wyonella Smith. "He was his closest friend. I'm sure there were things he shared with Jack that he didn't share with anyone [else]. And when he got sick, he wanted Jack to be there."[51]

During one of Saperstein's hospital stays, he sent Jackson on a strange errand to buy the legs of a department store mannequin. Then Jackson and Saperstein brightened the hospital room by propping the legs under the drapes, as if a female visitor was hiding there.[52] Saperstein seemed determined to live to the fullest until his time ran out.

Saperstein was admitted to Weiss Memorial Hospital on March 11, four days after his arrival in Chicago, and he spent four days in the hospital before his scheduled prostate surgery. "He was supposed to come home the next day," said his sister Leah. Instead, Saperstein experienced a violent coughing fit as he was being prepped for surgery, and he suffered a fatal heart attack. He was declared dead at 7:00 p.m. on March 15, 1966.[53]

Two of Saperstein's most loyal staffers, Marie Linehan and Wyonella Smith, were still working a long day in the downtown office when they got the phone call with the news. Sports promoter Syd Pollock wasn't even on speaking terms with Saperstein, but his son found him in tears after hearing the news. The Harlem Globetrotters were playing in Greensboro, North Carolina, when they heard. Red Klotz walked off the court and called it a night, but his Generals and the Trotters played on, as Saperstein would have wanted.[54]

Saperstein's grandchildren Lonni and Avi were watching a Huckleberry Hound cartoon in California when an announcer came on the television to report that the Globetrotters founder had died. That's how they found out that Papa Abe was gone.[55]

Sympathy and praise poured in to the family from celebrities such as Danny Kaye, Bill Veeck, and Prince Philip and from ordinary people who had been touched by the Polish tailor's son who had built an enormously influential sports business.

The irrationally ambitious Saperstein fell short on two personal career goals, however. He visited nearly ninety countries, not the hundred he aimed for. And he left the stage more than a decade before reaching his dream of celebrating the Globetrotters' fiftieth anniversary. Although the team's win-loss record was increasingly beside the point, Saperstein was always proud of it. And it was quite a mark: 8,680 victories and only 322 defeats during his lifetime.[56]

A different Saperstein accomplishment was pointed out by Connie Hawkins, the ABL's most valuable player who had gone on to the Globetrotters when the ABL folded. "He was a master at finding out if they really enjoyed the show," Hawkins said. "Lot of times people were really laughing but he'd come and give us heck because he'd say they weren't laughing enough. He always knew. He was a connoisseur of laughter."[57]

At his funeral, Rabbi Ernest M. Lorge of Chicago's Temple Beth Israel said: "What an utterly impossible task to try to speak about a legend. How do you deal with a legend?"[58] Perhaps the answer to the rabbi's question is to simply let the legend speak for himself. Less than a year before his death, Saperstein sized up his approach to life better than anyone else possibly could.

"I've been wrong," he said. "At times I've been crazy.

"The trick in life, though, is to keep venturing and hope that you'll be right more times than you're crazy."[59]

The Harlem Globetrotters have been sold six times since Abe Saperstein's death but continue to tour and appear on television.

EPILOGUE

Abe Saperstein left many legacies. The worldwide popularity of basketball is one of them. Every three-point shot scored in a game is another. The Harlem Globetrotters are yet another. In the nearly six decades since Saperstein's death, the Trotters have changed ownership six times, but they're still delighting audiences.

"Abe honestly believed that the Globetrotters would die when he left," said Joe Anzivino, a Saperstein aide who eventually ran the operation.[1] Saperstein's widow, Sylvia, tried to hand the team to her family's next generation, but there was resistance. "When Abe died, Sylvia said, 'I want Jerry to take over,' and Marie [Linehan], who was really the whole team, said if he takes over, we quit," recalled Abe's cousin, Gerald Saperstein.[2]

It wasn't the family's decision to make. Abe's last will and testament named his attorney Allan Bloch and Continental Bank as coexecutors, and they put the Globetrotters up for sale, citing the burden of inheritance taxes. The Sapersteins backed a bid by LIN Broadcasting, which promised to let the family buy a 20 percent share. Sports play-by-play announcer Jack Brickhouse tried to put together an investment group but made no formal offer. Metromedia, a television and radio chain that owned the Ice Capades, put in an initial $3 million bid for the team. But the winner was a group helmed by Potter Palmer IV, whose great-grandfather had been a key figure in the development of downtown Chicago. The $3.71 million price tag seemed high to some observers, but Palmer said, "It's the most profitable basketball team in the world."[3]

After administrative fees and taxes, about $2.6 million was available for Saperstein's heirs. His will gave 4 percent each to three loyal colleagues: his sister Fay, Inman Jackson, and Marie Linehan. The rest was divided among his widow, Sylvia, and his children Jerry and Eloise.[4]

Long after the team's sale, Saperstein's estate remained a battleground for lawyers. In 1970, the estate won a federal tax ruling allowing it to deduct about $235,000 in Saperstein's American Basketball League financing as business bad debts in 1961 and 1962. In another court case related to executor fees that lasted until 1974, testimony revealed a surprising fact: at the time of Saperstein's death, none of his top four stars were under a written contract. Coexecutor Bloch had to reach new deals with raises for Meadowlark Lemon, Fred "Curly" Neal, Robert "Showboat" Hall, and Hubert "Geese" Ausbie.[5]

Getting Saperstein into the Naismith Memorial Basketball Hall of Fame proved easier than settling the legal affairs. Linehan and sportswriter James Enright spearheaded a successful campaign in 1970, soliciting letters of support from DePaul coach Ray Meyer, Chicago Mayor Richard J. Daley, and highly respected basketball coach John Wooden of the University of California at Los Angeles.[6]

Saperstein's friend Inman Jackson eventually made the Hall, too—also posthumously. Jackson, who died in 1973, reached the Hall in 2022 along with Sonny Boswell and Runt Pullins after they were cited by a committee formed to recognize overlooked Black players from the early years. Those inductions meant that Saperstein's Globetrotters had enough Hall of Famers to field two teams plus two substitutes—or three subs, if you included Saperstein himself. The other inductees from the Saperstein-era Trotters are Wilt Chamberlain, Sweetwater Clifton, Chuck Cooper, Pop Gates, Connie Hawkins, Marques Haynes, Goose Tatum, Mannie Jackson, and Meadowlark Lemon. Separately, the Globetrotters were enshrined as a team in 2002.[7]

It wasn't long after Saperstein's 1971 induction that Black denunciations of the Globetrotters grew sharper. Connie Hawkins, the former ABL and Trotters star who had praised Saperstein as "a connoisseur of laughter" after his death, participated in a book by David Wolf called *Foul! The Connie Hawkins Story* that clotheslined the Saperstein legacy. In a chapter titled "Tomming for Abe," Hawkins complained: "What we were doing out there was acting like Uncle Toms. . . . Grinnin and smilin and dancin around, and that's the way a lot of white people like to think we really are."[8]

Lacy J. Banks, a Black sportswriter for Saperstein's hometown *Chicago Sun-Times*, provided a chilly welcome before a Trotters performance in 1973: "The slapstick antics, falsetto voices, rubbery-limb motions, toothy grins, and yelping dialogue are as modern America as Aunt Jemima and Little Black Sambo, and equally defaming to many Blacks."[9]

Saperstein wasn't around to take these blows, but members of his family were, even though they maintained friendships with many ex-players and their wives and children. After Saperstein's death, daughter Eloise ran the Abe Saperstein Foundation, which created programs to help urban children through basketball activities. The foundation ran clinics attended by more than fifteen thousand kids and held a summer basketball camp for two hundred. It also operated summer leagues at Chicago State University on the South Side and Malcolm X College on the Near West Side.[10] One of the young people helped by Eloise was Isiah Thomas, who rose to fame with the Detroit Pistons. In Thomas's Hall of Fame induction speech in 2000, he cited people who had supported him as a youngster. "There was a woman by the name of Eloise Saperstein who would give money to the Boys Club, who would take care of us as kids, buy us hot dogs and hamburgers," Thomas said.[11]

Eloise also became a sports agent, with clients including the Chicago Bulls' Quintin Dailey and Loyola star Alfredrick Hughes.[12]

Eloise's closeness with Chicago's Black sports community was demonstrated by a recommitment ceremony she hosted for the Chicago Bulls' Norm Van Lier and his wife at her home in Chicago's northern suburb of Lincolnwood. Jesse Jackson presided over the ceremony, which was attended by hundreds of guests. Eloise's friendships with Black people didn't please all the neighbors, though. The family recalls an incident when an anti-Black slur was spray-painted on Eloise's pink Cadillac.

Eloise died in 2018. Her brother Jerry died three years later. Though Jerry didn't fulfill his father's ambitions for him with the Globetrotters, he did follow a career in sports promotion. Jerry held various roles with World Team Tennis, minor league hockey, indoor soccer, and management of New York's Madison Square Garden. And in a gimmick that his father would certainly have enjoyed, Jerry founded a barnstorming basketball team called the American Giants in which all players are seven-footers or taller.[13]

Abe's widow, Sylvia, married George Kahn in 1978, moved to Florida, and died in 1993.

The resentment toward the Globetrotters expressed by Connie Hawkins and others was far from universal among Black people in the decades after Saperstein's death. Barack Obama recalled that, as a child in Honolulu, he appreciated the Globetrotters as a source of racial pride. "I, growing up, was living in Hawaii, which didn't have many African-Americans, and when the Globetrotters came into town, it was just a wonderful, fun-filled afternoon, but it had, I think, a deeper meaning to it," said the forty-fourth president of the United States.[14]

The Globetrotters increased their television visibility in the years after Saperstein's death with a Saturday morning cartoon show, a Saturday morning variety show called *The Harlem Globetrotters Popcorn Machine*, and even a made-for-TV movie called *The Harlem Globetrotters on Gilligan's Island*. Decades after those programs, NBC launched a show called *Harlem Globetrotters: Play It Forward* in 2022 to highlight the players' achievements on and off the court.

But the Trotters have not developed the kind of ownership continuity they had under Saperstein.

The Potter Palmer group, which bought the Globetrotters a year after Saperstein's death, sold the team nine years later to Metromedia, one of the companies it had outbid in 1967. Metromedia sold the team a decade later to International Broadcasting. After International filed for bankruptcy protection, the Trotters were purchased in 1993 by a group headed by former Globetrotter Mannie Jackson, giving the team Black ownership for the first time. Jackson sold controlling interest in 2005 to the private equity firm Shamrock Capital Growth Fund, run by Roy Disney, nephew of Walt Disney. Eight years later, the team was acquired by Herschend Family Entertainment, which runs theme parks such as Dollywood and Silver Dollar City.[15]

Marie Linehan stayed with the team for two decades after her beloved boss's death, moving to Los Angeles when the headquarters shifted there and assuming a loftier title of vice president of administration. She died in 1990.

The Globetrotters have made a few moves to modernize their act over the years. In 1985, they added their first woman player, Lynette Woodard.[16] In

2010, they built upon Saperstein's groundbreaking three-point shot with a four-point shot. At first, it was taken at designated spots thirty-five feet out on each end of the court, but it was later refined to be like the three-point semicircles, except farther out, thirty feet from the basket.[17]

The Globetrotters continue to do the Magic Circle to the tune of "Sweet Georgia Brown," but there's plenty of hip-hop too. The team was always family friendly, but today's version seems even more focused on kids, who are invited on the court to shoot baskets, dance, and make TikTok videos. The players all have cool nicknames like Jet, Spider, Bulldog, and Torch. But many old traditions survive. The Washington Generals are still losers, and ancient routines have survived, including the ball-on-a-string, the stinky shoe, and the football game.

Only occasionally in recent decades have Saperstein's contributions to sports been prominently recalled. A 1999 ABC program called *SportsCentury: Most Influential People* included the Trotters boss. Boston sportswriter Bob Ryan continues to denounce the three-point shot as "the gimmick of a promoter named Abe Saperstein." And the Trotters boss was a character in the 2023 Nathaniel Clifton biopic *Sweetwater*, which showed Saperstein driving the team bus, which he didn't do in real life.[18]

At the height of Saperstein's fame, the *Ann Arbor (Michigan) News* wrote: "The busy Saperstein hasn't found time to author a book yet. But it should be a dandy when it comes."[19] Unfortunately, it never did. Saperstein was always too busy making history, so this book will have to do.

Saperstein basked in the publicity when his Globetrotters brought a little warmth to the Cold War by playing in the Soviet Union.

ACKNOWLEDGMENTS

The idea for this book came from a friend, author Richard Cahan, who also provided wise counsel along the way. He and Michael Williams were our photo editors for this project.

Abra Berkley, Abe Saperstein's namesake granddaughter, is a dedicated keeper of her family's story. She shared memorabilia about her grandfather and was a knowledgeable resource on his career. We want to express our deep appreciation to her and other Saperstein grandchildren: Lonni Berkley, Avi Berkley, Lanier Saperstein, and Adam Saperstein, as well as additional family members we met through Abra.

Ben Green, author of the most comprehensive book on the Harlem Globetrotters, *Spinning the Globe*, was remarkably generous with his time and resources. Ben's benevolence should serve as a model for how history writers treat researchers who come after them. *Spinning the Globe* benefited from Globetrotters tour notes compiled by the late Seattle sportswriter J. Michael Kenyon, and Ben shared those notes with us.

Librarians and archivists made this book possible. Our research at the Dolph Briscoe Center for American History at the University of Texas in Austin was helped greatly by reference archivist Erin Harbour, library assistant Marisa Jefferson, and duplication services coordinator Aryn Glazier. Rachel Wells, a reference librarian at the Baseball Hall of Fame, shared content from the Giamatti Research Center. Peter Burtch of the Northwestern University Library tracked down old magazine articles about the Globetrotters. Helen McGettrick, a reference librarian at Chicago's Newberry

Library, helped us hunt for information on Saperstein, as did Julie Lynch of the Chicago Public Library's Sulzer Regional Library. Other research centers that supported our work were the Regenstein Library at the University of Chicago, the Skokie (Illinois) Public Library, the Evanston (Illinois) Public Library, and the National Archives and Records Administration in College Park, Maryland. We also thank Mark's spouse, Lisa Jacob; offspring Katherine Jacob, and friend Sue Simek, all of whom are librarians who helped us locate hard-to-find information.

We're grateful for the sharp readers who volunteered to go through our manuscript and offer constructive advice. They include Sherman Jenkins, P. Wayne Moore, Lorraine Forte, and the aforementioned Richard Cahan and Michael Williams. Mark's secret resource was his Chicago writers support group, especially Mark Caro, who shared insightful storytelling tips, and Jonathan Eig, who was a terrific coach during the research. Others in the writers group who gave steady encouragement: James Finn Garner, Pat Byrnes, Lou Carlozo, Jim Powers, Keir Graff, and Paul Erickson. We also received invaluable advice from history writers Robert Loerzel, Adam Selzer, and Marianne Mather. Lawrence Downes, whose father worked at the *Honolulu Star-Bulletin*, tracked down Hawaiian records for us. Matt O'Connor delved into Cook County (Illinois) Circuit Court records to support our research into legal issues involving Saperstein's estate.

We offer special thanks to our editor at Rowman & Littlefield, Christen Karniski; our R&L production editor, Andrew Yoder; our copy editor, Erin McGarvey; and our agent, Gary Heidt, of Signature Literary Agency. Our friend Ted Weinstein offered helpful tips for promoting this book.

A host of helpful people connected us with interview subjects and information. Hilary Shenfeld arranged our interview with her father, Gerald Saperstein, Abe's first cousin. Carmen Del Giudice connected us with former Globetrotter Emory Luck. Nancy Franke Wilson and Jimmy Erickson helped us arrange an interview with Don Shelby, who recalled seeing the Globetrotters in the 1950s. Chris Lauten, Northwestern University's director of basketball operations, connected us with former DePaul University basketball coach Joey Meyer. Nancy Pinion of the Jesse Owens Museum and Memorial Park in Oakville, Alabama, led us to Marlene Rankin, Jesse Owens's daughter. Kathie Linehan gave us a family perspective on her mother-in-law, key Saperstein aide Marie Linehan. Joshua Wetterhahn shared a senior honors thesis about Abe Saperstein that he wrote while at Northwestern University, featuring an interview with Marques Haynes.

Helpful advice and observations were given by sports public relations expert Tom Isaacson, an associate professor at Northern Michigan University, and Steve Dittmore, dean of the College of Education and Health Sciences at Baldwin Wallace University and coauthor of the textbook *Sport Public Relations*. Cleveland-area history experts Scott Longert and Sean Martin helped us try (but fail) to find any trace of an Abe Saperstein link with the Cleveland Rosenblums basketball team. We also thank Lani Anzivino, daughter of former Globetrotters executive Joe Anzivino, whom Saperstein hired in 1961, and Bob Pritchard, president of the Hinckley (Illinois) Historical Society.

No, Abe Saperstein could not really palm a basketball. He used a sports sticky spray to hold onto the ball.

PHOTO CREDITS

Saperstein brought tennis stars Karol Fageros and Althea Gibson on tour with the Globetrotters in 1959.

NOTES

The following abbreviations are used for sources in the notes.

AP: Associated Press
CD: Chicago Defender
CDN: Chicago Daily News
CST: Chicago Sun-Times
CT: Chicago Tribune
DBC: Dolph Briscoe Center for American History, University of Texas
    at Austin
INS: International News Service
NA: National Archives of the United States
PC: Pittsburgh Courier
UP: United Press
UPI: United Press International

CHAPTER 1

1. Michael Schumacher, *Mr. Basketball: George Mikan, the Minneapolis Lakers and the Birth of the NBA* (New York: Bloomsbury, 2007), 114.

2. Wendell Smith, Wendell Smith's Sports Beat, *PC*, 7 Jan. 1950; "Trotters Return Here in 2 Weeks," *Lodi (CA) News-Sentinel*, 12 Jan. 1952; Ken McConnell, Before and After, *Vancouver Province*, 23 Dec. 1948.

3. Don Hayner and Tom McNamee, *The Stadium: 1929-1994, the Official Commemorative History of the Chicago Stadium* (Chicago: Performance Media, 1993).

4. Hayner and McNamee, *The Stadium.*

5. Gene Graff, "16,000 to See Pro Cage Bill," *CST*, 19 Feb. 1948; "Trotters Spill Lakers in Last Second 61-59," *Minneapolis Tribune*, 20 Feb. 1948; ad in *CT*, 19 Feb. 1948. Adjusted for inflation, the top reserved-seat price of $3 and the $1.20 general admission would be about $40 and $16 in 2024 dollars.

6. Author interview with Frank Rose, 22 Jan. 2022.

7. Charles Leavelle, "Brick Slayer Is Likened to Jungle Beast," *CT*, 5 June 1938.

8. Luther H. Gulick, "The Psychological Effects of Basket Ball for Women," in *Line Basket Ball or Basket Ball for Women*, by Senda Berenson (New York: American Sports Publishing, 1901), 12.

9. Charles Einstein, INS, "Harlem Globetrotters Start on Second Half Million Miles," *Scrantonian (PA) Tribune*, 23 Dec. 1945.

10. Leonard Lewin, *New York Mirror*, reprinted in *St. Croix Avis* (Virgin Islands), 9 Oct. 1963.

11. Hayner and McNamee, *The Stadium.*

12. Schumacher, *Mr. Basketball*, 43–44.

13. Ben Green, *Spinning the Globe: The Rise, Fall, and Return to Greatness of the Harlem Globetrotters* (New York: Amistad, 2005), 201.

14. Buster Miller, Sports Parade, *New York Age*, 15 March 1941.

15. "Capacity House Expected for Big Cage Show," *Daily Oklahoman*, 1 Feb. 1948.

16. Green, *Spinning the Globe*, 250-51.

17. Jim Litke, AP, "Best Game Nobody Remembers," *Orangeburg (SC) Times and Democrat*, 20 Feb. 2003.

18. Schumacher, *Mr. Basketball*, 115.

19. Author interview with Gerald Saperstein, 10 Nov. 2022; Don Babwin, AP, "No Joke—60 Years since Globetrotters Beat the Lakers," *Rapid City (SD) Journal*, 18 Feb. 2008.

20. Arch Ward, In the Wake of the News, *CT*, 26 Dec. 1946.

21. Sid Ziff, "Physician Gets Call," *Los Angeles Times*, 27 Feb. 1962.

22. "Trotters' Pressley Out to Stop Mikan," *CDN*, 18 Feb. 1948.

23. "Trotters Top Lakers with Rally, 61-59," *CT*, 20 Feb. 1948.

24. Green, *Spinning the Globe*, 203.

25. "Mikan Co., Stags Face Tough Foes," *Chicago Herald-American*, 19 Feb. 1948.

26. Green, *Spinning the Globe*, 203–4; Schumacher, *Mr. Basketball*, 115–16.

27. Pete Sallaway, Sports Mirror, *Victoria (BC) Times Colonist*, 20 Jan. 1941.

28. Green, *Spinning the Globe*, 204–5.

29. UP, "Pro Basketball Changes Sought," *Pittsburgh Press*, 6 Jan. 1950.

30. Don Bryant, Point Blank, *Lincoln (NE) Journal Star*, 11 Jan. 1959.

31. Green, *Spinning the Globe*, 204–5.

32. Schumacher, *Mr. Basketball*, 224; "George Mikan," Basketball-reference .com, www.basketball-reference.com/players/m/mikange01.html (accessed 3 June 2022).

33. Green, *Spinning the Globe*, 205.

34. Schumacher, *Mr. Basketball*, 115.

35. "Trotters Top Lakers with Rally, 61–59," *CT*, 20 Feb. 1948.

36. John Christgau, *Tricksters in the Madhouse: Lakers vs. Globetrotters, 1948* (Lincoln, NE: Bison Books, 2007), 49.

37. Bruce Weber, "Marques Haynes, 89, Dies; Dribbled as a Globetrotter and Dazzled Worldwide," *New York Times*, 22 May 2015. The game in which Haynes dribbled out the entire fourth quarter was in Mexico City in 1946 when he was playing for Saperstein's Kansas City Stars.

38. Green, *Spinning the Globe*, 206.

39. Christgau, *Tricksters*, 148–49. No video or audio record of the 1948 Lakers-Globetrotters game exists, and Christgau's book sometimes takes literary license with the play-by-play of the game. But Christgau interviewed Marques Haynes and presumably got a firsthand account of his conversation with Saperstein.

40. Hayner and McNamee, *The Stadium*.

41. Litke, "Best Game"; Christgau, *Tricksters*, 169.

42. Christgau, *Tricksters*, 161.

43. Green, *Spinning the Globe,* 208–9; Schumacher, *Mr. Basketball*, 118; Edgar C. Greene, "Trotters Win in Last Second, 61–59," *Chicago Herald-American*, 20 Feb. 1948.

44. "Last Second Win by Globetrotters Gives 17,823 'Biggest' Thrill," *CD*, 28 Feb. 1948.

45. Green, *Spinning the Globe*, 209; Jeff Coplon, "Champs and Tramps," *Sports Heritage,* November–December 1987. We're accepting Globetrotters player Vertes Zeigler's version of Saperstein's bonuses. Teammate Sam Wheeler claimed the bonuses were $1,000, but that seems rich for Saperstein or any other sports owner of that time.

46. Green, *Spinning the Globe*, 209.

47. Greene, "Trotters Win."

48. Edward P. Sainsbury, UP, "Ezzard Charles' Kayo Punch Kills 20-Year-Old Light Heavy," *Dayton Herald*, 21 Feb. 1948.

49. Litke, "Best Game."

50. Eric Nusbaum, "How the Harlem Globetrotters Integrated the NBA," *Sports Stories* newsletter, vol. 7, Nov. 5, 2019, https://sportsstories.substack.com/p/how-the-harlem-globetrotters-integrated (accessed 23 Jan. 2023).

51. Green, *Spinning the Globe*, 209.

52. "'Privileged Few' Hit in Jackson Day Talk; Southern Revolt, Wallace Not Mentioned," *Staunton (VA) News-Leader*, 20 Feb. 1948.

53. Author interview with Frank Rose, 22 Jan. 2022.

54. Coplon, "Champs and Tramps."

55. Murray Rose, AP, Sports Roundup, *Key West (FL) Citizen*, 14 Jan. 1953.

CHAPTER 2

1. "Abe Saperstein, a Biography," Joseph J. Anzivino Collection, DBC, 98-166/2.

2. "Tour through Whitechapel," *Minneapolis Daily Times*, 5 Feb. 1898.

3. "King Feasts London Poor," *Boston Evening Transcript*, 5 July 1902.

4. Ben Green, *Spinning the Globe: The Rise, Fall, and Return to Greatness of the Harlem Globetrotters* (New York: Amistad, 2005), 14–15. Green's book is by far the best source on Saperstein's family during the early years. He interviewed three of Saperstein's siblings, all of whom had died by the time we began our research.

5. Green, *Spinning the Globe*, 15.

6. "Lomza History," Virtual Shtetl, https://sztetl.org.pl/en/towns/l/680-lomza/99-history/137628-history-of-community (accessed 20 Nov. 2022).

7. James L. Haley, *Wolf: The Lives of Jack London* (New York: Basic Books, 2010), 140–50.

8. Jack London, *The People of the Abyss* (New York: Macmillan, 1903), 192.

9. Green, *Spinning the Globe*, 16.

10. Green, *Spinning the Globe*, 16–17.

11. Author interview with Guy Saperstein, 1 Feb. 2022; "Abe Saperstein, a Biography," Anzivino Collection, DBC, 98-166/2. Some biographical information describes Abe as Louis and Anna's oldest child, but another child was born before Abe and died at an early age, most likely before the family's immigration to the United States. The name and the sex of that child is unknown.

12. Green, *Spinning the Globe*, 17; Eloise Saperstein Berkley, unpublished manuscript, 21.

13. Author interview with Roy Raemer, 13 March 2023.

14. Author interview with Guy Saperstein, 1 Feb. 2022.

15. Green, *Spinning the Globe*, 18. Roy Raemer, son of Abe's sister Leah, told us that as his grandmother Anna got older, she picked up some English, speaking it with a heavy accent.

16. Green, *Spinning the Globe*, 19.

17. James Enright, "No Free Throws at Abe's Feed, Old Pals Pay 50 Bucks a Plate," *Sporting News*, 12 Dec. 1964.

18. Dave Zinkoff with Edgar Williams, *Around the World with the Harlem Globetrotters* (Philadelphia: MacRae Smith, 1953), 20.

19. Henry Ford, "The International Jew: The World's Foremost Problem," *Dearborn Independent*, 3 Sept. 1921.

20. Green, *Spinning the Globe*, 20–21.

21. Eloise Saperstein Berkley, unpublished memoir, 22; Green, *Spinning the Globe*, 21.

22. *Red & White*, Lake View High School yearbook, March 1920; John P. Carmichael, The Barber Shop, "Globetrotters Mark 33d Years Jan. 2," *CDN*, 21 Dec. 1959.

23. Al Warden, Patrolling the Sport Highway, *Ogden (Utah) Standard-Examiner*, 5 Jan. 1947; Dave Quinn, "Illinois All-State Teams, 1933–1993," Basketball Museum of Illinois, https://basketballmuseumofillinois.com/history/527-all-state-teams/ (accessed 21 Nov. 2022).

24. Pat Harmon, Red Peppers, *Cedar Rapids (IA) Gazette*, 6 Jan. 1949; Abe Saperstein, "Globetrotter Takes Tip from Biblical Job," *Windsor (Ontario, Canada) Star*, 17 April 1957; email to the authors from Sammi Merritt, Transcript and Verification Unit, Office of the Registrar, University of Illinois Urbana-Champaign, 12 May 2022.

25. Green, *Spinning the Globe*, 22–23. The home on Hermitage was too far south to be in what most people consider Ravenswood. Even so, the family considered Ravenswood its home neighborhood, and some or all of its previous homes may have been in Ravenswood proper. Also, the Saperstein children went to Ravenswood Elementary School. The Hermitage house is now demolished, but a weather-beaten historical marker reminds people that Saperstein once lived there.

26. Green, *Spinning the Globe*, 23.

27. Green, *Spinning the Globe*, 23–24.

28. "Bring Colored Stars to Butte," *Montana Standard*, 12 Feb. 1934; "Max Rosenblum," Encyclopedia of Cleveland, Case Western Reserve University, https://case.edu/ech/articles/r/rosenblum-max (accessed 22 Nov. 2022).

29. Author interview with Guy Saperstein, 1 Feb. 2022.

30. Author interview with Lanier Saperstein, 24 Feb. 2022.

CHAPTER 3

1. Ben Green, *Spinning the Globe: The Rise, Fall, and Return to Greatness of the Harlem Globetrotters* (New York: Amistad, 2005), 24.

2. Nicholas Lemann, *The Promised Land: The Great Black Migration and How It Changed America* (New York: Vintage Books, 1992), 16; Robert Loerzel, "Blood in the Streets," *Chicago* magazine, Aug. 2019.

3. Green, *Spinning the Globe*, 33; Terry Bohn, "Walter Ball," Society for American Baseball Research, https://sabr.org/bioproj/person/walter-ball/ (accessed 22 Nov. 2022).

4. "African-American Pioneers," Pro Football Hall of Fame, www.profootball-hof.com/news/2004/02/news-african-american-pioneers/ (accessed 25 Nov. 2022).

5. "Savoy Big Five," Black Fives Foundation, www.blackfives.org/teams/savoy -big-five/ (accessed 23 Nov. 2022).

6. Robert W. Peterson, *Pigskin: The Early Years of Pro Football* (New York: Oxford University Press, 1997), 175–77; Kenan Heise, "Football Legend 'Fritz' Pollard," *CT*, 14 May 1986.

7. Fritz Pollard, Sports Closeup, *Jackson (MS) Advocate*, 27 June 1953.

8. Alan Ward, On Second Thought, *Oakland Tribune*, 3 Feb. 1949.

9. "Big Darktown Ballroom Taken by Gothamites," *CT*, 20 Feb. 1927; David W. Kellum, "Howard U Beaten in Chicago," *CD*, 7 Jan. 1928.

10. "Individual History of Savoy Big Five Basketball Players," *Savoyager*, 3 March 1928, Abe Saperstein Papers, DBC, 2.325/P14c; Pollard, Sports Closeup.

11. "Red Triangles Beat Giles Post, 42 to 24," *La Crosse (WI) Tribune*, 16 Feb. 1928.

12. Green, *Spinning the Globe*, 38–39.

13. "Red Triangles Beat Giles Post, 42 to 24,"; "Savoys Give Evanston a Good Licking," *CD*, 21 April 1928.

14. Green, *Spinning the Globe*, 37–39.

15. "Havre All-Stars Have Six Games Scheduled for Next Three Weeks," *Great Falls (MT) Tribune*, 1 Feb. 1922; "Globe Trotters Start," *Lima (OH) News*, 7 Jan. 1920.

16. Michael Strauss, "Real Founder of the Globe Trotters," *Sports Quarterly Basketball Special, 1973–74* (New York: Counterpoint, 1973), 58–59, 112–13; Green, *Spinning the Globe*, 44–49.

17. Murray Nelson, "Tommy Brookins: Pioneer in Two Worlds," in *Before Jackie Robinson: The Transcendent Role of Black Sporting Pioneers*, ed. Gerald R. Gems (Lincoln: University of Nebraska Press, 2017), 222–28.

18. Pollard, Sports Closeup.

19. "'Very Special' Notes Regarding Origin of Harlem Globetrotters," Saperstein Papers, DBC, 2.325/P14c. The Globetrotters' origin report may have been written by Saperstein aide Marie Linehan. She wrote other short papers on Trotters history that have a similar writing style.

20. "First Harlem Globetrotter Team" and "#1 Harlem Globetrotters team," Saperstein Papers, DBC, 2.325/P14c.

21. Green, *Spinning the Globe*, 35.

22. "Recall First Game of Globetrotters Here," *Hinckley (IL) Review*, 5 March 1959.

23. "High Score Is Collected by Hinckley Five," *DeKalb (IL) Chronicle*, 19 Jan. 1929; "Hinckley Is Winner over Colored Five," *DeKalb (IL) Chronicle*, 23 Jan. 1929.

24. J. Michael Kenyon, "Chron 1928–1940," notes and game listings shared with Ben Green, who shared them with us. Kenyon died in 2017.

25. "Hoop Team Wants Game: Harlem Globe Trotters Would Like to Visit Pacific Northwest," *Oregonian* (Portland), 13 Nov. 1928; "Globe Trotters to Engage 151st Quintet Dec. 27," *Minneapolis Tribune*, 16 Dec. 1928. A team called the Harlem Big Five did operate out of New York City, but it had a different coach and different players.

26. "Al (Runt) Pullins, One of the Original Harlem Globetrotters, Guides His Own Sepia Court Specialists," *Helena (MT) Independent Record*, 18 Nov. 1952.

27. Green, *Spinning the Globe*, 42–43.

CHAPTER 4

1. Charles Bartlett, "Trotters Got Start in Illinois Hamlet," *Fond du Lac (WI) Commonwealth Reporter*, 27 Oct. 1965.

2. Ben Green, *Spinning the Globe: The Rise, Fall, and Return to Greatness of the Harlem Globetrotters* (New York: Amistad, 2005), 53.

3. Jerry Leslie, "Sioux Cityan Recalls Giving Helping Hand," *Sioux City (IA) Journal,* 31 Jan. 1968.

4. Nelson George, *Elevating the Game: Black Men and Basketball* (New York: HarperCollins, 1992), 44; Green, *Spinning the Globe*, 62.

5. Bartlett, "Trotters Got Start"; Ray Schwartz, Sports with Schwartz, *Provo (UT) Herald*, 30 Dec. 1956; Eloise Saperstein Berkley, unpublished memoir, 25.

6. Bartlett, "Trotters Got Start."

7. Red Smith, Views of Sports, *Indianapolis News*, 25 Nov. 1948; Green, *Spinning the Globe*, 61.

8. Leo Fischer, "Nomads of the Hardwood Floor," *Esquire*, April 1939.

9. Green, *Spinning the Globe*, 51; Schwartz, Sports with Schwartz.

10. Green, *Spinning the Globe*, 58; Edgar Williams, "They Clown but They Win," *Philadelphia Inquirer*, 26 Feb. 1950; Bernard J. Duffy, "Death of Saperstein Recalls Early Start," *Winona (MN) Daily News*, 22 March 1966; Bob Hoenig, Inside Outlook, *Los Angeles Citizen-News*, 25 Jan. 1950.

11. Author interview with Frank Rose, 22 Jan. 2022.

12. Hal Tate, I've Got News for You, *Austin News* (Chicago), 17 May 1961.

13. Larry Boeck, "Trotters Traveled Hard Road to Top," *Louisville Courier-Journal*, 2 April 1950.

14. Green, *Spinning the Globe*, 52–53.

15. Green, *Spinning the Globe*, 55–57.

16. U.S. Census, 1910, 1920, and 1930.

17. *Northwest Monitor*, 31 Jan 1933, quoted in Damion L. Thomas, *Globetrotting: African American Athletes and Cold War Politics* (Urbana: University of Illinois Press, 2012), 54–55; "Accurate-Shooting Globe Trotters Rally to Beat Barnsdalls," *Winona (MI) Republican-Herald*, 1 Feb. 1933; AP, 2 Feb. 1933, quoted by J. Michael Kenyon, "Chron 1928–1940."

18. Dick Hackenberg, Please Note . . . , *Moorhead (MI) Daily News*, 5 Sept. 1933.

19. "Captain of 'Globetrotters' Tells of Discrimination," *Producers News* (Plentywood, MT), 9 Feb. 1934.

20. "Captain of 'Globetrotters' Tells of Discrimination," *Producers News*.

21. Green, *Spinning the Globe*, 54.

22. "New York Harlem Globe Trotters Come Here Feb. 10," *Rapid City (SD) Journal*, 30 Jan. 1933.

23. Hackenberg, Please Note.

24. Hackenberg, Please Note; Elliot Cushing, Sports Eye View, *Rochester (NY) Democrat and Chronicle*, 3 Dec. 1944.

25. Dale M. Brumfield, "House of David Hoops Team Held Court, *News Leader* (Staunton, VA), 17 July 2017.

26. UP, "Babe Zaharias, 42, Dies after Long Cancer Fight," *Philadelphia Inquirer*, 28 Sept. 1956; Bernard J. Duffy, The Duffer's Lane, *Winona (MN) Republican-Herald*, 23 Dec. 1933; "Globe Trotters Toy with Didrikson to Win, 37–20," *Winona (MN) Republican-Herald*, 23 Dec. 1933.

27. "Accurate-Shooting Globe Trotters Rally to Beat Barnsdalls."

28. "Colored Team Battles Rock Island Quint," *Davenport (IA) Democrat and Leader*, 3 Dec. 1931; "Steely Quintet Battles Gotham Five on East High School Floor Tonight," *Waterloo (IA) Evening Courier*, 30 Jan. 1929; "Hoop Team Wants

Game: Harlem Globe Trotters Would Like to Visit Pacific Northwest," *Oregonian* (Portland), 13 Nov. 1928.

29. Carmichael, "Globetrotters Mark 33d Year Jan. 2"; Bartlett, "Trotters Got Start"; Jim Murray, "Globies Would Play Best in Celts' Bill Russell," *Passaic (NJ) Herald News*, 1 Feb. 1965.

30. "Knights Ready for Tilt with Bearded Stars," *Davenport (IA) Democrat and Leader*, 14 June 1925.

31. Thomas, *Globetrotting*, 63–66.

32. Bob Smith, "Saperstein Shocker—The Silent 700," *CDN*, 4 Jan. 1963.

33. Stew Hargesheimer, *Rochester (MN) Post Bulletin*, Feb. 1932, quoted by J. Michael Kenyon, "Chron 1928–1940."

34. "Globetrotters to Play Union Furniture Stars," *El Paso Times*, 29 Jan. 1967.

35. Phil Jackman, "Inman Jackson Was More Than a Player," *Baltimore Sun*, 13 April 1973.

36. Jackman, "Inman Jackson."

37. Green, *Spinning the Globe*, 68.

38. Green, *Spinning the Globe*, 52. Decades later, Pullins would claim that they split the proceeds six ways, not seven, with Saperstein getting only one share. But Green notes that Saperstein claimed he got two of the seven shares, an explanation that Green thought was more plausible given that Saperstein handled expenses. We agree.

39. Green, *Spinning the Globe*, 52, 62.

40. Bernard J. Duffy, "Death of Saperstein Recalls Early Start," *Winona (MN) Daily News*, 22 March 1966.

41. *Great Falls (MT) Tribune*, March 1933, quoted by J. Michael Kenyon, "Chron 1928–1940"; "Brewers Down Nationals with Crippled Quint," *St. Cloud (MN) Times*, 22 Jan. 1934; Green, *Spinning the Globe*, 68.

42. AP, "Globetrotters Find Gate Off about 20 Percent," *Washington Star*, 8 April 1958.

43. Bernard J. Duffy, The Duffer's Lane, *Winona (MN) Republican-Herald*, 24 May 1932.

44. Green, *Spinning the Globe*, 58, 66.

45. "Novel Quintet to Play Celts Here on Friday," *Davenport (IA) Democrat and Leader*, 22 Jan. 1929.

46. "Harlem Globe Trotters Will Invade West," *CD*, 29 Nov. 1930.

47. "New York Harlem Globe Trotters Come Here Feb. 10," *Rapid City (SD) Journal*, 30 Jan. 1933.

48. "Voyageurs Set for Invasion of Globe Trotters," *Winona (MN) Republican-Herald*, 6 March 1931; "Trotters Coming with Classy Quint," *Plentywood (MT) Herald*, 10 Jan. 1935.

49. Green, *Spinning the Globe*, 62.

50. "Globe-Trotters Play at Lake," *Mason City (IA) Globe-Gazette*, 22 Dec. 1930; "High Score Is Collected by Hinckley Five," *DeKalb (IL) Chronicle*, 19 Jan. 1929; "Colored Team Will Be Foe of Indees at Community Hi Gym," *Sterling (IL) Daily Gazette*, 22 Jan. 1929; "New York Renaissance," Naismith National Basketball Hall of Fame website, www.hoophall.com/hall-of-famers/new-york -renaissance/ (accessed 10 Dec. 2022).

51. Chester Washington, Says Ches, *PC*, 28 Jan. 1933; "New York Renaissance," Naismith National Basketball Hall of Fame website.

52. *Breckenridge (MN) Gazette Telegram*, Jan. 1933, quoted in Green, *Spinning the Globe*, 71.

CHAPTER 5

1. "Famous Globe Trotters to Invade Redfield and Aberdeen This Week," *Aberdeen (SD) American-News*, 5 Feb. 1933; "Detroit's Portside Passer," *PC*, 21 March 1936; Ben Green, *Spinning the Globe: The Rise, Fall, and Return to Greatness of the Harlem Globetrotters* (New York: Amistad, 2005), 78. According to Green, Saperstein's future father-in-law, Andrew Franklin, persuaded him to put his name on the jerseys. Saperstein eventually dropped his name from the uniform, reason unknown.

2. US Bureau of Labor Statistics Inflation Calculator, www.bls.gov/data/infla tion_calculator.htm (accessed 15 April 2024).

3. "Al (Runt) Pullins, One of Original Harlem Globetrotters, Guides His Own Sepia Court Specialists," *Helena (MT) Independent-Record*, 18 Nov. 1952.

4. Bernard J. Duffy, The Duffer's Lane, *Winona (MN) Republican-Herald*, 2 Feb. 1934.

5. "Harlem Globe Trotters Will Present Improved Team Here," *Helena (MT) Daily Independent*, 19 March 1934.

6. Green, *Spinning the Globe*, 78–79; "Harlem Globe Trotters Will Present," *Helena (MT) Daily Independent*.

7. "Al (Runt) Pullins, One of Original Harlem Globetrotters," *Helena (MT) Independent-Record*; "Globe Trotters Seek to Halt Infringement," *Minneapolis Star*, 12 Feb. 1934; Green, *Spinning the Globe*, 324.

8. "Harlem Globe Trotters Pause Here on Homeward Leg of Tour," *Billings (MT) Gazette*, 27 March 1934.

9. Author interview with Abra Berkley, 30 Nov. 2021.

10. Author interview with Abra Berkley, 30 Nov. 2021; 1940 US Census.

11. Author interview with Joyce Leviton, 27 Dec. 2021. Leviton's father, Buddy Franklin, was Sylvia Franklin's brother.

12. Eloise Saperstein Berkley, unpublished memoir, 27.

13. David Condon, In the Wake of the News, *CT*, 27 Jan. 1959. Some details of the blizzard story varied in Saperstein's repeated tellings, and author Claude Johnson of *The Black Fives* has even expressed doubts that it happened. But we believe that it likely did.

14. "Globetrotter Boss, Abe Saperstein, Remembers Team's Early Travels, Including Gun Toters in Montana," *Burlington (VT) Free Press*, 28 Oct. 1955.

15. David Condon, In the Wake of the News, *CT*, 27 Jan. 1959.

16. Red Smith, Views of Sports, *Indianapolis News*, 25 Nov. 1948.

17. Merle Jones, Egypt Sport Talk, *Southern Illinoisan*, 22 April 1952.

18. Green, *Spinning the Globe*, 86–89; "Harlem Trotters Are on Good List," *Spokane (WA) Chronicle*, 11 Feb. 1935.

19. AP, "Find Team Not Amateurs," *Spokane (WA) Spokesman-Review*, 19 Feb. 1935; Green, *Spinning the Globe*, 88–89.

20. Emmett Watson, Watson's Needle, *Seattle Post-Intelligencer*, 10 April 1957.

21. Stu Keate, Sports Shots, *Vancouver Province*, 12 Jan. 1942.

22. Ken Gunderman, Sez Me, *Escanaba (MI) Daily Press*, 5 April 1935; US Bureau of Labor Statistics Inflation Calculator, www.bls.gov/data/inflation_calculator.htm (accessed 13 Dec. 2022).

23. Inman Jackson, letter to the editor of an Iron Mountain, Michigan, newspaper, quoted by Green, *Spinning the Globe*, 83.

24. James Enright, "Saperstein Super-Duper Hoops Salesman," *Sporting News*, 22 Dec. 1962.

25. David Condon, In the Wake of the News, *CT*, 17 Feb. 1969.

26. "Broadway Clowns Rated with Harlem," *Vancouver Province*, 7 Feb. 1938.

27. "Harlem Globe Trotters Play Celtics March 25," *CD*, 19 March 1938.

28. Oney Fred Sweet, "Hunting New Thrills as an Understudy at the Amusement Parks," *CT*, 16 July 1915. It's unclear when the African Dip ended at White City, but it was operating in Chicago at the Century of Progress exhibition in 1933–1934.

29. "Harlem Globe Trotters and Celtics in Tie," *CD*, April 2, 1938; "Harlem Globe Trotters and Celtics Play 32–32 Tie," *CT*, 26 March 1938. The newspapers

differed on the final score—36-36 or 32-32—but the *Defender* wrote a more detailed story, so its report seems more reliable.

30. "Renaissance Calls Harlem Globetrotters 'Court Clowns'; Will Play Them 'Winner Take All' Game," *PC*, 14 Jan. 1939.

31. Green, *Spinning the Globe*, 105.

32. Green, *Spinning the Globe*, 97, 105, 110.

33. "Pro Basketball Title Tourney Opens Today," *CT*, 26 March 1939.

34. Green, *Spinning the Globe*, 107–20.

35. "Pro Basketball Title Tourney Opens Today," *CT*, 26 March 1939; Howard Martin, "Harlem Quintet Beats Harmon in Pro Tourney," *CT*, 27 March 1939.

36. Green, *Spinning the Globe*, 119.

37. Green, *Spinning the Globe*, 115–19.

38. Jeff Coplon, "Champs and Tramps," *Sports Heritage*, Nov.–Dec. 1987.

39. Sport Rays, *Bellingham (WA) Herald*, 9 April 1939.

40. Alan Gould, "Helen Stephens Is Best Athlete," *Lawrence (KS) Journal-World*, 15 Dec. 1936; "Helen Stephens Is Real Girl," *Harrisburg (PA) Telegraph*, 6 Aug. 1936.

41. "Outstanding Touring Cage Teams Will Meet Dominoes," *Victoria (BC) Daily Times*, 4 Jan. 1940.

42. Esther Bradley, St. Paul Society News, *St. Paul (MN) Recorder*, 3 Jan. 1936.

43. Bill Forst, Sports with Bill Forst, *Vancouver Province*, 21 Jan. 1937.

44. Pete Sallaway, Sports Mirror, *Victoria (BC) Times Colonist*, 20 Jan. 1940; "Joe Law," Boxrec.com, https://boxrec.com/en/box-pro/30138 (accessed 13 Dec. 2022).

45. Alf Cottrell, On the Sunbeam, *Vancouver Sun*, 4 Oct. 1944.

46. Bill Forst, In This Corner, *Vancouver Province*, 29 Jan. 1938; "Illinois Stars Meet Charlton in Soccer Today," *CT*, 6 June 1937.

47. Cottrell, On the Sunbeam.

CHAPTER 6

1. Todd Peterson, *Early Black Baseball in Minnesota: The St. Paul Gophers, Minneapolis Keystones, and Other Barnstorming Teams of the Deadball Era* (Jefferson, NC: McFarland, 2010), 196.

2. "Cleveland Black Friars, Managed by Saperstein of Harlem Globe Trotters, to Play Here Sunday," *Winona (MN) Daily News*, 24 May 1932.

3. Neil Lanctot, *Negro League Baseball: The Rise and Ruin of a Black Institution* (Philadelphia: University of Pennsylvania Press, 2004), 114.

4. "Sport: Satchel the Great," *Time*, 19 July 1948; Larry Tye, *Satchel: The Life and Times of an American Legend* (New York: Random House, 2009), 62.

5. Steven V. Roberts, "'Color Blind: The Forgotten Team That Broke Baseball's Color Line' by Tom Dunkel," *Washington Post*, 7 April 2013.

6. Tye, *Satchel*, 103; US Department of Labor, "National Income in 1935," *Monthly Labor Review*, 1936, https://heinonline.org/HOL/LandingPage?handle=hein.journals/month43&div=74&id=&page= (accessed 2 June 2, 2023).

7. Tye, *Satchel*, 65.

8. Larry Tye, "Master Entertainers," National Baseball Hall of Fame, https://baseballhall.org/discover-more/stories/baseball-history/master-entertainers (accessed 19 Feb. 2022).

9. Tye, *Satchel*, 93.

10. Tye, *Satchel*, 99.

11. Alan J. Pollock, *Barnstorming to Heaven: Syd Pollock and His Great Black Teams* (Tuscaloosa: University of Alabama Press, 2006), 65.

12. Tye, *Satchel*, 273.

13. "Satchel Paige," Negro Leagues Baseball Museum, https://nlbemuseum.com/history/players/paige.html (accessed 6 Feb. 2022).

14. Tye, *Satchel*, 95.

15. Timothy M. Gay, *Satch, Dizzy & Rapid Robert: The Wild Saga of Interracial Baseball before Jackie Robinson* (New York: Simon & Schuster, 2010), 2; Satchel Paige, *Maybe I'll Pitch Forever* (Lincoln: University of Nebraska Press, 1993), 115.

16. Paige, *Maybe I'll Pitch Forever*, 159–60.

17. Lanctot, *Negro League Baseball*, 169.

18. "Satchel Paige," Baseball Reference, www.baseball-reference.com/players/p/paigesa01.shtml (accessed 19 June 2022); Luke Epplin, *Our Team: The Epic Story of Four Men and the World Series That Changed Baseball* (New York: Flatiron Books, 2021), 69.

19. Neil Lanctot, "First Chapter: Negro League Baseball," *New York Times*, 16 May 2004.

20. "All-Nations Baseball Club Opposes Eagles at New Ball Park Tonight," *St. Cloud (MN) Times*, 7 July 1933; Rebecca T. Alpert, *Out of Left Field: Jews and Black Baseball* (New York: Oxford University Press, 2011), 48.

21. "Eagles Play All-Nations Sunday and Monday—Two Leagues End Slate." *St. Cloud (MN) Times*, 11 Aug. 1933.

22. Cathy Nelson Price, "Baseball's Integration Spurred by House of David, Negro League Contests," *Midland (MI) Daily News*, 7 Aug. 2007, www.ourmidland.com/news/article/Baseball-s-integration-spurred-by-House-of-David-7013103.php (20 June 2022).

23. "Madison Blues Take Berth in New Tri-State Baseball League," *La Crosse (WI) Tribune*, 22 March 1938; "Blues' Stars Worry about Wages," *Capital Times* (Madison, WI), 29 May 1938; UP, "Midwest Baseball League Announced," *The Gazette* (Cedar Rapids, IA), 23 March 1941.

24. Larry Powell, *Black Barons of Birmingham: The South's Greatest Negro League Team and Its Players* (Jefferson, NC: McFarland, 2009), 47–48.

25. Alf Cottrell, "Can He Carry Paige's Satchel?" *Vancouver Sun*, 14 Jan. 1946; Frank Thompson, Baseball Reference, www.baseball-reference.com/bull pen/Frank_Thompson_(thompfr04) (accessed 21 Feb. 2023).

26. "Monarchs Win Game; Tatum Wins Crowd," *Tulsa World*, 1 May 1947.

27. John Holway, *Voices from the Great Black Baseball Leagues* (Mineola, NY: Dover, 2010), 182.

28. Gordon Graham, Graham Crackers, *Journal and Courier* (Lafayette, IN), 27 July 1945.

29. Powell, *Black Barons of Birmingham*, 42; Ben Green, *Spinning the Globe: The Rise, Fall, and Return to Greatness of the Harlem Globetrotters* (New York: Amistad, 2005), 162.

30. "Trotters Vie Here Sunday," *Cincinnati Post*, 23 Sept. 1944; Al Warden, "Davidites, Trotters Drive Blues Away," *Standard-Examiner* (Ogden, UT), 19 Aug. 1944; Shaun O'Neill, "'Double Duty,' Negro Leagues' 2-Way Star," Major League Baseball, 18 Feb. 2021, www.mlb.com/news/double-duty-radcliffe-negro -leagues (accessed 9 Feb. 2022); "Trotters, Davidites Due Here Friday," *Medford (OR) Mail Tribune*, 8 Aug. 1954; Alan Ward, On Second Thought, *Oakland Tribune*, 15 Aug. 1954.

31. Pete Sallaway, *Times-Colonist* (Victoria, BC), 15 Jan. 1946; "Guide to the West Coast Negro Baseball Association Collection," Online Archive of California: African American Museum and Library at Oakland, https://oac.cdlib.org/findaid/ ark:/13030/c8125tf5/ (6 March 2022).

32. William J. Baker, *Jesse Owens: An American Life* (New York: The Free Press, 1986), 153–54.

33. Todd Anton and Bill Nowlin, *When Baseball Went to War* (Chicago: Triumph Books, 2008), 144.

34. "Cannibal Nine to Play Here," *Indianapolis News*, 30 June 1936.

35. Buck O'Neil and David Conrads, *I Was Right on Time: My Journey from the Negro Leagues to the Majors* (New York: Simon & Schuster, 1996), 12; Norm King, "Abe Saperstein," Society for American Baseball Research, 2017; Richard Goldstein, "Buck O'Neil, Negro Leagues Pioneer, Is Dead at 94," *New York Times*, 7 Oct. 2006.

36. Lanctot, *Negro League Baseball*, 108.

37. Brian Carroll, "Black Baseball's 'Funmakers': Taking the Miami Ethiopian Clowns Seriously," Society for American Baseball Research, https://sabr.org/journal/article/black-baseballs-funmakers-taking-the-miami-ethiopian-clowns-seriously/ (accessed 4 Feb. 2022).

38. Cum Posey, Posey's Points, *PC*, 21 Nov. 1942.

39. Lanctot, *Negro League Baseball*, 108; Martha Ackmann, *Curveball: The Remarkable Story of Toni Stone, the First Woman to Play Professional Baseball in the Negro League* (Chicago: Chicago Review Press, 2010), 92–93; Lanctot, *Negro League Baseball*, 109–10.

40. Lanctot, *Negro League Baseball*, 114; Marcus Hayes, Knight-Ridder Newspapers, "Negro League Classic Was Big Event—East-West Game Outdrew Major Leagues' All-Stars," *Seattle Times*, 7 July 1996.

41. "East-West All Star Game (Summaries)," Center for Negro League Baseball Research, www.cnlbr.org/Portals/0/RL/East-West%20All%20Star%20Game%20Summaries.pdf (accessed 22 Feb. 2023).

42. Lanctot, *Negro League Baseball*, 114, 145–46.

43. Lanctot, *Negro League Baseball*, 114, 112.

44. Cumberland Posey, "Posey Exposes Flaws of Sepia Baseball," *PC*, 23 Aug. 1941, 16.

45. C. W. Posey, Facts about Sports, *Weekly Review* (Birmingham, AL), 9 Sept. 1944; Lanctot, *Negro League Baseball*, 115.

46. Alpert, *Out of Left Field*, 87. Burley was a Black journalist who sometimes wrote under the name of Don Deleighbur.

47. Don Deleighbur, "Cum Posey vs. Abe Saperstein or the Inside Story of Promotional Warfare Going on in Negro Baseball," *Indianapolis Recorder*, 29 July 1944.

48. C. W. Posey, *Weekly Review* (Birmingham, AL), 2 Sept. 1944; Lanctot, *Negro League Baseball*, 122.

49. Wendell Smith, Smitty's Sports-Spurts, *PC*, 16 May 1942.

50. Alf Cottrell, "Abe's in Town—But on Holiday," *Vancouver Sun*, 26 Sept. 1944.

51. Pollock, *Barnstorming to Heaven*, 96. The team was called the Cincinnati Ethiopian Clowns for a time.

52. Pollock, *Barnstorming to Heaven*, 155.

53. Lanctot, *Negro League Baseball*, 145; Alpert, *Out of Left Field*, 86; Graham, Graham Crackers.

54. Doron Goldman, "1933–1962: The Business Meetings of Negro League Baseball," Society for American Baseball Research, https://sabr.org/journal/article/

1933-1962-the-business-meetings-of-negro-league-baseball/ (accessed 15 Nov. 2023).

55. Bill Forst, In This Corner, *Vancouver Province*, 21 Jan. 1939.

56. Pollock, *Barnstorming to Heaven*, 383; Alexa Brown, "Shortstops: Real Clowning Around," National Baseball Hall of Fame, https://baseballhall.org/discover/shortstops/real-clowning-around (accessed 19 Feb. 2023).

57. Jack Patterson, 'Round the Sports Map, *Vancouver Sun*, 17 Sept. 1938.

58. Bernie Swanson, "Crutchers Weren't Fooling," *Minneapolis Tribune*, 2 Aug. 1944.

59. Holway, *Voices from the Great Black Baseball Leagues*, 182, 186; Michael Bamberger, "Man of a Century Double-Duty Radcliffe, Nemesis of Ty Cobb, Close Friend of Satchel Paige, a Negro Leagues Legend, Remains the Life of the Party as He Celebrates His 100th Birthday," *Sports Illustrated*, 15 July 2002.

60. Lanctot, *Negro League Baseball*, 145.

61. William J. Marshall, Effa Manley interview, Louie B. Nunn Center for Oral History, University of Kentucky Libraries, 19 Oct. 1977, https://nunncenter.net/ohms-spokedb/render.php?cachefile=1977oh079_chan041_ohm.xml (accessed 12 Feb. 2022).

CHAPTER 7

1. Ben Green, *Spinning the Globe: The Rise, Fall, and Return to Greatness of the Harlem Globetrotters* (New York: Amistad, 2005), 122.

2. Dan Walton, Sports-Log, *Tacoma (WA) News Tribune*, 14 Feb. 1942.

3. Buster Miller, Sports Parade, *New York Age*, 30 March 1940.

4. Green, *Spinning the Globe,* 129–34; "Globe Trotters Five Eliminates New York Rens in Pro Tourney," *CD*, 23 March 1940.

5. Jake Frong, The Press Box, *Dayton Journal*, 21 March 1940.

6. Fay Young, The Stuff Is Here, *CD*, 23 March 1940.

7. Green, *Spinning the Globe*, 135; "Globe Trotters Cop World Cage Crown," *CD*, 30 March 1940; "Globe Trotters and Bruins Win; Reach Final," *CT*, 20 March 1940.

8. Stanley Frank, "Crossroads Champs," *Collier's*, 8 Feb. 1941.

9. *Chicago Herald-American*, quoted in Green, *Spinning the Globe*, 137.

10. "Globe Trotters Cop World Cage Crown," *CD*, 30 March 1940; "Harlems Beat Bruins to Win Basket Title," *CT*, 21 March 1940.

11. Frank, "Crossroads Champs."

12. "Pro Cage Champs Are Impressed by All-Star Lineup," *Oshkosh (WI) Daily Northwestern*, 31 Oct. 1940; Green, *Spinning the Globe*, 138–39.

13. "To Present Miss Bronze America When All-Stars Meet the Globe Trotters," *CD*, 16 Nov. 1940.

14. John C. Day, "College All-Stars Win 44–42 Overtime Game from Globe Trotters," *CD*, 7 Dec. 1940; "Oshkosh, College All-Stars Both Are Winners," *Oshkosh (WI) Daily Northwestern*, 30 Nov. 1940; "All-Stars Beat Pros, 44 to 42, in Overtime," *CT*, 30 Nov. 1940.

15. Wendell Smith, "'Dream Game' Thrills 22,000 as All-Stars Nip 'Trotters," *PC*, 7 Dec. 1940.

16. Bill Reddy, Keeping Posted, *Syracuse (NY) Post-Standard*, 21 May 1949.

17. Green, *Spinning the Globe*, 141–42.

18. Green, *Spinning the Globe*, 140–41; James Doherty, "Gibby's: Mecca of Horse Fans and Politicians," *CT*, 12 Jan. 1950; Gene Kessler, "Pensive, Tear Clash to Wait," *Chicago Times*, 27 June 1944.

19. Green, *Spinning the Globe*, 150–51.

20. Ole Nosey [pseud.], Everybody Goes When the Wagon Comes, *CD*, 22 March 1941; Fay Young, The Stuff Is Here, *CD*, 22 March 1941.

21. Sport Rays, *Bellingham (WA) Herald*, 18 Jan. 1942.

22. Dan Walton, Sports-Log, *Tacoma News Tribune*, 14 Feb. 1942.

23. *Spokane Daily Chronicle*, quoted in J. Michael Kenyon, "Chron, 1940–1949."

24. Green, *Spinning the Globe*, 198.

25. Smith, "Saperstein Shocker—The Silent 700," *CDN*.

26. Buster Miller, The Sports Parade, *New York Age*, 15 March 1941.

27. Alex Shults, *Seattle Times*, Dec. 1940, quoted in Green, *Spinning the Globe*, 147; Alf Cottrell, On the Sunbeam, *Vancouver Sun*, 14 Jan. 1944.

28. Hal Straight, Sport Rays, *Vancouver Sun*, 13 Jan. 1940. Despite Saperstein's insulting comments about Joe Louis, he later participated in a fundraiser when the boxer faced tax problems.

29. Red Smith, Views of Sports, *Indianapolis News*, 25 Nov. 1948; Murray, "Globies Would Play Best in Celts' Bill Russell," *Passaic (NJ) Herald News*.

30. Green, *Spinning the Globe*, 171.

31. Eloise Saperstein Berkley, unpublished memoir, 40–41.

32. Frank, "Crossroads Champs."

33. Author interview with Don Shelby, 17 Aug. 2023.

34. Dan Walton, Sports-Log, *Tacoma News Tribune*, 13 Jan. 1942; US Bureau of Labor Statistics Inflation Calculator, www.bls.gov/data/inflation_calculator.htm (accessed 15 April 2024).

35. "War Changes Personnel of Harlem Globe Trotters," *Detroit Tribune*, 24 Oct. 1942; Green, *Spinning the Globe*, 170.

36. Stu Keate, Sports Shots, *Vancouver Province*, 16 Jan. 1942.

37. Green, *Spinning the Globe*, 163–64.

38. "Harlem Five on Tour for 16th Season," *Dayton Herald*, 10 Dec. 1942.

39. Green, *Spinning the Globe*, 164.

40. Dan Walton, Sports-Log, *Tacoma News Tribune*, 12 April 1957.

41. Harry Borba, Side Lines, *San Francisco Examiner*, 28 Jan. 1943; "Globe Trotters Nip Monterey, 39 to 36," *San Luis Obispo (CA) Tribune*, 23 Jan. 1943.

42. C. W. Wilson, "Trotting Globetrotters Irk Chewelah Reader," *Spokane Spokesman-Review*, 30 Jan. 1945.

43. Green, *Spinning the Globe*, 172.

44. Pete Sallaway, Sports Mirror, *Victoria (BC) Times Colonist*, 29 Dec. 1944.

45. Dan Walton, Sports-Log, *Tacoma News Tribune*, 12 April 1957.

46. Sport Rays, *Bellingham (WA) Herald*, 5 Dec. 1943.

47. Green, *Spinning the Globe*, 169.

48. Alex Shults, From the Scorebook, *Seattle Times*, 6 Jan. 1944.

49. Shults, From the Notebook.

50. *Chicago Daily News*, "Basketball Rates High with Sports Fans South of the Border," 15 May 1943.

51. Laurie J. Schmidt, "Benchmarks: April 1, 1946, Hawaii Tsunami Ushers in a Pacific-Wide Warning System," *Earth*, 6 July 2016, www.earthmagazine .org/article/benchmarks-april-1-1946-hawaii-tsunami-ushers-pacific-wide-warning -system/ (accessed 25 April 2023); Bert Nakaji, Bert's Sports Dirt, *Hawaii Tribune-Herald*, 11 April 1946; K. S. Vandergrift, Schofield's Red Dust, *Honolulu Advertiser*, 16 April 1946; "Trotters Pick All-Opponent Hawaii Case Five," *Honolulu Star-Bulletin*, 17 April 1946.

52. Gus Russo, *The Outfit* (New York: Bloomsbury, 2001), 232–33; Cesar Brioso, "Jackie Robinson's Groundbreaking Moment Didn't Start in the U.S.; It Began in Cuba," *USA Today*, 4 Feb. 2022; "Globetrotters Head for Cuban Cage Tournament," *CD*, 22 Feb. 1947; "Globetrotters to Hawaii, March 27," *CD*, 8 March 1947; Green, *Spinning the Globe*, 196.

53. Green, *Spinning the Globe*, 174–87.

54. Jimmy Powers, The Powerhouse, *New York Daily News*, 26 Nov. 1948.

55. "Buie Wowed as One-Armed Globetrotter," *Arkansas Democrat-Gazette*, 1 March 2021.

56. Green, *Spinning the Globe*, 188–90; Author interview with Kathie Linehan, 30 March 2023; Emmett Watson, Watson's Needle, *Seattle Post-Intelligencer*, 10 April 1957.

57. "About Wendell Smith," National Baseball Hall of Fame, https://baseballhall.org/discover-more/stories/wendell-smith/345 (accessed 26 Dec. 2023); Dave Hoekstra, "Wyonella Smith—A Chicago Love Story," 2 Dec. 2020, www.davehoekstra.com/2020/12/02/wyonella-smith-a-chicago-love-story/ (accessed 26 Dec. 2022).

CHAPTER 8

1. Bill Veeck with Ed Linn, *Veeck as in Wreck: The Autobiography of Bill Veeck* (Chicago: University of Chicago Press, 2001), 171.
2. Bill Veeck, "It's Hail, Farewell to an Old Sports Buddy," *CST*, 20 March 1966.
3. Wirt Gammon, "Well, What Would Saperstein Do?" *Chattanooga Daily Times*, 1 July 1956; Neal Acocella, "Baseball's Showman," ESPN Classic, 20 Aug. 1996, www.espn.com/classic/veeckbill000816.html (accessed 17 Feb. 2022); Eric Chesterton, "In 1951, Bill Veeck Let the Fans Manage the St. Louis Browns on Grandstand Managers Night," Cut4, Major League Baseball, 24 Aug. 2017, www.mlb.com/cut4/in-1951-bill-veeck-let-the-fans-manage-the-st-louis-browns-on-grandstand-manager (accessed 6 March 2022).
4. Gammon, "Well, What Would Saperstein Do?"
5. Veeck, *Veeck as in Wreck*, 177–78; Hank Greenberg and Ira Berkow, *Hank Greenberg: The Story of My Life* (Chicago: Ivan R. Dee, 1989), 258.
6. Jack Patterson, 'Round the Sports Map, *Vancouver Sun*, 17 Sept. 1938.
7. Author interview with Joyce Leviton, 27 Dec. 2021. Saperstein raised his family at 2948 West Eastwood in the Ravenswood Manor neighborhood on Chicago's North Side. This was about two miles northwest of the home at 3828 Hermitage where Saperstein lived with his parents as a young man.
8. Rich Westcott, "Philadelphia Phillies Team Ownership History," Society for American Baseball Research, 1 Oct. 2018, https://sabr.org/bioproj/topic/philadelphia-phillies-team-ownership-history/ (accessed 5 July 2022); Gary Bedingfield, "Baseball in World War II," Baseball in Wartime, www.baseballinwartime.com/baseball_in_wwii/baseball_in_wwii.htm (accessed 5 July 2022); Veeck, *Veeck as in Wreck*, 171.
9. Veeck, *Veeck as in Wreck*, 171; Larry Gerlach, David Jordan, and John Rossi, "A Baseball Myth Exploded: Bill Veeck and the 1943 Sale of the Phillies," The National Pastime, Society for American Baseball Research, vol. 18, 1998, https://sabr.org/research/article/a-baseball-myth-exploded-bill-veeck-and-the-1943-sale-of-the-phillies/ (accessed 5 March 2022); Jules Tygiel, "Revisiting Bill Veeck and the 1943 Phillies," *Baseball Research Journal*, 2006, https://sabr.org/journal/

article/revisiting-bill-veeck-and-the-1943-phillies/ (accessed 12 May 2022); Robert
D. Warrington and Norman Macht, "The Veracity of Veeck," *Baseball Research
Journal*, fall 2013, https://sabr.org/journal/article/the-veracity-of-veeck/ (accessed
6 July 2022).

10. Joseph Thomas Moore, *Larry Doby: The Struggle of the American League's
First Black Player* (Mineola, NY: Dover Publications, 2011), 39; Tygiel, "Revisiting Bill Veeck and the 1943 Phillies."

11. Ken McConnell, "Chicago Abe Succeeds," *Vancouver Province*, 14 Jan.
1944.

12. Shirley Povich, "Veeck: We'd Have Walked Away with the Championship,"
Boston Globe, 7 June 1953.

13. Associated Negro Press, "Veeck Planned to Use Tan NL Team," *CD*, 14
Aug. 1954.

14. "Sees Negroes in Majors," *Kansas City Star*, 17 Aug. 1943.

15. Robert Peterson, *Only the Ball Was White: A History of Legendary Black
Players and All-Black Professional Teams* (New York: Oxford University Press,
1970), 16–17.

16. Benjamin Rader, *Baseball: A History of America's Game* (Urbana: University
of Illinois Press, 1992), 51.

17. "A Color Line in Baseball: The St. Louis Browns Refuse to Play with the
Cuban Giants," *New York Times*, 12 Sept. 1887.

18. Jules Tygiel, *Baseball's Great Experiment: Jackie Robinson and His Legacy*
(New York: Oxford University Press, 1997), 15–16.

19. Larry Tye, *Satchel: The Life and Times of an American Legend* (New York:
Random House, 2009), 85–86; "Rogers Hornsby," National Baseball Hall of Fame,
https://baseballhall.org/hall-of-famers/hornsby-rogers (accessed 6 Feb. 2022); Tye,
Satchel, 96.

20. "Demand Removal of Powell from Baseball for Radio Slur," *CD*, 6 Aug.
1938.

21. Chris Lamb, "Public Slur in 1938 Laid Bare a Game's Racism," *New York
Times*, 27 July 2008, www.nytimes.com/2008/07/27/sports/baseball/27powell
.html (accessed 8 March 2022).

22. Curley Grieve, *San Francisco Examiner*, 23 Jan. 1943.

23. "Hank Casserly Says," *Capitol-Times* (Madison, WI), 11 May 1945.

24. Alf Cottrell, "Wandering Hoop Salesman in Town," *Vancouver Sun*, 11
Jan. 1946.

25. Red McQueen, "A Negro on Every Major League Team," *Honolulu Advertiser*, 2 Aug. 1947.

26. Maury Allen, *Dixie Walker of the Dodgers: The People's Choice* (Tuscaloosa: University of Alabama Press, 2010), 158.

27. Peterson, *Only the Ball Was White*, 198.

28. Peterson, *Only the Ball Was White*, 80.

29. Lonnie White, "Owners' Success Wasn't Strictly by the Numbers," *Los Angeles Times*, 28 July 2006, www.latimes.com/archives/la-xpm-2006-jul-28-sp -negroleagueowners28-story.html (accessed 10 March 2022).

30. Marie Linehan letter to lawyer Norman Waite Jr., ca. June 1970, Saperstein Papers, DBC, Box 2.325/P14c.

31. Wendell Smith, Wendell Smith's Sports Beat, *PC*, 2 April 1966.

32. Author interview with Abra Berkley, 7 Dec. 2021.

33. McQueen, "A Negro on Every Major League Team."

34. Neil Lanctot, *Negro League Baseball: The Rise and Ruin of a Black Institution* (Philadelphia: University of Pennsylvania Press, 2004), 114.

35. "Jackie Robinson to Speak at Abe Saperstein Dinner," *Alabama Tribune*, 22 March 1957, 2.

36. Moore, *Larry Doby*, 40.

37. "Negro Player Eyed by Seals," *Spokane (WA) Spokesman-Review*, 30 July 1947; "Minor Leagues Also Seeking Negro Stars," *Alabama Tribune*, 8 Aug. 1947; "Samuel Jethroe," Negro Leagues Baseball Museum, https://nlbemuseum .com/history/players/jethroe.html (accessed 31 March 2022).

38. Hy Turkin, "Veeck, Grabiner Buy Cleveland Indians," *New York Daily News*,19 June 1946.

39. Curley Grieve, Sports Parade, *San Francisco Examiner*, 23 Jan. 1943.

40. Luke Epplin, *Our Team: The Epic Story of Four Men and the World Series That Changed Baseball* (New York: Flatiron Books, 2021), 117; Michael Beschloss, "The Struggles of Satchel Paige," *New York Times*, 3 Oct. 2014.

41. Epplin, *Our Team*, 219.

42. Epplin, *Our Team*, 219; Satchel Paige, *Maybe I'll Pitch Forever* (Lincoln: University of Nebraska Press, 1993) 196–98.

43. Epplin, *Our Team*, 221.

44. Epplin, *Our Team*, 223; Lanctot, *Negro League Baseball*, 337.

45. Paul Schmanska, "Sport Survey," *Lewiston (ME) Daily Sun*, 24 July 1948, 8.

46. Paige, *Maybe I'll Pitch Forever*, 198.

47. AP, "Satchel Paige Hurls, Two Land in Jail," *Dothan (AL) Eagle*, 15 Aug. 1948; Veeck, *Veeck as in Wreck*, 116.

48. Mark Stewart, "Minnie Miñoso," Society for American Baseball Research, 24 Dec. 2021, https://sabr.org/bioproj/person/minnie-minoso/ (accessed 8 July 2022).

49. Tye, *Satchel*, 173.

50. Tim Kelly, *The Legend of Red Klotz: How Basketball's Loss Leader Won Over the World—14,000 Times* (Margate, NJ: ComteQ, 2013), 232.

51. A. S. Young, Sportivanting, *Cleveland Call and Post*, 15 May 1948.

52. Fay Young, *CD*, 15 May 1948.

53. Young, Sportivanting, *Cleveland Call and Post*; Lanctot, *Negro League Baseball*, 232–36.

54. Tye, *Satchel*, 164.

55. Merle Jones, "Trotters' Saperstein Colorful in His Own Right," *Southern Illinoisan*, 22 April 1952.

CHAPTER 9

1. Chester Washington, Ches' Sez, "Suggesting Resolutions," *PC*, 2 Jan. 1937.

2. John O'Donnell, Sports Chats, *Davenport (IA) Democrat and Leader*, 17 July 1942.

3. Joe Sephus, Joe Sephus's Cullings, *Cumberland (MD) Times*, 5 March 1941.

4. Jack Gallagher, Sporttalk, *Houston Post*, 29 Dec. 1956; Jack Sweeney, "Rough Acres Awaits Sweeney after All-Star Game Tonight," *San Diego Union*, 2 Aug. 1963.

5. Sec Taylor, Sittin' in with the Athletes, *Des Moines Register*, 18 Aug. 1952.

6. Jack Stevenson, AP, "Jumping Jupiter (with Pouch) New Threat to Wilt the Stilt," *North Hollywood (CA) Valley Times*, 10 Jan. 1957.

7. Al Warden, Patrolling the Sport Highway, "Newspapermen Praise Globetrotters," *Ogden (UT) Standard Examiner*, 20 Feb. 1942.

8. Harry Borba, Side Lines, *San Francisco Examiner*, 29 Jan. 1944; Sid Ziff, The Inside Track, *Los Angeles Mirror News*, 26 Jan. 1952.

9. "Black Magic to Cure Polio," *Spokane (WA) Spokesman-Review*, 19 Jan. 1945.

10. "Old-Timers on Trotters Payroll," *Munster (IN) Times*, 11 Oct. 1960.

11. "Globetrotter Ace Facing Law Suit," *PC*, 15 Dec. 1945.

12. Peter Vecsey, "Hall of Famer Haynes Talks Family, Life in Hoops," *New York Post*, 19 June 2011.

13. Meadowlark Lemon with Jerry B. Jenkins, *Meadowlark* (Nashville: Thomas Nelson Publishers, 1987), 154.

14. Author interview with Mannie Jackson, 11 May 2023.

15. Mark Johnson, *Basketball Slave: The Andy Johnson Harlem Globetrotter/ NBA Story* (Mantua, NJ: JuniorCam Publishing, 2010), 36–37.

16. Author interview with Hallie Bryant, 21 Oct. 2021. Bryant did not remember the name of the city where Saperstein skipped playing because of the hotel dispute.

17. Author interview with Mannie Jackson, 11 May 2023.

18. Author interview with Bobby Hunter, 18 Oct. 2021.

19. "Abe Saperstein Called in to Give Pep Talk to Slugger," *PC*, 18 Aug. 1951.

20. Beatrice Michaels Shapiro, "No-Lose Situation," *CT*, 3 March 1995.

21. Lemon, *Meadowlark*, 152, 156.

22. Tim Kelly, *The Legend of Red Klotz: How Basketball's Loss Leader Won Over the World—14,000 Times* (Margate, NJ: ComteQ, 2013), 244.

23. Cottrell, On the Sunbeam, *Vancouver Sun*, 14 Jan. 1946.

24. Chuck Menville, *The Harlem Globetrotters: An Illustrated History* (New York: David McKay, 1978), 24–25.

25. Author interview with Gerald Saperstein, 10 Nov. 2022.

26. Bruce Carter, "Fishing and Basketball," *Honolulu Star-Bulletin*, 27 Jan. 1963.

27. Author interview with Burt Tucker, 23 Jan. 2022. Saperstein's niece Sylvia "Ducky" Zolott supported this view in a separate interview March 7, 2022.

28. Cards from Berkley family collection, 1955–1958.

29. Author interview with Roy Raemer, 13 March 2023.

30. Text from Joyce Leviton to the authors, 27 Dec. 2021; author interview with Guy Saperstein, 1 Feb. 2022.

31. Author interview with Joyce Leviton, 27 Dec. 2021.

32. Text from Joyce Leviton to the authors, 27 Dec. 2021.

33. Author interview with Lonni Berkley, 16 Dec. 2021.

34. Author interview with Lonni Berkley, 16 Dec. 2021.

35. Author interview with Burt Tucker, 23 Jan. 2022; Abe Saperstein letter to Eloise Saperstein, 25 May 1956.

36. Author interview with Guy Saperstein, 1 Feb. 2022.

37. Author interview with Lanier Saperstein, 24 Feb. 2022.

38. Author interview with Abra Berkley, 30 Nov. 2021.

39. Shapiro, "No-Lose Situation."

40. Shapiro, "No-Lose Situation."

41. Author interview with Burt Tucker, 23 Jan. 2022.

42. AP, "Mrs. Abe Saperstein Leads Globetrotters," *Bismarck (ND) Tribune*, 2 July 1966.

43. AP, "Mrs. Abe Saperstein."

44. AP, "Mrs. Abe Saperstein."

NOTES

CHAPTER 10

1. Peter C. Bjarkman, *Encyclopedia of Pro Basketball Team Histories* (New York: Carroll & Graf, 1994), xvi, 466. The NBA considers the debut of the BAA in 1946–1947 to be the NBA's start as far as records and anniversaries.

2. Wendell Smith, Wendell Smith's Sports Beat, *PC*, 7 Jan. 1950.

3. Red Harmon, Red Peppers, *Cedar Rapids Gazette*, 6 Jan. 1949.

4. Clifton Brown, "Sweetwater Clifton, 65, Is Dead; Was Star on Knick Teams of 50's," *New York Times*, 2 Sept. 1990.

5. Ben Green, *Spinning the Globe: The Rise, Fall, and Return to Greatness of the Harlem Globetrotters* (New York: Amistad, 2005), 212–15.

6. Joe Hendrickson, Sports Opinions, *Minneapolis Tribune*, 2 March 1949.

7. "Results of Harlem Globetrotters–Minneapolis Lakers Games," Association for Professional Basketball Research, www.apbr.org/trotters-lakers.html (accessed 27 Dec. 2022); Abe Saperstein letter to Lakers General Manager John Kundla, 11 Jan. 1958, Anzivino Collection, DBC, 98-166/14.

8. Green, *Spinning the Globe*, 229.

9. Ron Thomas, *They Cleared the Lane* (Lincoln: University of Nebraska Press, 2002), 16.

10. Thomas, *They Cleared the Lane*, 21.

11. Thomas, *They Cleared the Lane*, 24.

12. George Sullivan, "The Celtics, Chuck Cooper, and the Struggling NBA," *New York Times*, 27 April 1980; Nelson George, *Elevating the Game: Black Men and Basketball* (New York: HarperCollins, 1992), 95–96.

13. *Harlem Globetrotters: The Team That Changed the World*, documentary written by Anne Kreiter (Chicago: TeamWorks Media/MJA, 2005).

14. Jerry Nason, "Globe Trotters' Boss, Riled by Cooper Deal, Bars Visits to Boston," *Boston Globe*, 27 April 1950.

15. "Cooper, Bluitt Would Prefer NBA," *Quincy (MA) Patriot-Ledger*, 17 April 1950; "Celtics Get Rights to Rebound Artist Cooper," INS, *Quincy (MA) Patriot-Ledger*, 4 May 1950; Roger Barry, "Macauley's Class Spoilers Zollner's 'Stop Him' Plot," *Quincy (MA) Patriot-Ledger*, 13 Dec. 1950.

16. "Stars Top Trotters, Cooper in Game," *Pittsburgh Sun-Telegraph*, 6 April 1950; Ritter Collet, Journal of Sports, *Dayton Journal Herald*, 22 Feb. 1950; Clif Keane, "Globe Trotters, Celtics in Garden Twin Bill," *Boston Globe*, 1 March 1951; Green, *Spinning the Globe*, 229–32.

17. Green, *Spinning the Globe*, 228; "History of Harlem Globetrotter Uniform," Anzivino Collection, DBC, 98-166/2.

18. Joe Anzivino, Up Front in the Sports World, "Globetrotters May Visit Honolulu in January," *Honolulu Star-Bulletin*, 10 Nov. 1950; "Fire Escape Gang Loots Skyscraper," *CT*, 1 Nov. 1954.

19. Green, *Spinning the Globe*, 211–23.

20. Green, *Spinning the Globe*, 216–20; AP, "11,275 Milwaukee Fans See Trotters Beat All-Stars," *Washington Star*, 19 April 1951; Louis Effrat, "Knicks Top Royals, 80–73, Tying Series," *New York Times*, 19 April 1951; Green, *Spinning the Globe*, 219.

21. Dick Cullum, Cullum's Column, *Minneapolis Tribune*, 9 March 1950.

22. Green, *Spinning the Globe*, 218–23; Ray Meyer, "Trotters Revive Exciting Memories," *CST*, 19 Feb. 1985.

23. Meyer, "Trotters Revive Exciting Memories."

24. Thomas, *They Cleared the Lane*, 100; Green, *Spinning the Globe*, 230.

25. Thomas, *They Cleared the Lane*, 100, Green, *Spinning the Globe*, 231.

26. Elliot Cushing, Sports Eye View, *Rochester (NY) Democrat and Chronicle*, 11 June 1950; AP, "Saperstein Buys Chicago Cagers," *Birmingham (AL) News*, 19 June 1950; AP, "Abe Saperstein Quits NBA," *Meriden (CT) Record-Journal*, 26 Sept. 1950; Robert Cromie, "Bruins Fold as Saperstein Drops Plans," *CT*, 26 Sept. 1950.

27. Wendell Smith, Wendell Smith's Sports Beat, *PC*, 22 Dec. 1951.

28. Walt Dobbins, I May Be Wrong, *Lincoln (NE) Journal Star*, 12 Jan. 1951.

29. Tim Kelly, *The Legend of Red Klotz: How Basketball's Loss Leader Won Over the World—14,000 Times* (Margate, NJ: ComteQ, 2013), 176; "Sportsdom's Most Exciting Exploits—with the Harlem Globetrotters," Anzivino Collection, DBC, 98-166/2.

30. "Trotters, Davidites Due Here Friday," *Medford (OR) Mail Tribune*, 8 Aug. 1954.

31. Neil Lanctot, *Negro League Baseball: The Rise and Ruin of a Black Institution* (Philadelphia: University of Pennsylvania Press, 2004), 372.

32. AP, "Veeck Now Working on Japanese Baseball Pact," *Daily Standard* (Sikeston, MO), 14 Feb. 1952.

33. AP, "Browns 'Ocean' out 2 Players," *Spokane (WA) Spokesman-Review*, 29 April 1952.

34. Robert L. Burnes, The Bench Warmer, *St. Louis Globe-Democrat*, 17 Aug. 1954.

35. "Forty-Niner Grid Club May Be Sold," *(Salinas) Californian*, 22 Jan. 1953; Dave Lewis, Once over Lightly, *Long Beach (CA) Independent*, 5 Feb. 1964.

36. Dick Hackenburg, Post Sportem, *CDN*, 5 Jan. 1950.

37. Jerry Liska, AP, "Harlem Globe Trotters Put Cage Show on Road," *Escanaba (MI) Daily Press*, 16 Oct. 1953; Murray Rose, AP, "Seton Hall's Walter Dukes Inks Contract with Harlem Globetrotters at $25,000 a Year," *Bangor (ME) Daily News*, 9 June 1953; Green, *Spinning the Globe*, 271–72. Saperstein sold Walter Dukes's rights to the New York Knicks in 1955.

38. *Harlem Globetrotters: America's Court Jesters*, produced and written by Greg Weinstein (New York: A&E Network, 1999), www.youtube.com/watch?v=EV _YTl1rkj8 (accessed 30 May 2023). Haynes's claim about Saperstein saying Black people needed less money than white people came in the A&E documentary and in an interview with author Ben Green, both long after Saperstein's death. Thus the Trotters owner never had the opportunity to confirm or deny it.

39. Green, *Spinning the Globe*, 253–59.

40. AP, "Ex-Trotter Sued by Abe Saperstein," *Oakland Tribune*, 30 Jan. 1964; "Abe Saperstein Wins Suit from Marques Haynes," *San Francisco Examiner*, 4 Feb. 1954.

41. Green, *Spinning the Globe*, 274–76.

42. Green, *Spinning the Globe*, 277; Michael Haupert, "MLB's Annual Salary Leaders since 1874," Society of American Baseball Research, https://sabr.org/research/article/mlbs-annual-salary-leaders-since-1874/ (accessed 30 Dec. 2022); U.S. Bureau of Labor Statistics Inflation Calculator, www.bls.gov/data/inflation_calculator.htm (accessed 15 April 2024).

43. Green, *Spinning the Globe*, 278–81.

44. "Globetrotters to Play Here Next January," *Honolulu Advertiser*, 2 Feb. 1956.

45. AP, "Globetrotters Getting along Nicely without Goose Tatum," *Massillon (OH) Independent*, 3 April 1955.

46. Bruce Weber, "Meadowlark Lemon Dies at 83; Harlem Globetrotters' Dazzling Court Jester," *New York Times*, 29 Dec. 2015; Michael Carlson, "Meadowlark Lemon Obituary," *Guardian*, 29 Dec. 2015. According to Ben Green, Globetrotters veteran Josh Grider gave Lemon the nickname "Meadowlark."

47. Saperstein Enterprises promotional files, Anzivino Collection, DBC, 98 -166/10.

48. "Globe Trotters, Bevo Francis Play Thursday at Fenway," *Boston Globe*, 25 July 1954; "Trotters Hope Cubs See Light," *CDN*, 17 Aug. 1954; Green, *Spinning the Globe*, 279.

49. Curley Grieve, Sports Parade, *San Francisco Examiner*, 22 Feb. 1955.

50. Aram Goudsouzian, *King of the Court: Bill Russell and the Basketball Revolution* (Berkeley: University of California Press, 2010), 64; Paul Miller, "Globetrotter Vet Says Saperstein Was Clean," *Everett (WA) Herald*, 9 Jan. 1976; Bill Russell

with Bill McSweeny, *Go Up for Glory* (New York: Dutton, 1966), 40–43. Russell blamed Saperstein for the NBA resisting integration, and he said in a 2020 foreword to *Go Up for Glory* that he delayed accepting his Hall of Fame selection "because it had inducted people like Saperstein." But in 2019 when Russell accepted his ring, he gave another reason for the delay—that he wanted Chuck Cooper to go into the hall before him.

51. Abe Chanin, The Spectator, *Arizona Daily Star*, 7 March 1956; Green, *Spinning the Globe*, 288.

52. Bob Brachman, "'Bill Russell Not for Sale,' Dad Says," *San Francisco Chronicle*, 13 April 1956. Various figures for the Trotters' offer to Russell were floated in the press, including a hard-to-believe $50,000. The amount cited by Russell's father seems most credible.

53. Bob Gibson with Phil Pepe, "Gibson Hoped Future Was with Basketball," *Miami News*, 9 Oct. 1968; "Bob Gibson," National Baseball Hall of Fame, https://baseballhall.org/hall-of-famers/gibson-bob#:~:text=He%20later%20served%20as%20a,%2C%20talent%2C%20respect%2C%20dedication (accessed 29 April 2023).

54. Gary M. Pomerantz, *Wilt, 1962: The Night of 100 Points and the Dawn of a New Era* (New York: Three Rivers Press, 2006), 45; Kelly, *The Legend of Red Klotz*, 209; "How the NBA Draft Became a Lottery," *Seattle Times*, 21 May 2007; UPI, "'Wilt the Stilt' Signed by Trotters for $65,000," *Boston Globe*, 18 June 1958.

55. *CT* photo, June 21, 1958; Green, *Spinning the Globe*, 291.

56. Jimmy Breslin, Newspaper Enterprise Association, "Trotters Make It Real Big with Wilt the Stilt," *Anderson (IN) Daily Bulletin*, 1 Jan. 1959.

57. Joe Bostic, The Scoreboard, *New York Age*, 23 Aug. 1958.

58. Marlowe Branagan, Tower Lights, "Silent Partner of Saperstein Enterprises Gives Us a Visit," *Oregon Journal*, 4 July 1950; Marion E. Jackson, World of Sports, *Alabama Tribune*, 29 Nov. 1957; author interview with Emory Luck, former Globetrotters and Bombers player, 10 April 2023.

59. AP, "'The Stilt' Finds Pro Basketball Rather 'Roughhouse' but Likes It," *St. Louis Post-Dispatch*, 10 Jan. 1960.

60. Green, *Spinning the Globe*, 300.

61. Marie Linehan letter to Norman Waite Jr., ca. June 1970, Saperstein Papers, DBC, 2.325-P14c; Green, *Spinning the Globe*, 309.

62. "Discuss New Pro Cagers," *CDN*, 24 March 1960.

63. Harry Grayson, Newspaper Enterprise Association, The Scoreboard, *Kingston (NY) Daily Freeman*, 24 June 1956.

64. Jerry Holtzman, "Saperstein Sees NBA Expansion to Coast in '59," *Sporting News*, 7 Jan. 1959.

65. UPI, "Chicago May Get Pro Cage Team Franchise from NBA," *Alexandria (LA) Town Talk*, 24 Jan. 1959.

66. "Los Angeles Dickers for Pro Cage Team," *Spokane (WA) Spokesman-Review*, 30 Jan. 1959.

67. "Los Angeles Dickers," *Spokane (WA) Spokesman-Review*.

68. Bob Ingram, As I Was Saying, *El Paso (TX) Herald-Post*, 22 Feb. 1960.

CHAPTER 11

1. Eloise Saperstein Berkley, unpublished memoir, 6.

2. Jimmy Cannon, Jimmy Cannon Says, *Newsday* (New York), 11 July 1952.

3. Wirt Gammon, Just between Us Fans, *Chattanooga (TN) Daily Times*, 1 July 1956.

4. Haskell Cohen, "Abe Saperstein's Globetrotters Tour the Basketball World," *Chicago Sentinel*, 2 Oct. 1947; James E. Doyle, The Sport Trail, *Cleveland Plain Dealer*, 27 March 1952; Ben Green, *Spinning the Globe: The Rise, Fall, and Return to Greatness of the Harlem Globetrotters* (New York: Amistad, 2005), 191.

5. Robert Pincus, "Star at the Stripe Forever," *Orlando Sentinel*, 10 July 1999; AP, "Globetrotter Harold 'Bunny' Levitt Dies at 96," ESPN.com, 3 May 2006, www.espn.com/nba/news/story?id=2432591 (accessed 1 Sept. 2022); Green, *Spinning the Globe*, 95, 169, 191, 317.

6. Cannon, Jimmy Cannon Says, 11 July 1952; "Game Set at 8:15 at Coliseum," *El Paso Times*, 9 April 1952; "Trotter Owner Gives Fans Money's Worth," *Logan (UT) Herald Journal*, 4 Jan. 1954; "Globetrotters Bring 6 Top Acts of Vaudeville, Also," *Sterling (IL) Daily Gazette*, 24 March 1964; "Gipson, Hall, Milton Stars of Trotters," *Honolulu Star-Bulletin*, 7 Feb. 1965.

7. Jim Waltzer and Tom Wilk, *Tales of South Jersey: Profiles and Personalities* (New Brunswick, NJ: Rutgers University Press, 2001), 20–23.

8. "Trotters Need 3 Wins for New Mark," *Ogden (UT) Standard-Examiner*, 15 Jan. 1951.

9. "Hula Girls Will Not Perform at Creighton Uni.," *Beatrice (NE) Daily Sun*, 19 March 1948.

10. "Harlem Globetrotters Play in Sun Devil Gym Tonight," *Arizona Republic*, 9 Feb. 1961; "Cash Instead of Cups," *Fresno Bee*, 20 Oct. 1959; AP, "Former Tennis Champ Karol Short, 53," 13 April 1988, https://apnews.com/article/94d6aa255eb6c91b1ac9b862d0f71aee (accessed 7 Sept. 2022).

11. Frank Gianelli, "Trotters Are Annual Show," *Arizona Republic*, 29 Jan. 1960.

12. John Gaspar, "Tennis Victimized by Abe Saperstein," *Daily Calumet (IL)*, 11 Dec. 1959; John Grasso, *Historical Dictionary of Tennis* (Lanham, MD: Scarecrow Press, 2011), 115.

13. Al Del Greco, For the Record, *Hackensack (NJ) Record*, 22 Dec. 1959.

14. Eric Barrow, "Jesse Owens' Glory Fleeting, His Legacy Lost in the Pack," *Baltimore Sun*, 26 Feb. 2007; "From Horse-Racer to Speech Writer: Jesse Owens' Life after the Olympic Games," Olympics.com, 30 March 2021, https://olympics.com/en/news/from-horse-racer-to-speech-writer-jesse-owens-life-after-the-olympic-games (accessed 7 Sept. 2022).

15. "Jesse Owens Loses Race to Horse," *Salt Lake Tribune*, 28 Aug. 1945; "Cincinnati, Harlem Crews Set to Battle," *Quad City Times*, 28 May 1948.

16. Haskell Cohen, Jews in Sports, *Southern Jewish Weekly*, 20 Aug. 1948.

17. "From Horse-Racer to Speech Writer," Olympics.com.

18. Author interview with Marlene Rankin, 22 Jan. 2022.

19. *The Harlem Globetrotters*, imdb.com, www.imdb.com/title/tt0043621/ (accessed 8 Sept. 2022); "Thomas Gomez," imdb.com, www.imdb.com/name/nm0327089/?ref_=fn_al_nm_1 (accessed 8 Sept. 2022).

20. *Carmen Jones*, imdb.com, www.imdb.com/title/tt0046828/ (accessed 8 Sept. 2022); Green, *Spinning the Globe*, 235.

21. *The Harlem Globetrotters*, directed by Phil Brown (Culver City, CA: Columbia Pictures, 1951), www.youtube.com/watch?v=3sIxwmQakVw (accessed 23 March 2023).

22. Francis Stann, Win, Lose or Draw, *Washington Star*, 4 April 1953.

23. *Go, Man, Go!*, imdb.com, www.imdb.com/title/tt0047032/?ref_=fn_al_tt_1 (accessed 9 Sept. 2022).

24. *Go, Man, Go!*, directed by James Wong Howe (West Hollywood, CA: Sirod Productions, United Artists, 1954), www.youtube.com/watch?v=l2O5xLpgYfQ (accessed 23 March 2023).

25. Bosley Crowther, "Harlem Globetrotters Perform in a Sports Romance, 'Go, Man, Go!' at the Globe," *New York Times*, 10 March 1954; Lawrence Van Gelder, "Dane Clark, Actor, 85, Dies; Starred in World War II Films," *New York Times*, 16 Sept. 1998.

26. Dinitia Smith, "Alfred Palca, 78, Screenwriter Blacklisted after Basketball Film," *New York Times*, 22 June 1998; Green, *Spinning the Globe*, 264–65.

27. Beatrice Loayza, "James Wong Howe: A Gutsy Cinematographer Finally Gets His Due," *New York Times*, 27 May 2022; Robert Hanley, "James Wong Howe Dies; Noted Cinematographer," *New York Times*, 16 July 1976.

28. Tom Callahan, *Gods at Play: An Eyewitness Account of Great Moments in American Sports* (New York: W. W. Norton, 2022), 36–37.

29. UP, "Trotter Coach Plans Auto Thrill Show," *Dayton (OH) Journal Herald*, 16 March 1955; Dick Hackenburg, "Abe, 'Trotters Still Cover World, Spread U.S. Image,'" *CST*, reprinted in *Corpus Christi (TX) Times*, 14 May 1965; "Abe Saperstein's Interests Varied," *Hanover (PA) Evening Sun*, 7 March 1956.

30. John L. Clark Jr., "Archie Bleyer and the Lost Influence of Stock Arrangements in Jazz," *American Music* 27, no. 2 (summer 2009), 138–79; *Who's Who in American Jewry* (New York: Jewish Biographical Bureau, 1927), 52. The song's lyrics were written by a third person, Kenneth Casey, but the version used by the Globetrotters didn't use the lyrics.

31. Tom McEwen, The Morning After, *Tampa Tribune*, 28 Feb. 1975; Greg Basse, "Ed P. Hamman, 81, Noted Sports Clown," *Tampa Bay Times*, 12 Jan. 1989; Marie Linehan, "'Sweet Georgia Brown' History" (17 June 1971) and "History of 'Sweet Georgia Brown': Brother Bones Arrangement" (19 April 1984), Anzivino Collection, DBC, 98-166/2. Two accounts written by Marie Linehan thirteen years apart conflict in regard to whether Albert Van Court brought the song to Saperstein or just made the deal with him to use it. The heard-it-in-a-store story varies as to who heard the song. Player Bobby Milton said Trotters advance man Harry Hannin was in a department store in Winnipeg, Canada, in 1950 when he heard the tune. But "Circus Ed" Hamman, a clown who toured with the team, claimed he heard the song in a "dime store" and introduced it to the team.

32. "Funeral Set for 'Brother Bones,'" *Independent* (Long Beach, CA), 18 June 1974; J. D. Kailer, The Scoreboard, *Albuquerque Journal*, 18 Feb. 1953.

33. News releases for Harlem Globetrotters Varieties of '55, Saperstein Papers, DBC, 2.325-P14c.

34. Tom Bolger, The Morning After, *Toledo (OH) Times*, 17 Dec. 1954.

35. Browsin' Around column, *Ottumwa (IA) Courier*, 11 March 1955.

36. Advertisement for "World of Music," *Cincinnati Enquirer*, 8 Jan. 1961; Charles Irish, "Only Handful Turns Out for Music World," *Sacramento (CA) Bee*, 20 Feb. 1961.

37. Dick Becker, I May Be Wrong, *Lincoln (NE) Journal*, 14 Nov. 1960.

38. R. G. Lynch, Maybe I'm Wrong, *Milwaukee Journal*, 6 April 1953.

39. Sid Ziff, The Inside Track, *Los Angeles Mirror News*, 27 Jan. 1956.

40. Harry Keck, "Abe Saperstein Doing Facelift for Marciano and Manager," *Pittsburgh Sun-Telegraph*, 23 Dec. 1955; Dick Beddoes, From Our Tower, *Vancouver Sun*, 28 Dec. 1955.

41. "Globetrotters Send TV Star 'Get Well' Message," *Phoenix Sun*, 2 Aug. 1956.

42. Clancy Loranger, It Says Here, *Vancouver Province*, 6 Jan. 1943; "Sun Ra and His Arkestra," Artyard Records website, https://artyardrecords.co.uk/sun-ra -and-his-arkestra/ (accessed 11 Sept. 2022).

43. "Protégé of Abe Saperstein to Play Role of 'Cindy Lou,'" *Indianapolis Recorder*, 22 May 1954; "Olga James Our Newest Rising Star," *PC*, 11 Dec. 1954; "Olga James to Make TV Debut at Cage Tilt," *Jet*, 17 March 1955; Louis Calta, "'Mr. Wonderful' Opening Tonight," *New York Times*, 22 March 1956; Notes of Eloise Saperstein Berkley's recollections, Saperstein Papers, DBC, 2.325-P14c; John S. Wilson, AP, "Cannonball Adderley, Jazzman, Dead," *New York Times*, 9 Aug. 1975.

44. "Hadda Brooks," *New York Sun*, 27 Sept. 1952; Suzanne Herel, "Hadda Brooks, the 'Queen of Boogie,' Dies," *San Francisco Chronicle*, 23 Nov. 2002.

45. Author interview with Avi Berkley, 7 Dec. 2021.

46. Author interview with Bobby Hunter, 18 Oct. 2021.

47. Washington Post-Los Angeles Times News Service, "Actress Terry Moore Wins Part of Hughes' Wealth," *Nashua (NH) Telegraph*, 26 May 1983.

48. Ed Sullivan, Little Old New York, *New York Daily News*, 12 Feb. 1953.

49. Howard V. Millard, Bait for Bugs, *Decatur (IL) Daily Review*, 29 June 1955; "The Fabulous Mr. Saperstein," 1955–1956 Harlem Globetrotters program; Maury White, "Daughter Gets Ermine Bathing Suit," *Des Moines (IA) Tribune*, 21 Dec. 1955.

50. Marie Linehan letter to Norman Waite Jr., ca. June 1970, Saperstein Papers, DBC, 2.325-P14c.

51. Green, *Spinning the Globe*, 299.

52. "These Hawaiian hula dancers . . ." (photo caption), *Idaho Statesman*, 29 Jan. 1953.

53. "First Delegate's Grandchild Wins Miss Hawaii Contest," *Honolulu Star-Bulletin*, 5 July 1954.

54. "California Miss Winner of Miss America Crown," *Wichita Eagle*, 12 Sept. 1954.

55. "Named Queen," *CT*, 10 Feb. 1955.

56. "Ex-Isle Beauty Queen Dodges Process Servers," *Honolulu Advertiser*, 29 Jan. 1957; "Annulment Suit Reveals Marriage," *Honolulu Star-Bulletin*, 29 Jan. 1957.

57. "Globetrotters Play in Barre on March 13th," *Montpelier (VT) Evening Argus*, 28 Feb. 1958; Eddie Sherman, Backstage, *Honolulu Advertiser*, 15 Jan. 1959.

58. Eddie Sherman, *Honolulu Star-Bulletin*, 8 Feb. 1961.

59. "Wife Charged in Slaying of Dairy Owner," *Honolulu Advertiser*, 1 Dec. 1983; Ken Kobayashi, "Friend of Toledo Takes Wife's Side," *Honolulu Advertiser*, 7 Feb. 2022.

60. Lee Catterall, "Expert Defines Mrs. Toledo as Battered Woman," *Honolulu Star-Bulletin*, 14 July 1984; Floyd K. Takeuchi, "Mrs. Toledo Called 'Battered Wife,'" *Honolulu Advertiser*, 14 July 1984. In a June 9, 2022, author interview with John Edmunds, Kapi Toledo's attorney, Edmunds explained that Walker testified about the Saperstein details instead of Kapi Toledo herself because Mrs. Toledo had speech problems as the result of a stroke and it was unclear whether she could testify. She ended up testifying later in the trial, he said. In a separate author interview on June 6, 2022, Walker stood by her testimony. She and Edmunds both said they considered Kapi Toledo's account to be credible.

61. "Princess Gertrude Kapi'olani Toledo," death notice, *Honolulu Star-Bulletin*, 2 Jan. 2007.

62. Emails to authors from Celine Kapi'olani, 22 April 2022 and 10–11 May 2022.

CHAPTER 12

1. Haskell Cohen, "I'll Take Abe Saperstein, You Can Have Mike Jacobs," *Jewish Post* (Indianapolis, IN), 9 March 1945.

2. Haskell Cohen, "Sid Luckman Works Himself into Shape with the Chicago Bears," *Chicago Sentinel*, 28 Aug. 1948; Elliot Cushing, Sports Eye View, *Democrat and Chronicle* (Rochester, NY), June 27, 1950.

3. Don Becker, "On the Inside," *Tri-City Herald* (Pasco, WA), 29 June 1950; Elliot Cushing, Sports Eye View, *Democrat and Chronicle* (Rochester, NY), 27 June 1950.

4. "Explore Passenger Flight by Era," National Air and Space Museum, https://airandspace.si.edu/explore/stories/passenger-flight (accessed 19 Sept. 2023); Janet Bednarek, "Longing for the 'Golden Age' of Air Travel? Be Careful What You Wish For," CNN, 28 Feb. 2023, www.cnn.com/travel/article/golden-age-of-air-travel-downsides/index.html (accessed 19 Sept. 2023); "ASN Aviation Safety Database: 1949," Flight Safety Foundation, http://aviation-safety.net/database/year/1949/1 (accessed 20 Sept. 2023).

5. Gene Kessler, "Bookies' Tip: Mr. Trouble," *CST*, 3 May 1950; Eric Whitehead, Eric Whitehead's Fanfare, *Vancouver Province*, 10 Aug. 1950.

6. *Diário de Coimbra* (Coimbra, Portugal), excerpted in *Quad City Times* (Davenport, IA), 15 May 1950.

7. Pat Harmon, The Mailbag, *Cedar Rapids (IA) Gazette*, 25 June 1950.

8. Jack Geyer, "Globetrotters Have Greatest Campaign," *Los Angeles Times*, 19 Jan. 1951.

9. Geyer, "Globetrotters Have Greatest Campaign."

10. Ben Green, *Spinning the Globe: The Rise, Fall, and Return to Greatness of the Harlem Globetrotters* (New York: Amistad, 2005), 225; Emery Pearce, "Jive-and-Juggle Now, Auntie," *Daily Herald* (London, UK), 16 May 1950.

11. Wales Thomas, "TV Talks Past the Anti-Advert. Rule," *Manchester (UK) Evening News*, 19 May 1950.

12. "The New Studio," *Guardian*, 22 May 1950; "Amateurs Got £4671 Each," *Evening Standard* (London, UK), 13 May 1950; "You Too Can Become a Basket-Ball Star," *Middlesex County Times* (Ealing, London, UK), 27 May 1950.

13. Green, *Spinning the Globe*, 225.

14. Ned Cronin, *Los Angeles Daily News*, 20 Jan. 1951; Benjamin Hoffman, "Globetrotters on Ice, All Tricks Included," *New York Times* blog, 30 Jan. 2010, https://archive.nytimes.com/offthedribble.blogs.nytimes.com/2010/01/30/globe-trotters-on-ice-all-tricks-included (accessed 8 May 2023).

15. Hank Casserly, Hank Casserly Says, *Capital Times* (Madison, WI), 3 June 1950; "Italian Communist Paper Blasts Globe Trotters for Burlesquing 'Russian Sport of Basketball,'" *Louisville Courier-Journal*, 25 July 1950; Pat Harmon, The Mailbag, *Cedar Rapids (IA) Gazette*, 25 June 1950.

16. "Italian Communist Paper Blasts Globe Trotters," *Louisville Courier-Journal*.

17. Oscar Fraley, UP, "Curve Ball Pitching Gets New 'Phenom' of Giants," *El Paso (TX) Herald-Post,* 27 April 1957.

18. Author interviews with Abra Berkley, 30 Nov. 2021 and 16 Dec. 2021. Berkley, who heard the story from her mother, Eloise, was uncertain where the hotel incident occurred but thought it might have been in Berlin.

19. Joe M. Butler, The Sportscope, *Scranton (PA) Times*, 12 July 1961.

20. Dave Zinkoff with Edgar Williams, *Around the World with the Harlem Globetrotters* (Philadelphia: MacRae Smith, 1953), 137–38.

21. Al Warden, Tid-Bits from the Sports World, *Ogden (UT) Standard-Examiner*, 8 June 1950.

22. Richard Goldstein, "Tony Lavelli, 71, Musician with a Memorable Hook Shot," *New York Times*, 13 Jan. 1998.

23. Pearce, "Jive-and-Juggle Now, Auntie."

24. Ned Cronin, "Globetrotters Sport's Greatest Road Show," *Sporting News*, 14 Feb. 1951; Cronin, "Globetrotters Sport's Greatest Road Show."

25. Cronin, "Globetrotters Sport's Greatest Road Show."

26. Wendell Smith, "Basketball Reports from Gay Paree . . ." *PC*, 24 June 1950.

27. Smith, "Basketball Reports from Gay Paree."

28. Green, *Spinning the Globe*, 236.

29. Bob Bialek, "Parade of Youth Reporter Meets Lavelli in Ecuador," *Hartford Courant*, 22 July 1951; Joe Anzivino, "Hawaiian Entertainers Are 'Wowing' Europe; Globetrotters Setting New Attendance Marks," *Honolulu Star-Bulletin*, 28 May 1951; "50,041 See U.S. Fives Play in Rio's Stadium," *New York Times*, 7 May 1951.

30. Tim Cohane, "The Harlem Globetrotters: Basketball's Goodwill Ambassadors," *Look*, 1 Jan. 1952.

31. Green, *Spinning the Globe*, 236–37.

32. Bob Panella, "Globetrotters—They Meet the Mighty," *Los Angeles Evening Citizen News*, 1 Feb. 1952; Green, *Spinning the Globe*, 237.

33. Zinkoff, *Around the World*, 127.

34. Zinkoff, *Around the World*, 80; AP, "75,000 in Berlin Hail Jesse Owens," *New York Daily News*, 23 Aug. 1951.

35. Earl Wilson, "Around the World with Earl Wilson," *Spokesman-Review* (Spokane, WA), 25 Aug. 1951.

36. Red Smith, "Abe Saperstein Mulls Over Some Highlights in Harlem Globetrotters' First 25 Years," *Philadelphia Inquirer*, 26 Oct. 1951; Earl Wilson, It Happened One Night, *Camden (NJ) Courier-Post*, 17 Aug. 1951.

37. Zinkoff, *Around the World*, 148–49; "World Loves Basketball," *Daily Chronicle (DeKalb, Illinois)*, 16 Oct. 1952; UP, "Globetrotters Show Tricks to Pope Pius," *Birmingham (AL) Post-Herald*, 2 Aug. 1952.

38. Maxwell Stiles, "Harlem Globetrotters Figure in Some Amazing Incidents," *Los Angeles Mirror*, 31 Jan. 1961; Ned Cronin, Cronin's Corner, *Los Angeles Times*, 10 Sept. 1956; John P. Carmichael, "Our Teams Put Chicago on Top in Sports," *CDN*, 21 Nov. 1963.

39. Zinkoff, *Around the World*, 144.

40. Newspaper Enterprise Association, "Farouk Would Pack Them in as a Wrestler," *Chillicothe (MO) Constitution-Tribune*, 30 Aug. 1952.

41. Playing cards with the photo of Saperstein and Naguib are in the Berkley family collection; Glenn Fowler, "Mohammed Naguib, First President of Egypt, Dies," *New York Times*, 29 Aug. 1984.

42. "'Globetrotters' Barnstorm Europe," *Gulf Informer* (Mobile, AL), 23 June 1951; 1951 Harlem Globetrotters Lavazza Avvenimenti Sportivi early basketball card, www.ebay.com/itm/334470576189 (accessed 15 Nov. 2023).

43. Zinkoff, *Around the World*, 119.

NOTES

44. AP, "Globe Trotters to Discontinue World Tours," *Morning Call* (Allentown, PA), 20 Oct. 1952; "Post-Season Tours," Saperstein Papers, DBC, 2.325/P14c.

45. Sports in a Nutshell, *Minneapolis Star*, 27 May 1952; "Portable Hardwood Readied for Globetrotters Tomorrow," *Troy (NY) Record*, 30 July 1954.

46. "Trotters Are Another Rags-to-Riches Story," *Minneapolis Tribune*, 28 March 1954; Zinkoff, *Around the World*, 155.

47. "Portable Hardwood Readied for Globetrotters Tomorrow," *Troy Record*; Jerry Jurgens, "Biggest Cage Show on Earth," *Daily Times* (Davenport, IA), 24 Aug. 1954.

48. Bob Whiting, "Globetrotters Still Sensations in 4th Summer Tour of Europe," *Morning Call* (Paterson, NJ), 8 July 1953; Abe Saperstein with Bill Fay, "'Round the World with the Globetrotters," *Collier's*, 31 Jan. 1953.

49. "Globetrotters Play Here on Sept. 3," *Capital Times* (Madison, WI), 8 Aug. 1955; John P. Carmichael, "Trotters Aid U.S. Cause in Red Nations," *CDN*, 21 Dec. 1960.

50. Ned Cronin, Cronin's Corner, *Los Angeles Times*, 10 Sept. 1956.

51. "Saperstein Reports Basketball Growth," *Honolulu Star-Bulletin*, 3 Oct. 1956.

52. "Trotters' Prosperity Attributed to Farm Aid," *Wichita Eagle*, 30 Dec. 1956; Harry Missildine, "Globetrotters Return Sunday Afternoon," *Spokesman-Review* (Spokane, WA), 3 Dec. 1958.

53. "Abe Wants Games in Red China," *CDN*, 17 Nov. 1960.

54. Paul Pinckney, "'Royals, Pistons Erred in Shifts'—Abe Saperstein," *Sporting News*, 15 Jan. 1958.

55. "Trotters Have Come Long Way since Cage Debut 30 Years Ago Tonight," *St. Joseph (MO) News-Press*, 7 Jan. 1957.

56. Zinkoff, *Around the World*, 201.

57. "About the Globetrotters," *Sun-Advocate* (Price, UT), 12 March 1959.

58. "About the Globetrotters," *Sun-Advocate*.

59. Tony Weitzel, "Philco Puzzle for TV Makers Here," *CDN*, 13 Feb. 1962.

60. Wendell Smith, Wendell Smith's Sports Beat, *PC*, 12 Jan. 1963.

61. Wendell Smith, "Athletic Possibilities in Africa Tremendous but Talent Must Be Developed—Saperstein," *PC*, 11 Jan. 1964.

62. Dave Lewis, "Could Win Lots with All-World Team," *Independent* (Long Beach, CA), 26 Jan. 1953.

63. "Thrill upon Thrill for Basketball's Fabulous Ambassadors," Saperstein Papers, DBC, 2.325/P14c; Dick Hackenberg, "Abe, 'Trotters Still Cover World, Spread U.S. Image," *CDN*, 14 May 1965.

64. Rube Samuelsen, "But This Is Different," *Citizen-News* (Hollywood, CA), 16 Aug. 1952.

65. Tommy Holmes, "Trotters Must Explain Their Game Is Comedy," *Dayton Journal Herald*, 27 July 1959.

66. Lewis F. Atchison, Atchison's Angle, *Washington Star*, 7 March 1961.

67. David Condon, In the Wake of the News, *CT*, 26 Jan. 1960; "Stamps, Coins & Hobbies," *CT*, 3 Jan. 1960.

68. Al Abrams, "Whirl Around the World of Sports," *Pittsburgh Post-Gazette*, 30 Jan. 1960.

69. Ed Sullivan, "An American Abroad," *New York Daily News*, 12 July 1965.

70. Estele Atwell, What to Wear, "Abe Saperstein Knows Secret of Traveling Light," *CT*, 13 Dec. 1964.

71. Tony Weitzel, "Late Mayor Kelly's Credo: Boss or Be Bossed," *CDN*, 11 March 1952.

72. Abe Saperstein travel logs, 23 May 1963 and 21 June 1963, Saperstein Papers, DBC, 2.325/P14c.

73. Hedda Hopper, "Simcox Given Role with Stewart," *Pittsburgh Press*, 1 Aug. 1964.

74. Hackenberg, "Abe, 'Trotters Still Cover World."

75. Hackenberg, "Abe, 'Trotters Still Cover World."

76. Zinkoff, *Around the World*, 66.

77. Roy Schwartz, Sports with Schwartz, *Daily Herald* (Provo, UT), 30 Dec. 1956.

78. Author interview with Joyce Leviton, 27 Dec. 2021.

79. Author interview with Hallie Bryant, 21 Oct. 2021.

80. "Trotters Are Another Rags-to-Riches Story," *Minneapolis Tribune*, 28 March 1954.

CHAPTER 13

1. Robert S. Bird and Ogden R. Reid, "U.S. Propaganda Effort Called Feeble Compared to Russians'," *Richmond Times-Dispatch*, 11 Aug. 1950.

2. Damion L. Thomas, *Globetrotting: African American Athletes and Cold War Politics* (Urbana: University of Illinois Press, 2012), 82; Peter Irons, *Jim Crow's Children: The Broken Promise of the Brown Decision* (New York: Penguin, 2002), 137.

3. AP, "Text of Gen. Eisenhower's Foreign Policy Speech in San Francisco," delivered 8 Oct. 1952, https://timesmachine.nytimes.com/timesmachine/1952/10/09/84263486.pdf (accessed 18 May 2022); Thomas, *Globetrotting*, 97.

4. Letter from Secretary of State Dean Acheson to American Legation, Damascus, 28 July 1952, NA, 811.453/7-2852; Thomas, *Globetrotting*, 48–49.

5. Jimmy Cannon, Jimmy Cannon Says, *Newsday* (Long Island, NY), 11 July 1952.

6. "Abe Saperstein Relates His Top Thrill in Sports," Harlem Globetrotters publicity, 1961, Anzivino Collection, DBC, 13/98-166.

7. AP, "Clean Bill of Health Is Given Sugar Ray by German Officials," *Washington Star*, 25 June 1951; UP, "Berlin Papers Mostly Critical of Sugar Ray," *Boston Globe*, 25 June 1951.

8. Telegram from Dean Acheson to US embassies in Berlin and Frankfurt, June 28, 1951, NA, 811.4535/6-2851; telegram from US embassy in Berlin to Dean Acheson, 18 July 1951, NA, 811.4535/7-1851.

9. Edwin Pope, "Memories of Abe," *Miami Herald*, 2 Feb. 1969.

10. Cobey Black, Who's News, *Honolulu Star-Bulletin*, 9 Feb. 1967.

11. Richard Kasischke, AP, "Jesse Owens Receives Ovation at Scene of Olympic Honors," *Johnson City (TN) Press*, 23 Aug. 1951.

12. UP, "Jesse Owens Sends Berlin on 'Hero Spree,'" *Binghamton (NY) Press*, 23 Aug. 1951.

13. Pope, "Memories of Abe."

14. UP, "Jesse Owens Sends Berlin on 'Hero Spree.'"

15. Abe Saperstein, "When Berlin Went Wild at a Basketball Game," *CDN*, 17 Dec. 1951.

16. Author interview with Marlene Rankin, 22 Jan. 2022.

17. Telegram from U.S. embassy in West Berlin, West Germany, to US State Department, 23 Aug. 1951, NA, 811.4535/6-2751.

18. Drew Pearson, "Oil Lobby Hired Special Planes to Thwart Governor Pat Brown's Severance Pay Plan," *Honolulu Star-Bulletin*, 22 June 1959; Jack Anderson, Washington Merry-Go-Round, *Daily Press* (Newport News, VA), 22 June 1959.

19. Al Del Greco, For the Record, *The Record* (Hackensack, NJ), 5 Dec. 1958.

20. Bob Considine, INS, "Harlem Globetrotters . . . Potent Ambassadors," *Omaha World Herald*, 7 July 1952.

21. Peter Lisagor, "Globetrotters Swing Indonesians to Our Side," *Lincoln (NE) Sunday Journal and Star*, 23 May 1954.

22. Considine, "Harlem Globetrotters . . . Potent Ambassadors."

23. *Harlem Globetrotters: The Team That Changed the World*, documentary written by Anne Kreiter (Chicago: TeamWorks Media/MJA, 2005).

24. John Kuenster, "Yanquis No, Cagers In," *CDN*, 11 Aug. 1962.

25. David Condon, "Rate Russian Basket Squad," *CT*, 1 Sept. 1956; Robert Cromie, "Trotters' European Tour Turns Commie Faces Red," *CT*, 25 Sept. 1951.

26. Paul Spiers, "Bob Kennedy Is Opposed to Concessions to Russia," *Holyoke (MA) Daily Transcript*, 21 Oct. 1955.

27. Steve Snider, "Saperstein Sends Two Crews on Cage Tour," *Honolulu Advertiser*, 21 May 1956; "Saperstein Reports Basketball Growth," *Honolulu Star-Bulletin*, 3 Oct. 1956; Red McQueen, "Trotters to Show in Russia," *Honolulu Advertiser*, 26 June 1959.

28. Red McQueen, "Trotters Tops in Sports," *Honolulu Advertiser*, 4 March 1961.

29. Pearson, "Oil Lobby Hired Special Planes to Thwart Governor Pat Brown's Severance Pay Plan."

30. AP, "Soviet Reaction Mixed on Globetrotters," *Daily Missoulian* (Missoula, MT), 8 July 1959.

31. Tommy Holmes, "Trotters Must Explain Their Game Is Comedy," *Dayton Journal Herald*, 27 July 1959.

32. Lewis F. Atchison, Atchison's Angle, *Washington Star*, 7 March 1961.

33. Cobey Black, Who's News, *Honolulu Star-Bulletin*, 9 Feb. 1967.

34. Wendell Smith, Wendell Smith's Sports Beat, *PC*, 1 Aug. 1959; Black, Who's News.

35. C. B. Fletcher, On the Local Scene, *Leaf-Chronicle* (Clarksville, TN), 10 Nov. 1960.

36. Larry Desautels, Batting Around, *Aberdeen (SD) American-News*, 1 Jan. 1967.

37. John Mooney, "Russians Savvy Trotters," *Salt Lake Tribune*, 3 Aug. 1959.

38. Smith, Wendell Smith's Sports Beat, 1 Aug. 1959.

39. Thomas, *Globetrotting*, 103–6.

40. Testimony by Douglas N. Batson to the US Appropriations Subcommittee on Departments of State and Justice and the Judiciary and Related Agencies, Supplemental Appropriation Bill for 1957, 14 June 1956, 700.

41. Letter from William O. Boswell, administrative officer at US embassy in Rome, to Abe Saperstein, 13 June 1955, Saperstein Papers, DBC, 2.325/P14c; Letter from Thomas L. Cannon, US Information Agency, to Abe Saperstein, 9 Dec. 1953, DBC, 2.325/P14c.

42. Curley Grieve, "State Department Gets Abe behind Iron Curtain," *San Francisco Examiner*, 19 Jan. 1961.

43. Bob Considine, INS, "'Trotters Spread Good Will," *Salt Lake Tribune*, 6 July 1952.

44. "Poland, Hungary and Roumania Visited by Trotters: List at 80," Harlem Globetrotters publicity, 1961, Anzivino Collection, DBC, 13/98-166.

45. Letter from Abe Saperstein to Mary Stewart French, US State Department, 14 Dec. 1954, NA, 811.4533/12-1454.

46. Letter from Mary Stewart French, US State Department, to Abe Saperstein, 26 Jan. 1955, NA, 811.4533/12-1454.

47. Drew Pearson, *Drew Pearson Diaries, 1949–1959* (New York: Holt, Rinehart, and Winston, 1974), 406.

48. Cable from US Information Agency to US embassy in Tripoli, Libya, 27 Nov. 1957, NA.

49. Letter from US consul general in Casablanca, Morocco, to US Information Agency, 30 Dec. 1957, NA.

50. US Information Agency, typed note with handwritten "not sent," archived with cable received from US embassy in Rabat, Morocco, 27 Nov. 1957.

51. Pearson, *Drew Pearson Diaries*, 406.

52. Cable from US embassy in Rabat, Morocco, to US Information Agency, 20 Dec. 1957, NA.

53. Sec Taylor, "Million-Dollar Idea," *Des Moines Register*, 18 Aug. 1952.

54. Wendell Smith, "A Visitor Drops In from Istanbul," *PC*, 23 Aug. 1952.

55. Wendell Smith, "'Athletic Possibilities in Africa Tremendous but Talent Must Be Developed'—Saperstein," *Pittsburgh Courier*, 11 Jan. 1964.

56. AP, "Globe Trotters Abroad Prove Non-Exploitation of Negroes," *South Bend (IN) Tribune*, 8 July 1952.

57. Mooney, "Russians Savvy Trotters."

58. Thomas, *Globetrotting*, 95.

59. *Harlem Globetrotters: The Team That Changed the World*, Kreiter.

60. "Crushing Soviet Lies," *PC*, 29 April 1950.

61. Julia Ioffe, "The History of Russian Involvement in America's Race Wars," *The Atlantic*, 21 Oct. 2017.

62. Letter from Scott McLeod, US ambassador to Ireland, to Abe Saperstein, 10 Oct. 1958, Saperstein Papers, DBC, 2.325/P14c.

63. Paul Zimmerman, "Trotters Big Hit in Africa," *Los Angeles Times*, 31 Jan. 1964.

64. *Harlem Globetrotters: The Team That Changed the World*, Kreiter.

65. Mark Langill, "Dodgers—International Baseball Overview," WalterOMalley.com, www.walteromalley.com/en/dodger-history/international-relations/Overview_Page-1#foot-note-1 (accessed 1 June 2022).

66. Thomas, *Globetrotting*, 44.

67. "Memorandum for Mr. Joseph Feeney: Proposed 1952 World Tour of the Cleveland Indians and Brooklyn Dodgers Baseball Clubs," 15 May 1952, NA, 811.4533/5-1552.

68. Cable from the US embassy in Athens, Greece, to the US State Department, 29 July 1952, NA, 811.4533/7-1952; "World Tour for Two Clubs," UP, *Greenville (OH) Daily Advocate*, 8 July 1952.

69. AP, "Trotters Back after World Trip; Lost Player in Hole in Floor," *St. Louis Post-Dispatch*, 7 Oct. 1952.

70. Bill Furlong, "Latins Still Like Trotters," *CDN*, 16 May 1958.

71. David Condon, In the Wake of the News, *CT*, 25 June 1963.

72. United States Information Service, Letter from C. Edward Wells, Public Affairs Officer at US embassy (Tehran), to Abe Saperstein, 3 Aug. 1955, Saperstein Papers, DBC, 2.325/P14c.

73. Letter from Waldemar J. Gallman, US ambassador to Iraq, to Abe Saperstein, 27 July 1955, Saperstein Papers, DBC, 2.325/P14c.

74. David Condon, In the Wake of the News, *CT*, 17 April 1964.

75. Gene Ward, Ward to the Wise, *New York Daily News*, 22 Aug. 1963.

CHAPTER 14

1. General League Bulletin, 5 July 1961, Anzivino Collection, DBC, 98-166/2; AP, "Sears Jumps Knicks, Signs with Comets," *Chattanooga Times*, 26 April 1961.

2. General League Bulletin, 5 July 1961.

3. Abe Saperstein letter to John Rex Allen, 26 April 1959, Anzivino Collection, DBC, 98-166/2.

4. Bill Furlong, "Tiny Titans Waging Pro Basketball Battle," *CDN*, 4 May 1961.

5. Max Kase, Briefkase, *New York Journal-American*, 20 March 1966.

6. Tom Hopkins, Sportraitures, *Honolulu Star-Bulletin*, 21 Jan. 1962.

7. Al Warden, The Sports Highway, *Ogden (UT) Standard-Examiner*, 8 May 1959.

8. AP, "New Pro League May Be Formed," *Hagerstown (MD) Daily Mail*, 22 March 1960; AP, "Abe Saperstein Starts New Pro Court League," *Hackensack (NJ) Record*, 22 April 1960.

9. Lyall Smith, "After Naismith, There's Lil' Abe," *Detroit Free Press*, 8 Nov. 1961.

10. "George McKeon," *San Francisco Examiner*, 15 Nov. 1976.

11. Rudy Cernkovic, UPI, "Rens Owner Ready for Season," *New Castle (PA) News*, 29 Aug. 1961.

12. AP, "Tapers Beat the Drum for Gala ABL Opener," *Kansas City Times*, 2 Nov. 1961.

13. AP, "Boston Celtics Owner Calls Sharman 'Quitter,'" *Johnson City (TN) Press-Chronicle*, 25 Oct. 1961.

14. "'We're Out to Get Top Players' Steinbrenner," *Cleveland Call and Post*, 18 Feb. 1961; AP, "Cleveland Cage Team Turns Pro," *Great Falls (MT) Tribune*, 28 March 1961.

15. AP, "Ames Housewife to Officiate at Globetrotters Tilt," *Mason City (IA) Globe-Gazette*, 22 Dec. 1959.

16. "Bud Hoeber Dies; Promoted Midget Auto Races Here," *St. Louis Post-Dispatch*, 10 July 1961; Murry R. Nelson, *Abe Saperstein and the American Basketball League 1960–1963* (Jefferson, NC: McFarland, 2013), 3, 8.

17. Nelson, *Abe Saperstein and the American Basketball League*, 2–3; ABL Bulletin, 24 June 1961, and Constitution of the American Basketball League, Anzivino Collection, DBC, 98-166/2.

18. Richard Dozier, "Andy Phillip Named Coach of Chicago ABL Team," *CT*, 24 April 1961.

19. Arne Harris, "Welcome, American Basketball League," Harlem Globetrotters program 1961–1962; Seerat Sohi, "How the NBA Was Saved on the Back of a Napkin," *Sports Illustrated*, 28 Aug. 2017, www.si.com/nba/2017/08/28/nba-shot-clock-history-invention-leo-ferris-george-mikan (accessed 5 Jan. 2023).

20. "Constitution of the American Basketball League," Anzivino Collection, DBC, 98-166/2.

21. AP, "Steers Lose to S.F. Late," *Kansas City Times*, 4 Jan. 1962; AP, "Boy Steals Ball, Steers Lose Game," *Garden City (KS) Telegram*, 4 Jan. 1962.

22. Nelson, *Abe Saperstein and the American Basketball League*, 58, 65–67; Wells A. Trombley, "Leonardo Protests: It's Hard to Lose Money . . . ," *Valley Times* (North Hollywood, CA), 9 Aug. 1961. George Yardley scored his 2,000 points in a season while with the Detroit Pistons and later was traded to the Syracuse Nationals.

23. UPI, "Oaks Will Open ABL Season against Steers," *Fresno (CA) Bee*, 14 Nov. 1962; Nelson, *Abe Saperstein and the American Basketball League*, 91, 121.

24. David Wolf, *Foul! The Connie Hawkins Story* (New York: Holt, Rinehart and Winston, 1972), 106.

25. Abe Saperstein telegram to George Steinbrenner, 17 March 1962, Anzivino Collection, DBC, 98-166/3.

26. Nelson, *Abe Saperstein and the American Basketball League*, 125, 132–33, 136–38; "They Just Want to Know What Pipers Are Doing," *CDN*, 19 Feb. 1962; AP, "ABL to Vote Today on Cleveland Status," *Baltimore Sun*, 20 Feb. 1962.

27. AP, "Pipers' Owner Defends Lucas' Actions," *Cincinnati Enquirer*, 18 May 1962; Nelson, *Abe Saperstein and the American Basketball League*, 140.

28. AP, "Podoloff Admits Merger Talks," *Baltimore Sun*, 6 July 1962.

29. AP, "Saperstein Ponders Fate of American Cage League," *Poughkeepsie (NY) Journal*, 12 July 1962; UPI, "Saperstein Calls a Foul," *Philadelphia Inquirer*, 13 July 1962; Si Burick, Si-ings, *Dayton Daily News*, 2 Aug. 1962.

30. AP, "Big Jerry Lucas Is Prize Pawn in Pro Cage Squabble," *Mitchell (SD) Republic*, 1 Aug. 1962; Fritz Kreisler, "Lucas Sits It Out for $30,000," *Kansas City Times*, 18 Sept. 1962; Jim Schottelkotte, "ABL One of Abe's Few Failures," *Cincinnati Enquirer*, 16 March 1966.

31. Marie Linehan letter to Bill Sharman, 30 July 1962, Anzivino Collection, DBC, 98-166/2.

32. Wendell Smith, Sports Beat, *PC*, 17 Nov. 1962.

33. Hopkins, Sportraitures, 21 Jan. 1962; Paul Pinckney, "Trotters Save ABL," *Rochester Democrat and Chronicle*, 25 March 1962; AP, "Basketball Loop Lost $1.5 Million," *Birmingham News*, 12 April 1962. In various interviews, Saperstein put the ABL's first-year loss at $1 million or $1.5 million.

34. League Bulletin, 27 July 1962, Anzivino Collection, DBC, 98-166/2.

35. League Bulletin, 25 Sept. 1962, Anzivino Collection, DBC, 98-166/2.

36. AP, "ABL Introducing Doubleheaders," *Oneonta (NY) Star*, 13 Nov. 1962; Abe Saperstein letter to Bill Sharman, 26 Dec. 1962, Anzivino Collection, DBC, 98-166/2; Tapers owner Paul Cohen telegram to Abe Saperstein, 11 Nov. 1962, Anzivino Collection, DBC, 98-166/2.

37. David Condon, In the Wake of the News, *CT*, 31 Dec. 1962.

38. Newspaper Enterprise Association, "New League Folds, but Not Saperstein, Globetrotters," *Nashua (NH) Telegraph*, 10 Jan. 1963; "Estate of Saperstein v. Commissioner," US Tax Court, 23 July 1970. In the NEA story, Saperstein said the league's owners lost $1.75 million. Ben Green put the total loss of all owners at $1.5 million. The 1970 tax filing by Saperstein's estate cited a debt by the Chicago Majors to Saperstein of nearly $190,000 as of 31 Dec. 1962 and an additional unrecoverable $56,000 that Saperstein lent to the ABL and its other teams. Green gives a higher figure of $300,000 as Saperstein's total loss.

39. Condon, In the Wake of the News, *CT*, 31 Dec. 1962.

40. Hy Zimmerman, Sports Hy-Lites, "The Little Big Man; Human Long Shot," *Seattle Times*, 17 March 1966.

CHAPTER 15

1. "Basketball Basics: The Evolution of the Game," Hooptactics.com, https://hooptactics.net/premium/basketballbasics/bb8rulesevolution.php (accessed 3 July 2022).

2. "Our Inquiring Reporter," *Vancouver Sun*, 22 Jan. 1937.

3. Bob Ingram, As I Was Saying, *El Paso Herald-Times*, 9 Jan. 1958.

4. Jack Donald, *San Francisco Call-Bulletin*, quoted in Bob Wood, Sports Splinters, *Uniontown (PA) Morning Herald*, 3 Feb. 1953.

5. Seymour S. Smith, "3-Point Goal: Good or Bad?" *Baltimore Sun*, 11 Feb. 1962.

6. McQueen, Hoomalimali, *Honolulu Advertiser*, 25 Jan. 1958.

7. Earl Kirmser, The Sporting Thing, *Winona (MN) Republican-Herald*, 27 Oct. 1936.

8. Ed Honeywell, Between the Bounces, *Tacoma (WA) News Tribune*, 2 Feb. 1949.

9. Bill Fuchs, "New League May Curb Giants in Basketball," *Washington Star*, 19 Dec. 1960.

10. Bob Ingram, As I Was Saying, *El Paso Herald-Post*, 22 Feb. 1960, quoting Saperstein interview by Scripps-Howard *Washington News*.

11. Nick Greene, *How to Watch Basketball Like a Genius: What Game Designers, Economists, Ballet Choreographers, and Theoretical Astrophysicists Reveal about the Greatest Game on Earth* (New York: Abrams, 2021), 67–70.

12. Louis Effrat, "Columbia Defeats Fordham, 73 to 58," *New York Times*, 8 Feb. 1945.

13. Charles Monagan, "Three-for-All," *Dartmouth Alumni Magazine*, Nov.–Dec. 2018.

14. Ben Cohen, "How George Steinbrenner and the Harlem Globetrotters Changed the NBA Forever," *Wall Street Journal*, 13 Feb. 2020.

15. Scott Ostler, "Three-Point Play Hasn't Bombed Yet," *Los Angeles Times*, 3 Jan. 1980.

16. Cohen, "How George Steinbrenner." It's not known which basketball court in Chicago they went to.

17. Author interview with Joey Meyer, 18 Jan. 2022.

18. Jerry Crowe, "How Basketball Became Three-Dimensional," *Los Angeles Times*, 6 May 2008, www.latimes.com/archives/la-xpm-2008-may-06-sp-crowe6-story.html (accessed 7 July 2022).

19. Stuart Miller, "A Basketball League Where Steinbrenner and 3-Pointers Started," *New York Times*, 24 Dec. 2011.

20. Crowe, "How Basketball Became Three-Dimensional."

21. Abe Saperstein note and sketch on three-point rule, Anzivino Collection, DBC, 98-166/2.

22. Crowe, "How Basketball Became Three-Dimensional."

23. Charles Chamberlain, AP, "Three-Point Shot Is Here to Stay," *Durham (NC) Herald*, 15 April 1962; Murray R. Nelson, *Abe Saperstein and the American Basketball League, 1960–1963: The Upstarts Who Shot for Three and Lost to the NBA* (Jefferson, NC: McFarland, 2013), 36; Ron Thomas, *They Cleared the Lane: The NBA's Black Pioneers* (Lincoln: University of Nebraska Press, 2002), 169.

24. Bob Lieb, *Shooting Threes and Shaking the Basketball Establishment: The Short, Chaotic Run of the American Basketball League* (Haworth, NJ: St. Johann Press, 2014), 58; "NBA League Average 3-Point Percentage 2023," Statmuse .com, www.statmuse.com/nba/ask/nba-league-average-3-point-percentage-2023 (accessed 29 Oct. 2023). Jackson started the season with the Tapers and was traded to the Majors.

25. Smith, "3-Point Goal: Good or Bad?"

26. Smith, "3-Point Goal: Good or Bad?"

27. Smith, "3-Point Goal: Good or Bad?"

28. Smith, "3-Point Goal: Good or Bad?"

29. Crowe, "How Basketball Became Three-Dimensional."

30. Art Rosenbaum, "The Three-Pointer: Pro and Con," *San Francisco Chronicle*, 2 July 1979.

31. Daniel Wilco, "How the New 3-Point Line Might Affect College Basketball," NCAA.com, 8 Nov. 2019, www.ncaa.com/news/basketball-men/article/2019-10 -03/how-new-3-point-line-might-affect-college-basketball (accessed 7 July 2022).

32. Author interview with Bobby Hunter, 18 Oct. 2021.

33. Stephen Babb, "How the 3-Point Shot Has Revolutionized the NBA," Bleacher Report, 1 Aug. 2013, https://bleacherreport.com/articles/1715367-how -the-3-point-shot-has-revolutionized-the-nba (accessed 6 Feb. 2023).

34. "2023 NBA Season Summary," Basketball-reference.com, www.basketball -reference.com/leagues/NBA_2023.html (accessed 29 Oct. 2023).

35. Babb, "How the 3-Point Shot."

36. Tom Anderson, From Up Close, *Knoxville Journal*, 25 Jan. 1963.

37. Kyle Given, Two Men in Sports, *Monrovia (CA) News-Post*, 8 Jan. 1965.

38. L. H. Gregory, Greg's Gossip, *Oregonian (Portland, OR)*, 29 Jan. 1963.

CHAPTER 16

1. Author interview with Frank Rose, 22 Jan. 2022.

2. Al Heim, "Won't Be the Same without Abe," *Cincinnati Enquirer*, 26 March 1966.

3. Ben Green, *Spinning the Globe: The Rise, Fall, and Return to Greatness of the Harlem Globetrotters* (New York: Amistad, 2005), 312.

4. AP, "NBA Players' Union Recognized by Owners," *East Liverpool (OH) Evening Review*, 19 April 1957; Karol Stronger, AP, "Trotters Backed," *Spokane (WA) Spokesman-Review*, 3 Dec. 1971.

5. John Mooney, Sports Mirror, *Salt Lake Tribune*, 14 Aug. 1966; Mooney said Troy Collier agreed to shave his beard but LeRoy Walker refused, left for a week, and came back to ask for his job back but "his change came too late." Mooney was apparently unaware that Walker played for the Trotters a few months later, sans beard.

6. Leonard Lewin, *New York Mirror*, reprinted in *St. Croix Avis* (Virgin Islands), 9 Oct. 1963.

7. Lewin, *New York Mirror*.

8. "The Texas Poll Tax," Texas Women's Foundation, https://txwf.org/the-texas-poll-tax/ (accessed 16 Jan. 2023); Kenneth McCaleb, Conversation Piece, *Corpus Christi Times*, 11 Feb. 1965.

9. Wendell Smith, "Inman Jackson, Globetrotters' Newest Coach, Determined to Combine Hilarity with Ability," *PC*, 26 Oct. 1963; Martha M. Hamilton, "Long before Charlottesville, 'Great Replacement Theory' Found Its Champion in a Racist Senator," *Washington Post*, 15 Nov. 2021.

10. Ed Levitt, "Mr. Globe Trotter," *Oakland Tribune*, 12 Jan. 1966.

11. New York Times News Service, "Harlem Globetrotters Join Janitors' Union," *Miami News*, 1 June 1974; Green, *Spinning the Globe*, 389.

12. Smith, "Inman Jackson." Jackson had served as a Globetrotters coach for decades, but Smith and Saperstein seemed to be highlighting Jackson's elevation to head coach of the main unit.

13. Author interview with Mannie Jackson, 11 May 2023.

14. "Satch Paige? He's on Globe Trotter Staff," *CT*, 27 Oct. 1964.

15. Terry Smith, Fairways, *Sydney (Australia) Morning Herald*, 1 Feb. 1976.

16. Green, *Spinning the Globe*, 310. The World Series of Basketball ran from 1950 to 1962, with two years off in 1959 and 1960 because of the Pan Am Games and the Olympics.

17. Dick Hackenberg, "Abe, 'Trotters Still Cover World, Spread U.S. Image," *CDN*, 14 May 1965; Green, *Spinning the Globe*, 310.

18. Green, *Spinning the Globe*, 310.

19. Green, *Spinning the Globe*, 311–12.

20. Murray Olderman, "Colts Score Touchdown," *Nashville Tennessean*, 10 Jan. 1964; "Podoloff Out, J. W. Kennedy In," *Baltimore Sun*, 1 May 1963.

21. "Losers Loot Best in Football," *Vancouver Sun*, 26 Jan. 1965.

22. Author interview with Don Shelby, 17 Aug. 2023.

23. Geoffrey Miller, AP, "Prince Philip's Taverners Nip Globetrotters in Mock Contest," *Appleton (WI) Post-Crescent*, 5 Nov. 1963.

24. AP, "Saperstein Plaque Unveiled in London," *Wisconsin State Journal*, 28 March 1963.

25. "Trotters Celebrating 39th Birthday," *Asbury Park (NJ) Press*, 15 Dec. 1964.

26. Green, *Spinning the Globe*, 302–4; "ABC Trails CBS in 2d Nielsen of Season," *Philadelphia Inquirer*, 26 Oct. 1965; "Hollywood Palace," 1965, https://m.youtube.com/watch?v=yh0cdEa6VO8 (accessed 18 Jan. 2023).

27. Green, *Spinning the Globe*, 304; "76ers, Minus Wilt, No Match for Celtics," *Portland (ME) Press Herald*, 17 Jan. 1966.

28. Abe Saperstein letter to Eloise Saperstein, 25 May 1956.

29. Author interview with Burt Tucker, 23 Jan. 2022.

30. Red Smith, "Abe Saperstein's Boy Jerry," *New York Times*, 3 Feb. 1978; Author interview with Lanier Saperstein, 24 Feb. 2022.

31. "Trotters Won't Play," *Ottumwa (IA) Courier*, 12 Dec. 1963.

32. Charles Einstein, "The Trotters Really Pack 'Em In—to One Million Tune," *Tipton (IN) Daily Tribune*, 9 March 1949.

33. C. V. Burns, "Abe Saperstein Dies," Sports Slants, *Cumberland (MD) News*, 20 Jan. 1951; AP, "Saperstein, Globetrotters Aide, Dies of Heart Attack," *Washington Star*, 15 Jan. 1951; author interview with Roy Raemer, 14 June 2023.

34. "Life Expectancy in the United States," University of California at Berkeley, https://u.demog.berkeley.edu/~andrew/1918/figure2.html (accessed 26 Jan. 2023).

35. AP, "Saperstein Released from Chicago Hospital," *St. Louis Post-Dispatch*, 28 May 1953.

36. AP, "Sudden Operation for Saperstein," *Des Moines Register*, 23 May 1957; Red McQueen, Hoomalimali, *Honolulu Advertiser*, 7 June 1957.

37. UPI, "Abe Saperstein Hospitalized," *Cincinnati Enquirer*, 12 Feb. 1963; "Trotter Coach Beats Pneumonia," *Daily Calumet (IL)*, 14 March 1963.

38. Green, *Spinning the Globe*, 312–13; Hackenberg, "Abe, 'Trotters Still Cover World"; Hack Miller, "Abe Answers Own Letter!" *Deseret News* (Salt Lake City, UT), 31 July 1965.

39. Abe Saperstein letter to Louis "Red" Klotz, 20 July 1965, Saperstein Papers, DBC, 2.325/P14c.

40. Tim Kelly, *The Legend of Red Klotz: How Basketball's Loss Leader Won Over the World—14,000 Times* (Margate, NJ: ComteQ, 2013), 248.

41. Jim Kearney, *Vancouver Sun*, 17 Sept. 1965; Ed Levitt, "Mr. Globe Trotter," *Oakland Tribune*, 12 Jan. 1966; Herb Lyon, Tower Ticker, *CT*, 10 Sept. 1965.

42. Author interview with Burt Tucker, 23 Jan. 2022.

43. Al Abrams, Sidelights on Sports, *Pittsburgh Post-Gazette*, 29 Dec. 1965.

44. Kelly, *The Legend of Red Klotz*, 247.

45. Abe Saperstein travel logs, Saperstein Papers, DBC, 2.325/P14c.

46. Eddie Sherman, *Honolulu Advertiser*, 16 March 1966.

47. Abe Saperstein travel logs, Saperstein Papers, DBC, 2.325/P14c; "January 29, 1966, Weather History in Chicago," Weather Spark, https://weatherspark .com/h/d/14091/1966/1/29/Historical-Weather-on-Saturday-January-29-1966-in -Chicago-Illinois-United-States#Figures-Temperature (accessed 30 Jan. 2023); Green, *Spinning the Globe*, 314.

48. Green, *Spinning the Globe*, 314; author interview with Abra Berkley, 16 Dec. 2021.

49. Author interview with Lonni Berkley, 16 Dec. 2021.

50. Abe Saperstein travel log, 7 March 1966, Saperstein Papers, DBC, 2.325/ P14c.

51. Green, *Spinning the Globe*, 314.

52. Green, *Spinning the Globe*, 314.

53. Green, *Spinning the Globe*, 315.

54. Green, *Spinning the Globe*, 315; Kelly, *The Legend of Red Klotz*, 250; Alan J. Pollock, *Barnstorming to Heaven: Syd Pollock and His Great Black Teams* (Tuscaloosa: University of Alabama Press, 2006), 384.

55. Author interview with Lonni Berkley, 16 Dec. 2021.

56. Hal Wood, *Honolulu Advertiser*, 16 March 1966. Like other official Globetrotters statistics, Saperstein's win-loss record should be taken with a grain of salt.

57. "An Emptiness without Abe," *CDN*, 7 April 1966.

58. Jack R. Griffin, "Last Tributes Paid to Trotters Founder," *CST*, 18 March 1966.

59. David Condon, In the Wake of the News, *CT*, 3 April 1965.

EPILOGUE

1. Ray Waddell, "Anzivino Aims to Maintain Ideals of Harlem Globetrotters' Founder," *Amusement Business*, 6 April 1992.
2. Author interview with Gerald Saperstein, 10 Nov. 2022.
3. AP, "Mrs. Abe Saperstein Leads Globetrotters," *Bismarck (ND) Tribune*, 2 July 1966; AP, "Harlem Globetrotters Sold to Chicago Group," *El Paso (TX) Times*, 9 June 1967; David Condon, In the Wake of the News, *CT*, 10 June 1967; John P. Carmichael, The Barber Shop, *CDN*, 11 Feb. 1969; "In Re Estate of Abraham M. Saperstein, Deceased, Sylvia Saperstein et al Respondents—Appellants vs. Martin L. Silverman et al Petitioners—Appellants," Appellate Court of Illinois, First District, Fourth Division, 27 Nov. 1974, No. 59064. The $3.71 million sale price would be almost ten times that amount today when adjusted for inflation.
4. "Executors' Second and Final Account in the Matter of the Estate of Abraham M. Saperstein, Deceased," Cook County (Illinois) Circuit Court, Probate Division, 1971; "Abe Saperstein Last Will and Testament," signed Aug. 13, 1951, and submitted in Cook County (Illinois) Circuit Court, Probate Division, after his death in 1966.
5. "Estate of Saperstein v. Commissioner," US Tax Court, 23 July 1970, Docket No. 3934-66; "Report of Proceedings in the Matter of the Estate of Abraham M. Saperstein," Cook County (IL) Circuit Court, Probate Division, 2 March 1973.
6. John Wooden letter to Ray Meyer, 21 Sept. 1970, and Marie Linehan letter to Kenneth "Tug" Wilson, 30 Sept. 1970, Anzivino Collection, DBC, 98-166/2.
7. "Hall of Famers," Naismith Memorial Basketball Hall of Fame website, www.hoophall.com/hall-of-famers/all/ (accessed 16 Feb. 2023). Pat Kennedy, who refereed for the Globetrotters for six years, is also in the Hall.
8. David Wolf, *Foul! The Connie Hawkins Story* (New York: Holt, Rinehart and Winston, 1972), 125.
9. Lacy J. Banks, "Trotters Offend Some," *CST*, 9 Feb. 1973.
10. AP, "Abe's Daughter Is Helping, Too," *Jacksonville (FL) Daily Journal*, 22 Oct. 1971; "Eloise Saperstein Berkley, Daughter of Globetrotters' Founder Abe Saperstein, Passes Away at Age 81," Harlem Globetrotters news release, 16 July 2018, www.prnewswire.com/news-releases/eloise-saperstein-berkley-daughter-of-globetrotters-founder-abe-saperstein-passes-away-at-age-81-300681547.html (accessed 17 Feb. 2023).
11. "Isiah L. Thomas' Basketball Hall of Fame Enshrinement Speech," YouTube.com, 8:44 mark, www.youtube.com/watch?v=8VnW3EE-4Mo (accessed 16 Feb. 2023).

12. "Eloise Saperstein Berkley," Harlem Globetrotters news release, 16 July 2018.

13. Red Smith, "Abe Saperstein's Boy Jerry," *New York Times*, 3 Feb. 1978; "Jerry Saperstein Remembered as a True American Giant of Sports Innovation," Big League Sports Entertainment news release, 16 Dec. 2021, www.einnews .com/pr_news/557870158/jerry-saperstein-remembered-as-a-true-american-giant -of-sports-innovation (accessed 17 Feb. 2023).

14. *Harlem Globetrotters: The Team That Changed the World*, documentary written by Anne Kreiter (Chicago: TeamWorks Media/MJA, 2005).

15. Timothy J. O'Brien, "Globetrotters Go All Out to Regain Glory," *Wall Street Journal*, 21 July 1994; "Roy Disney Firm Buys Interest in Globetrotters," *Merced (CA) Sun-Star*, 28 Sept. 2005.

16. "Lynette Woodard," Naismith Memorial Basketball Hall of Fame website, www.hoophall.com/hall-of-famers/lynette-woodard/ (accessed 16 Feb. 2023).

17. Mike Coppinger, "Going Deep: Harlem Globetrotters Add a Four-Point Line," *USA Today*, 22 Sept. 2016; Julian Lim, "From Way Downtown: Examining the Four-Point Shot in Basketball," Medium.com, 21 April 2017, https:// medium.com/@Julian_Lim/from-way-downtown-examining-the-four-point-shot -in-basketball-d2d55ee331e5 (accessed 16 Feb. 2023).

18. *ESPN 30 for 30: From Harlem with Love*, directed by Matthew Ogens (A Tool Production, 2014), https://vimeo.com/201076788 (accessed 15 Nov. 2023); Bob Ryan, @GlobeBobRyan on Twitter, 19 March 2023, https://twitter .com/GlobeBobRyan/status/1637585389627101187 (23 May 2023); *Sweetwater*, directed by Martin Guigui (Hollywood, CA: Sunset Pictures, Reserve Entertainment, Astrablu Media, Open River Entertainment, Pasaca Entertainment, 2023).

19. Dave Tefft, "Trotters Could Add a Story Hour to Their Entertainment Program," *Ann Arbor News*, 26 Nov. 1957.

SELECTED
BIBLIOGRAPHY

Allen, Maury. *Dixie Walker of the Dodgers: The People's Choice.* Tuscaloosa: University of Alabama Press, 2010.

Alpert, Rebecca T. *Out of Left Field: Jews and Black Baseball.* New York: Oxford University Press, 2011.

Bjarkman, Peter C. *The Encyclopedia of Pro Basketball Team Histories.* New York: Carroll & Graf, 1994.

Callahan, Tom. *Gods at Play: An Eyewitness Account of Great Moments in American Sports.* New York: W.W. Norton, 2022.

Christgau, John. *Tricksters in the Madhouse: Lakers vs. Globetrotters, 1948.* Lincoln, NE: Bison Books, 2007.

Epplin, Luke. *Our Team: The Epic Story of Four Men and the World Series That Changed Baseball.* New York: Flatiron Books, 2021.

Freedarko High Council. *The Undisputed Guide to Pro Basketball History.* New York: Bloomsbury, 2010.

Gay, Timothy M. *Satch, Dizzy & Rapid Robert: The Wild Saga of Interracial Baseball before Jackie Robinson.* New York: Simon & Schuster, 2010.

George, Nelson. *Elevating the Game: Black Men and Basketball.* New York: HarperCollins, 1992.

Goudsouzian, Aram. *King of the Court: Bill Russell and the Basketball Revolution.* Berkeley: University of California Press, 2010.

Green, Ben. *Spinning the Globe: The Rise, Fall, and Return to Greatness of the Harlem Globetrotters.* New York: Amistad, 2005.

Greene, Nick. *How to Watch Basketball Like a Genius: What Game Designers, Economists, Ballet Choreographers, and Theoretical Astrophysicists Reveal about the Greatest Game on Earth.* New York: Abrams, 2021.

Hayner, Don, and Tom McNamee. *The Stadium: 1929–1994, the Official Commemorative History of the Chicago Stadium.* Chicago: Performance Media, 1993.

Johnson, Claude. *The Black Fives: The Epic Story of Basketball's Forgotten Era.* New York: Abrams Press, 2021.

Johnson, Mark. *Basketball Slave: The Andy Johnson Harlem Globetrotter/NBA Story.* Mantua, NJ: JuniorCam Publishing, 2010.

Kelly, Tim. *The Legend of Red Klotz: How Basketball's Loss Leader Won Over the World—14,000 Times.* Margate, NJ: ComteQ, 2013.

Lanctot, Neil. *Negro League Baseball: The Rise and Ruin of a Black Institution.* Philadelphia: University of Pennsylvania Press, 2004.

Lemann, Nicholas. *The Promised Land: The Great Black Migration and How It Changed America.* New York: Vintage Books, 1992.

Lemon, Meadowlark, with Jerry B. Jenkins. *Meadowlark.* Nashville, TN: Thomas Nelson Publishers, 1987.

Lieb, Bob. *Shooting Threes and Shaking the Basketball Establishment: The Short, Chaotic Run of the American Basketball League.* Haworth, NJ: St. Johann Press, 2014.

McRae, Donald. *In Black & White: The Untold Story of Joe Louis and Jesse Owens.* London: Scribner, 2002.

Menville, Chuck. *The Harlem Globetrotters: An Illustrated History.* New York: David McKay, 1978.

Moore, Joseph Thomas. *Larry Doby: The Struggle of the American League's First Black Player.* Mineola, NY: Dover, 2011.

Nelson, Murray R. *Abe Saperstein and the American Basketball League, 1960–1963: The Upstarts Who Shot for Three and Lost to the NBA.* Jefferson, NC: McFarland, 2013.

Paige, Satchel. *Maybe I'll Pitch Forever.* Lincoln: University of Nebraska Press, 1993.

Peterson, Robert. *Only the Ball Was White: A History of Legendary Black Players and All-Black Professional Teams.* New York: Oxford University Press, 1970.

Pollock, Alan J. *Barnstorming to Heaven: Syd Pollock and His Great Black Teams.* Tuscaloosa: University of Alabama Press, 2006.

Pomerantz, Gary M. *Wilt, 1962: The Night of 100 Points and the Dawn of a New Era.* New York: Crown Publishers, 2005.

Powell, Larry. *Black Barons of Birmingham: The South's Greatest Negro League Team and Its Players.* Jefferson, NC: McFarland, 2009.

Russell, Bill, with Bill McSweeny. *Go Up for Glory.* New York: Dutton, 1966.

Schumacher, Michael. *Mr. Basketball: George Mikan, the Minneapolis Lakers and the Birth of the NBA.* New York: Bloomsbury, 2007.

Stark, Douglas. *Wartime Basketball: The Emergence of a National Sport during World War II.* Lincoln: University of Nebraska Press, 2016.

Thomas, Damion L. *Globetrotting: African American Athletes and Cold War Politics.* Urbana, Chicago: University of Illinois Press, 2012.

Thomas, Ron. *They Cleared the Lane: The NBA's Black Pioneers.* Lincoln: University of Nebraska Press, 2002.

Tye, Larry. *Satchel: The Life and Times of an American Legend.* New York: Random House, 2009.

Tygiel, Jules. *Baseball's Great Experiment: Jackie Robinson and His Legacy.* New York: Oxford University Press, 1997.

Veeck, Bill, with Ed Linn. *Veeck as in Wreck: The Autobiography of Bill Veeck.* Chicago: University of Chicago Press, 2001.

Wolf, David. *Foul! The Connie Hawkins Story.* New York: Holt, Rinehart and Winston, 1972.

Zarum, Dave. *NBA 75: The Definite History.* Buffalo, NY: Firefly Books, 2020.

Zinkoff, Dave, with Edgar Williams. *Around the World with the Harlem Globetrotters.* Philadelphia: MacRae Smith, 1953.

INDEX

Aaron, Henry (Hank), 70

ABA. *See* American Basketball Association

ABC. *See* American Broadcasting Company

Abdul-Jabbar, Kareem, 139

Abe Saperstein Foundation, 215

Abe Saperstein Sports Enterprises, 79, 88, 118

ABL. *See* American Basketball League

Acheson, Dean, 163–165, 174

Adderley, Cannonball, 142

Akron Pros, 27

Albuquerque, New Mexico, 140

Algiers, Algeria, 152

Algeria, 152

Algona, Iowa, 42

Allen, Steve, 205, 209

All-Nations Club (baseball), 63

All-Star Classic of 1940, 77–78

Amateur Athletic Union, 45, 52, 135, 203

American Basketball Association (ABA), 195–196

American Basketball League (ABL), 1961–62 championship series, 185
adoption of wider foul lane, 183
concerns about three-point shot, 194
demise of the league, 183–187
denounced as "a bunch of pirates," 182
doubleheader format, 187
explores merger with NBA, 185
financial distress of owners, 184, 186–187
formation of league, 177, 181–183
friction between Saperstein and owners, 184, 186, 194
loans to finance league, 214
original motivations of Saperstein, 180
shot clock differences with NBA, 183
stolen ball incident in San Francisco, 183
three-point shooting percentage, 195

three-point shot, origins of,
192–193
three-point shot, rule of, 183,
193–195
travel challenges for teams, 182–183
American Broadcasting Company
(ABC), 206, 217
American Giants, 215
Amman, Jordan, 171
Anderson, Bob, 28
Anderson, Gilbert, 20
Anderson (Indiana) Packers, 113
Anderson, Lawrence "Rock," 49, 73
Angola, 158
anti-Semitism, 17, 19, 20, 40, 50, 68,
151, 202
Antwerp, Belgium, 151
Anzivino, Joe, 204, 213
Arcadia, Wisconsin, 44
Argentina, 153, 174
Auerbach, Red, 116, 118, 204
Ausbie, Hubert "Geese," 214
Auschwitz, Poland, 17, 152
Australia, 105, 156, 157, 174,
203–204, 208

Babb, Sanora, 139
Babb, Stephen, 196–197
Ball, Walter, 25–26
Baltimore Bullets, 121, 129
Baltimore, Maryland, 79
Banks, Ernie, 135
Banks, Lacy J., 215
Barcelona, Spain, 109, 166
Barnsdall Millers, 39, 41
Barnum, P. T., 131
Baroudi, Sam, 13
Basketball Association of America, 8
Bates, Clayton "Peg Leg," 133–134

Baylor, Elgin, 183
Beatles, The, 142–143
Belafonte, Harry, 142
Belgium, 151
Bell, Puggy, 75
Bennett, Carl, 116–117
Benton Harbor, Michigan, 41
Bergmann, Richard, 134
Berkeley, California, 66
Berkley, Abra, 98, 111, 151
Berkley, Avi, 142, 209, 210
Berkley, Lonni, 110, 209–210
Berkley, Eloise Saperstein, 109,
143, 209
anti-Semitic incident in German
hotel, 151
birth of, 58
death of, 215
discussed as successor to father, 206
hosts ceremony for basketball
player, 215
incident in Miami Beach with Inman
Jackson, 83
inheritance from her father's
estate, 214
manages Abe Saperstein
Foundation, 215
pendant received from father, 151
racist incident in Illinois, 215
recalls relationship of parents,
111–112
recalls reaction of father to
losses, 56
relationship with father, 110–111
travels with father, 111, 151
weeps over Jackie Robinson's
struggle, 98
works as sports agent, 215
Berkley, Irwin, 142

Berlin, Germany, 57, 119, 135, 136, 151, 165–167, 170, 175

Bermuda, 109

Bernie, Ben, 139

Bibb, Oliver, 141–142

Bilbo, Theodore, 202, 205

Birmingham, Alabama, 173

Birmingham Black Barons, 64–65, 121

Bismarck, North Dakota, 61–62

Black, Timuel, 13, 173

Bleacher Report, 196

Bleach, Larry, 55–56

Bloch, Allan, 213–214

Blonsky, Katherine Saperstein, 18

Bogart, Humphrey, 137–138

Bologna, Italy, 151

Bostic, Joe, 127

Boston Brownskins, 58

Boston Celtics, 54, 116, 117–118, 126, 137, 182, 193, 204, 206

Boston Garden, 113, 117–118

Boston Globe, 117

Boston, Massachusetts, 114, 117–118

Boston Whirlwinds, 125

Boswell, Sonny, 74–76, 78–79, 84, 214

Bouncing Collegians, 134

Brando, Marlon, 137

Brazil, 119, 153, 186

Brickhouse, Jack, 213

British Broadcasting Company, 150

Britton, John, Jr., 122

Broadway Clowns, 49, 54

Brockton, Massachusetts, 141

Brookins, Tommy, 28–30, 147

Brooks, Hadda, 142, 143

Brooks, Mel, 206

Brooklyn Dodgers. *See* Los Angeles Dodgers

Brother Bones and His Shadows, 140

Brown, Hilary, 79

Brown University, 27

Brown, Walter, 117, 182

Brownstein, Phil, 90

Brownwood, Texas, 202

Bryant, Hallie, 107, 162

Buie, Boid, 89

Bull, Frank, 129

Burley, Dan, 68

Bushame, Frances Saperstein, 18

Butte, Montana, 47

Calloway, Cab, 110

Campanella, Roy, 101

Canada, 87, 147

Capri, Italy, 155

Carmen Jones (film), 137, 142

Caronia (ship), 152

Casablanca, Morocco, 152, 171

Castel Gandolfo (Italy), 154

Cathedral Grove (Vancouver), 53

CBS. *See* Columbia Broadcasting Service

"CBS Sports Spectacular" (TV), 206

Chamberlain, Wilt, *114*, 126–128, 179, 181, 184, 206
  college fame, 126
  commentary from Black press, 127
  courted to return to Globetrotters, 127
  fond memories of Globetrotters, 128
  frustration with "roughhouse tactics" in NBA, 127
  inducted into Hall of Fame, 214
  lucrative contract with Globetrotters, 126
  position played for Globetrotters, 127

Chandler, Albert Benjamin "Happy" Sr., 105
Chaplin, Charlie, 20
"The Charge of the Light Brigade" (song), 152
Charles, Ezzard, 13
Charlton Athletic, 58
Checkpoint Charlie (Berlin), 175–176
Chicago American, 55
Chicago American Giants, 69, 122
Chicago Bears, 3, 55, 76
Chicago Blackhawks, 3
Chicago Bombers, 79, 125, 127
Chicago Bruins, 76–77, 120
Chicago Bulls, 215
Chicago Coliseum, 56
Chicago Cubs, 18, 91, 125
Chicago Daily News, 58, 175
Chicago Defender, 12, 28–29, 45, 46, 54–55, 67, 68, 76–79, 94, 101
Chicago Harmons, 56, 76
Chicago Herald-American, 12, 77, 90
Chicago Herald-Examiner, 55
Chicago, Illinois,
    birthplace of Harlem Globetrotters, 1, 3
    Beige Room (jazz club), 142
    Bronzeville neighborhood, 25, 26
    influx of Black people into South Side, 25
    Kelvyn Park High School, 90
    Lake View High School, 21, 38
    Lane Technical High School, 28
    Lincoln Park, 33
    Madison Street Armory, 75
    Maxwell Street Market, 18–19
    race relations and incidents, 4, 25, 54

rapid growth in early 20th century, 18
    Ravenswood neighborhood, 17–20
    reaction to 1948 Globetrotters–Lakers game, 12–13
    Savoy Ballroom, 28
    Welles Park, 19, 25
    Wendell Phillips High School, 28, 45
    White City amusement park, 54–55
Chicago Majors, 120, 181, 183, 186
Chicago & Northwestern Railroad, 22
Chicago Packers (a.k.a. Zephyrs), 129, 181
Chicago Reds, 25
Chicago Stadium, 1, 186, 187
    description of, 5
    hosts 1948 Globetrotters–Lakers game, 106, 115
    hosts All-Star Classic tournament, 78
    hosts brutal boxing match, 13
    noise level inside, 3
    notable events hosted by, 3
    sightlines of fans, 5
    ticket prices, 3–4
Chicago Stags, 8, 120, 128
Chicago State University, 215
Chicago Sun-Times, 3, 215
Chicago Tribune, 4, 7, 28, 56, 76, 118, 160, 187
Chicago White Sox, 19, 95, 100
Chihuahua Dorados, 88
Chile, 153
China, 157
Chinese Exclusion Act, 138
Chinese Hong Wa Kues, 57
Churchill, Neil, 61

Cincinnati Crescents, 70
Cincinnati Gardens, 199
Cincinnati, Ohio, 68–69, 129
Cincinnati Royals, 129, 186
Clark, Dane (a.k.a. Bernard
    Zanville), 137
Cleveland Black Friars, 59
Cleveland Indians, 70, 98–100, 108, 174
Cleveland, Ohio, 22, 108, 181
Cleveland Pipers, 182, 184–186, 193
Cleveland Rosenblums, 22
Clifton, Nathaniel "Sweetwater," 2,
    115–117, 120, 137, 214, 217
Clinton, Iowa, 123
Coca-Cola, 199
Cohen, Haskell, 136
Cohen, Paul, x, 182
Cold War, The, xiii, 14, 163–164,
    168, 173–174
College All-Stars,
    attendance at games, 119
    compensation of players and
        coaches, 119–120
    games versus Globetrotters,
        119, 126
    head coach of, 119
    media criticism of Globetrotters
        series, 119
    participating players, 77–78
    termination of the series versus
        Globetrotters, 203
Collier's, 76
Colombia, 153
Columbia Broadcasting Service (CBS),
    124, 184, 206
Columbia Pictures, 137
Columbia University (New York), 193
Come Back, Little Sheba (film), 143
Comiskey Park (Chicago), 68, 69, 100

Congo, Democratic Republic of, 159
Connie Mack Stadium
    (Philadelphia), 125
Conquian (card game), 107
Considine, Bob, 167
Continental Bank, 213
Conway, Tim, 206
Cooper, Charles Henry "Chuck,"
    117–18, 137, 214
Cooper, Charles "Tarzan," 56, 75–76
Cottrell, Alf, 96
Cousy, Bob, 204
Cow Palace (San Francisco), 128
Creighton University, 126, 134
Crosby, Bing, 182
Cuba, 87, 88, 147
Cuban Giants, 94–95
Cugat, Xavier, 141
Cullum, Dick, 119
Cumberland, Roscoe "Duke," 73–74,
    79, 84, 137
Czechoslovakian Folk Dancers, 206

Dailey, Quintin, 215
Daley, Richard J., 214
Damone, Vic, 206
Dandridge, Dorothy, 137
"Darktown Strutters Ball" (song), 139
Davis, Bette, 61
Davis, Freeman, 140
Davis, Glenn, 143
Davis, Sammy, Jr., 142
Dean, Jay Hanna "Dizzy," 62
Decatur, Illinois, 85
Denver, Colorado, 114, 207
DePaul University, 5, 10, 78, 119, 125,
    193, 214, 220
Des Moines, Iowa, 37
Des Plaines, Illinois, 37

Detroit Eagles, 79
Detroit Free Press, 181
Detroit, Michigan, 9, 49, 55, 70, 76, 82
Detroit Pistons, 129, 215
Didrikson, Babe, 41
DiMaggio, Joe, 141
Disney, Roy, 216
Disney, Walt, 216
Doby, Larry, 98, 100
Douglas, Bob, 73, 75
Douglas, William O., 163
Dubonnet (French company), 155
Duffy, Bernard, 44, 49
Dukes, Walter, *60*, 122, 127
Durocher, Leo, 96, 206

East Berlin, Germany. *See* Berlin, Germany
Easter, George, 44, 49
Easter, Luke, 108
Eastern Professional Basketball League, 195
Eastern South Dakota State Teachers College, 41
East Germany. *See* Germany
East–West All-Star games. *See* Negro Leagues
Eau Claire, Wisconsin, 29–30
Eckman, Charlie, 43
Ecuador, 153
Effrat, Louis, 193
Egypt, 154–155, 174
Eisenhower, Dwight, 121, 163
Ellis Island (New York), 17
Elson, Bob, 19, 95
Empire State Building, 118, 120, 179
Enright, James, 53, 214

Esquire, 37
Essanay Studios (Chicago), 20
Ethiopian Clowns, 67, 69–70
Evans, Dale, 3
Evanston, Illinois, 110
"Eve of Destruction" (song), 205

Fageros, Karol, 134, *224*
Faggen, I. J. (Jay), 28–29
Fawks, Al, 76–77
Feeney, Joseph, 174
Feller, Bob, *93*, 100
Fenway Park (Boston), 125
Ferguson, Lester, 140
Finney, Gus, 49
Fisher, Eddie, 141
Florence, Italy, 170
Ford, Bill, 55, 57
Ford, Henry, 20
Fordham University, 193
Fort Lewis (Washington State), 10, 86
Fort Wayne (Indiana) Harvesters, 56
Fort Wayne (Indiana) Pistons, 116
Foul! The Connie Hawkins Story (book), 214–216
Frank, Aaron, 52
Franklin, Bernice, 109
Frazier, William "Razor," 49
French, Mary Stewart, 171
French Open (tennis), 134
Frick, Ford, 174
Fujii, Norikazu "Cannonball," 134

Gates, William "Pop," 56, 137, 214
Germany, 136, 151, 162, 165
    1951 appearance of Jesse Owens in Berlin, 165–167

basketball game sets attendance record, 119, 154

incident at hotel involving Eloise Saperstein, 151

Gibby's restaurant (Chicago), 79

Gibson, Althea, 134, *224*

Gibson, Bob, 126

Gibson, Hoot, 181

Giles Post American Legion (Chicago), 28

Glasgow, Montana, 51

Gomez, Thomas, 137–138

Gonzaga University, 80

Go, Man, Go! (film), *132*, 137–139

Gottlieb, Eddie, 116–117, 121, 126–128, 179, 184

Graziano, Rocky, 3

Great Depression, 35, 38, 44, 63, 66

Great Falls, Montana, 40, 44

Greece, 153

Green, Ben, 31, 73, 117, 143

Greenberg, Hank, *92*, 93

Greene, Edgar C., 12

Greensboro, North Carolina, 210

Grenoble, France, 150

Grieve, Curley, 125

The Guardian, 150

Gulick, Luther, 4

Hagan, Frank, 134

Hahn, Bob, 152

Halas, George, 55, 76

Hall, Robert "Showboat," 214

Hammond (Indiana) Pros, 26–27

Hampton, Lionel, 12

Hankyu Braves, 122

Hannin, Harry, 157

Harlem Globetrotters (a.k.a. Harlem Globe Trotters) baseball team, 65

Harlem Globetrotters (a.k.a. Harlem Globe Trotters) basketball team

1948 victory over Minneapolis Lakers, 12, 106, 115

1949 victory over Minneapolis Lakers, 115

1951 *The Harlem Globetrotters* film, 136–138

1954 *Go, Man, Go!* film, 137–139

attempts to form players union, 201–202

ball-handling and other skills, ix, 6, 8, 11, 39, 41, 44, 75, 87, 149

celebrities, appearances with, 135, 205–206

changes in uniform design, 118

clowning antics, 6, 14, 41–44, 80–81, 124, *133*, 168–169

creation of multiple Globetrotter teams, 123, 157

criticism of clowning as degrading, 14, 81, 127, 202

date of first game, 28, 31–33

early struggles with conditions on the road, 35–38

encounters with racism, 37, 40, 82–83, 150, 167

exodus of players in 1934, 47, 49

exodus of players in 1941, 79

expands its tours to new regions, 79, 87–88, 149–159

first game broadcast on television, 124

formation of, 3, 27–33

games played in the Soviet Union, 168–170

games versus the College All-Stars, 119, 126

greeted by Soviet leader, *164*, 169

halftime shows, 110, 133–136

impact of World War II, 84–87

increase in scoring per game, 74–75

length of schedule, 6, 45

Magic Circle, the, 42, 87, 126, 154, 202, 217

Mexico City tournament, 87

name of team, 3, 27, 147

other teams with similar name, 29

partying before a key game, 79

player revolt over money in 1941, 79

players inducted into Hall of Fame, 214

players' memories of Saperstein, 106–108, 202, 211

players' strike in 1971, 201

plays doubleheaders with pro teams, 116, 118, 186, 204

plays for segregated audiences, 4, 83, 127, 134

plays in tough conditions, 37, 150–151, 156

promotional efforts by European companies, 155

reception by foreign fans, 149–151, 153–154, 157–158, 162

reception by foreign media, 149–150, 154

reputation as champions, 46, 77

sales of the team after Saperstein's death, 213, 216

team induction into Hall of Fame, 214

television appearances and contracts, 124, 150, 205–206, 216

television ratings, 206

television shows, inspired by, 216

tours abroad, 149–162, 164–176

use of portable basketball floor, 149, 156, 170

wages/bonuses for players, 42, 47, 53, 84, 106–107, 119–120, 123–124

World Basketball Tournament of 1939, 55–57

World Basketball Tournament of 1940, 75–77

The Harlem Globetrotters (film), 136–138

Harlem Globetrotters Varieties of '55 (variety show), 140

Harlem Magicians, 124

Harvard University, 27

Hawaii Aliis, 183

Hawaiian All-Stars, 134

Hawaiian Surfriders, 125

Hawaii Chiefs, 183–184

Hawkins, Connie,
achieves stardom in ABL, 184
believes Globetrotters acted "like Uncle Toms," 214–215
cites Saperstein's ability to gauge fan reaction, 211
contrasts reception by foreign and U.S. fans, 167
inducted into Hall of Fame, 214

Hayes, Tom, 64

Haynes, Marques,
appears in Globetrotter films, 137
comical dribbling in France, 150–151

forms team with Goose Tatum, 124
influence on future NBA players,
139, 204
induction into Hall of Fame, 214
injury in 1948 Lakers game, 10–12
joins Globetrotters, 88–89
legal conflict with Saperstein, 106
plays against Globetrotters, 88
quits Globetrotters, 123
relations with Saperstein, 106, 123
Hayworth, Rita, 154
Hearne, Richard, 205
Hearst, William Randolph, 55
Hecht, Gerhard, 165
Heim, Al, 199
Helen Stephens' St. Louis Caging Co-
Eds, 57
"Hellzapoppin'" (musical), 141
Henry, Charlie, 66–67
Herschend Family Entertainment, 216
Hinckley, Illinois, 28, 31–33
Hines, Earl "Fatha," 140
Hinsdale, Illinois, 91
Hitler, Adolf, 135, 151, 166
Hobson, Howard, 192–193
Hoeber, Bud, 182
Holiday, Billie, 142
Holocaust, The, 17, 151–152
Holway, John, 67–68
Homestead Grays, 67
Honduras, 157
Hong Kong, China, 144, 156,
157, 158
Honolulu, Hawaii, 88, 145, 181, 183,
209, 216
Hope, Bob, 141
Hopper, Hedda, 161
Hornsby, Rogers, 95
Hotel Pennsylvania (New York), 135

House of David (baseball team), 42, 63
House of David (basketball team), 41,
56, 88, 125
Houston, Texas, 180
Hudson, Dick, 26–30
Hughes, Alfredrick, 215
Hughes, Howard, 143
Hunter, Bobby, 107, 142–143,
196, 202

Ice Capades, 139, 203–204, 208, 213
Illidge, Eric, 55
India, 154, 163, 174
Indiana Clark Twins, 125
Indianapolis Clowns. *See* Ethiopian
Clowns
Indianapolis, Indiana, 69
Indonesia, 167
International Broadcasting, 216
International Falls, Minnesota, 109
Iran, 156, 175
Iraq, 157, 175
Ireland, 173
Irish, Ned, 116
Iron and Oil Base Ball League, 95
Iron Mountain, Michigan, 43
Iron River, Michigan, 53
Italy, 151, 154, 155, 156
Isaacs, John, 73
Israel, 109, 155, 156

Jack the Ripper, 15
Jackson, Inman, *26*, *36*, 41, 45, 51, 54,
57, 76, 79, 82, 87
appears in 1951 film, 137
background of, 28, *39*, 45
childhood of, *39*
coaching and managerial roles, 53,
79, 85, 90, 203

developed the Globetrotters style of
play, 43
dropkick comic routine, 43
fight during a game in
Minneapolis, 39
fishing hobby, 109
friendship with Saperstein, 5, 50,
108–109, 209–210
gracious manner, 53, 80
incident in Miami Beach, 83
induction into Hall of Fame, 214
inheritance from Saperstein, 108
knowledge of Globetrotters'
origins, 31
managerial style, 53, 203
mentors new players, 43
performance in tournament game,
75–76
praise from Saperstein, 49–50, 203
pulls pranks on teammates and
Saperstein, 52–53, 108
recalls traveling with team in a
blizzard, 43
receipt of military draft notice, 87
role with Chicago Majors, 183
seen as quintessential Globetrotter,
49–50
strange errand performed for
Saperstein, 210
views on racism and civil rights,
39–40
wages from Globetrotters, 53
Jackson, Jesse, 7, 215
Jackson, Mannie, ix–xii, x, 107, 203,
214, 216
Jackson, Marion E., 127
Jackson, Tony, 195
James, Olga, 140, 142
Janssen, David, 206

Japan, 122, 147, 156, 158, 174, 208
Jethroe, Sam, 98–99
Johannesburg, South Africa, 159
Johnson, Andy, 107
Johnson, Earvin "Magic," 205
Johnson, Lester, 37
Johnson, Mark, 107
Johnston, Olin D., 13
Joliet, Illinois, 5
Jones, Chuck, 52
Jordan, 171
Jordan, Montana, 51
Juilliard School of Music
(New York), 142
The Jungle (book), 18

Kahn, George, 216
Kansas City, Missouri, 209
Kansas City Monarchs, 62–63, 65,
67, 100
Kansas City Stars, 88, 89, 123, 125
Kansas City Steers, 182–183, 185, 195
Kapiʻolani, Celine, 144–145
Kartens, Bob, 87
Kase, Max, 177–180
Keate, Stu, 84
Kennedy, John F., 105, 175
Kennedy, Pat, 55
Kennedy, Robert F., 168
Kennedy, Walter, 169, 204
Kenosha Badgers, 75
Kenyon, J. Michael, 32, 133, 219
Key Largo (film), 137
Khrushchev, Nikita, *164*, 169
Kim, Art, 183
King and Zerita, 140
King Constantine II of Greece, 154
King Edward VII of the United
Kingdom, 15

King Farouk of Egypt, 155
Klotz, Gloria, 108
Klotz, Red, 108, 121, 208–209, 210
Krueger, Ken, 182
Ku Klux Klan, 83, 95, 202

La Crosse, Wisconsin, 28
Lafayette (Indiana) Red Sox, 65
Landis, Kenesaw Mountain, 93
Langston College (Oklahoma), 88
Lansky, Meyer, 88
Lapchick, Joe, 120, 195
Las Vegas, New Mexico, 53
Lavazza (Italian company), 155
Lavelli, Tony, 152
Law, Joe, 58
Lawford, Peter, 206
Lemon, Meadowlark, 106, 108, 124,
    127, 214
Lenin Central Stadium (Moscow), 168
Leviton, Joyce, 50, 93, 110, 162
Levitt, Harold "Bunny," 133
Liebling, Abbott Joseph, 5
Lille, France, 156
Lima, Peru, 153
LIN Broadcasting, 213
Lincoln Army Air Field Wings, 85
Linehan, Bart Edward, 89
Linehan, Kathie, 90
Linehan, Marie, 128, 210
    background of, 89–90
    career after death of Saperstein, 216
    comments on actress Terry
        Moore, 143
    death of, 216
    explains absence of Saperstein, 186
    helps lead Hall of Fame
        campaign, 214
    hired by Saperstein, 89–90

    inheritance from Saperstein, 214
    marriage and family, 89–90
    praise from Saperstein, 90
    promotion, 216
    recalls Saperstein views of Jackie
        Robinson, 97
    scolds Saperstein for his soda
        habit, 199
    shouts at 1948 Lakers game, 14
    tells story about team's theme
        song, 139
    threatens to quit, 213
Lisbon, Portugal, 149
Litman, Lenny, 181–182, 184
Little Rock (Arkansas) school
    desegregation crisis, 171, 173
Lomza, Poland, 15, 17
London, England, 15, 17, 143, 150,
    158, 161
London, Jack, 17
Long Beach, California, 184
Long, Byron "Fat," 26, 31, 44
Long, Luz, 166
Lord's Taverners, 205
Lorge, Ernest M., 211
Los Angeles Angels, 178
Los Angeles, California, 5, 66, 119,
    128, 177–181, 183–184, 209, 216
Los Angeles Coliseum, 128
Los Angeles Dodgers, 88, 96, 174, 178
Los Angeles Jets, 178, 182–184
Los Angeles Lakers. See Minneapolis
    Lakers
Los Angeles Rams, 129
Louis, Joe, 82, 83
Loyola University (Chicago), 56,
    89, 215
Lucas, Jerry, 185–186
Luciano, Charles "Lucky," 88

Luxembourg, 153
Lynn, Harry, 181
Lyon, France, 167

McArthur, Douglas, 147
McGuire, Barry, 205
McKeon, George, 181
McLendon, John, 182
McMahon, Jack, 182, 195
McQueen, Red, 168
Madison Square Garden (New York),
    113, 116, 118, 215
Major League Baseball,
    criticism by Saperstein of the game's
        pace, 131–132
    historic racism, 94–95
    integration and Jackie Robinson, 96
    suspension of Jake Powell, 95
    troubles of Philadelphia Phillies, 93
Make Room for Daddy (TV), 141
Malcolm X, 202
Malcolm X College (Chicago), 215
Mandela, Nelson, 159
Manila, Philippines, 157, 159
Manley, Effa, 70–71
Mansfield, Jayne, 109
Maravich, Pete, 205
Marciano, Rocky, 141
Martin, J. B., 71
Martinez, Rosalita, 140–141
Mason & Anderson, 140
Maytag Washers (team), 41
Memphis, Tennessee, 127
Metromedia, 213, 216
Mexico, 87–88, 90, 110, 147, 161
Mexico City, Mexico 87, 206
Meyer, Joey, 194, 196
Meyer, Ray, 5, 10, 119, 193–194, 214
Miami, Florida, 67

Miami Beach, Florida, 83
Michigan State University, 206
Mikan, George, 1, 2, 8, 115
    college stardom at DePaul
        University, 5
    comments on portable playing
        court, 156
    commissioner of the ABA, 196
    development as a player, 5
    impressions of the Globetrotters, 7
    performance in 1948 game versus
        Globetrotters, 8–11
    physical appearance, 5
    poor eyesight of, 5
    praised by Saperstein, 115
    superstar in NBA, 5
Milan, Italy, 151
Miller, Buster, 81–82
Miller, Gertrude Kapiolani "Kapi,"
    background of, 144
    birth of daughter Celine, 144
    marriage to Robert Toledo, 144
    tells psychologist of affair with
        Saperstein, 145
    tours with the Globetrotters, 144
    trial for murder, 144–145
Millikan, Bud, 195
Milton, Bobby, 139, 203
Milwaukee Badgers, 27
Milwaukee Brewers, 91–92
Milwaukee, Wisconsin, 58, 119
Minneapolis Lakers, 106
    1948 game against Globetrotters,
        1–14, 115
    1949 game against
        Globetrotters, 115
    alleged interest in signing Marques
        Haynes, 120

discontinue series with
Globetrotters, 115
franchise moves to Los Angeles, 178
impact of Globetrotters series on
integration, 13, 117
post-1949 games against
Globetrotters, 115
stature/reputation of team, 1, 8,
11, 115
Minneapolis, Minnesota, 39, 40, 41,
83, 178, 204
Minnesota Marines, 26
Minnelli, Liza, 205
Miñoso, Minnie, 100
Minot, North Dakota, 44
Mitchum, Robert, 154
Monte Carlo, 152
Monterey, California, 86
Moore, Terry, 143
Morocco, 152, 158, 171, 172
Morrison, Shug, 142
Mozambique, 109, 158
"Mr. Wonderful" (musical), 142
Munich, Germany, 151
Municipal Stadium (Cleveland), 100
Musial, Stan, 182

Naguib, Mohammed, 155
Nagurski, Bronko, 41
Nanaimo, British Columbia, 53
Nancy, France, 150
Napastnikov, Vasily, 168
Naples, Italy, 156
Naismith, James, 4, 181, 189
Naismith Memorial Basketball Hall of
Fame, xi, 214–215
National Association of Base Ball
Players, 94
National Basketball Association (NBA),

1951 championship series, 119
adopts three-point shot, 196
alleged pressure to end Lakers–
Globetrotters series, 115
initial steps to integrate, 116–117
comparison of television ratings,
119, 206
criticism by Saperstein of quality of
play, 129
denies Saperstein a franchise,
128–129
doubleheaders played with
Globetrotters, 116, 204
expands to West Coast, 129
explores merger with ABL, 185
first superstar in league, 5
history and early franchises, 113
less popular than college
basketball, 77
low attendance at games, 119
offer of franchise that Saperstein
rejected, 179–180
racial composition, history of, 116
recognizes players' union, 201
relations with Saperstein, 117–118,
120–121, 128–129
shot clock rule, 183
television ratings, 206
National Basketball League, 7,
113, 116
National Broadcasting Company
(NBC), 216
National Football League (NFL), 3, 26,
105, 122
National Industrial Basketball League,
ix, 182
National Invitational Tournament, 5
NBA. *See* National Basketball
Association

NBC. *See* National Broadcasting
Company
Neal, Fred "Curly," 214
Negro Leagues (baseball), xiii, 25
1939 East–West All-Star game,
67–68
1943 East–West All-Star game,
62–63
criticized for ties to numbers
"racket," 96
Ethiopian Clowns join the
league, 69
financial stability of teams, 63
internal discord over Saperstein,
68–71
Negro American League, 59, 62,
63, 68–71
Negro National League, 62, 68–69
racial composition of fans, 62–63
role of Saperstein as booking/
publicity agent, 59, 68
Negro Major Baseball League of
America, 69
Nehru, Jawaharlal, 154
Netherlands, The, 109, 158
Newark Eagles, 62, 69, 70–71
Newberry, James, 122
New Mexico Highlands University, 53
Newton, Iowa, 42
New York Celtics, 54–55, 125
New York Daily News, 143
New York Herald-Tribune, 160
New York Journal-American, 177, 179
New York Knicks, 8, 116–120,
122, 177
New York Nationals, 43–44
New York, New York, ix, 79, 135, 142

New York Renaissance (a.k.a. Rens),
46, 54–57, 73, 75, 76, 78, 79–81,
85, 125, 181
New York Times, 29–30, 94, 138, 193
New York World's Fair (1964-65), 205
New York Yankees (baseball team), 65,
95, 101, 182
New York Yankees (basketball
team), 56
NFL. *See* National Football League
Nice, France, 150
Nippon Professional Baseball, 122
Nixon, Richard, 173, 175
Norfolk, Virginia, 134
North Carolina State University, 152
Novak, Mike, 56, 76
Nugent, Gerry, 94
Nusbaum, Eric, 13

Oakland, California, 66
Oakland Oaks, 184, 204
Obama, Barack, 216
Ocala, Florida, 92
O'Donnell, John, 104
Ohio State University, 185
Oklahoma City, Oklahoma, 88
Olympics. *See* United States Olympic
teams
O'Neil, John "Buck," 67
Oliver, William "Kid," *26*, 31
Olympic Stadium (Berlin), 165–166
Omaha, Nebraska, 123, 134
Oshkosh All-Stars, 57
Ottumwa, Iowa, 207
Owens, Jesse, xiii, 170, 203
1951 appearance in West Berlin,
165–167
conflict with Amateur Athletic
Union, 135

controversy over racing stunts, 66,
135–136
employment and financial
challenges, 135
encounters racism after Olympic
success, 135
jobs/roles provided by Saperstein,
xiii, 135
optimism about new Black baseball
league, 66
ownership of Black baseball
team, 66
relationship with Saperstein, 66,
135–136
self-image as "public relations
man," 136

Paar, Jack, 205
Paige, Satchel, xiii, *60*, 70, 99
appraisals of his talent, 99–100
breaks contracts, 62
demeanor on the field, 61
enters Major League Baseball,
xiii, 99
high-earning status, 101
monetizes his value, 61–62
pitches for Negro League teams, 64
pitches in barnstorming games, 63,
65, 95
reaction to Cleveland's signing, 100
represented by Saperstein, 61–63
similarities to Saperstein, 61
views on baseball integration, 94
works for the Globetrotters,
135, 203
Palais des Sports (Paris), 151
Palca, Alfred, 138
Palmer IV, Potter, 213
Panama, 153

Paris, France, 111, 120, 141, 143, 151,
152, 159
Pauley, Ed, 129
Pearl Harbor, attack on, 85
Pearson, Drew, 168, 171–172
The People of the Abyss (book), 17
People's Republic of China. *See* China
Perón, Eva, 153–154, 174
Perón, Juan, 153–154, 174
Peru, 153
Philadelphia 76ers, 206
Philadelphia Athletics, 99, 122
Philadelphia, Pennsylvania, 126, 184
Philadelphia Phillies, 91–94, 101
Philadelphia Warriors, 116, 121, 123
acquisition of Wilt Chamberlain,
126–128
move by franchise to West
Coast, 184
partial ownership by
Saperstein, 121
stance of owner on NBA
integration, 116
trade involving Marques
Haynes, 123
Philippines, 157, 159
Phillip, Andy, 183
Pinkard, Maceo, 139
Pittsburgh Courier, 46, 55, 69, 90,
103, 173
Pittsburgh Crawfords, 62
Pittsburgh, Pennsylvania, 79, 181
Pittsburgh Rens, 181–182, 184–186
Podoloff, Maurice, 115, 117, 120,
128–129, 177–181, 185, 204
Poitier, Sidney, 137
Pollard, Fritz, 26–28, 30
Pollard, Jim, 6
Pollock, Alan, 62, 70

Pollock, Syd, 62, 66–67, 69–70, 210
Polo Grounds (New York), 125
Ponce, Tony, 140
Pope Pius XII (a.k.a. Eugenio
  Pacelli), 154
Port Alberni, British Columbia, 53
Portland, Oregon, 66, 180, 209
Portland Rose Buds, 66
Portugal, 149, 160
Posey, Cumberland "Cum," 67–69
Powell, Jake, 95
Powelson, Carlos, 31
Pressley, Louis "Babe," 2, 9–10,
  55–56, 75, 79
  appears in 1951 film, 137
  clashes with Saperstein, 106
  highest-paid Globetrotter, 84
  leadership roles on team, 9, 90
Price, Bernie, 55, 77, 79, 108
Pricert, Raphael, 139
Prince Philip, Duke of Edinburgh, 202,
  205, 210
Providence Steam Roller, 27
Pullins, Al "Runt," 26, 31, 33, 39, 45,
  47, 49, 54, 79, 84, 214

Queen Narriman of Egypt, 154

Rabat, Morocco, 172
racism and racial climate,
  incidents involving Globetrotters,
    37, 40, 82–83, 150, 167
  Little Rock school desegregation
    crisis, 171, 173
  prosecution of Scottsboro boys, 39
  race-based assessments of athletes,
    4, 76, 95
  racial climate in Chicago, 4, 25, 54

  racial slur by baseball player in
    1938, 95
  reinforced by media narratives, 4,
    40, 76, 202
  segregated audiences for sporting
    events, 4, 83, 127, 134
  segregation in baseball, history of,
    94–95
  State Department cites its adverse
    impact, 163
  views of Naismith mentor, 4
Radcliffe, Ted "Double Duty,"
  64–65, 70
Raemer, Leah Saperstein, 16, 18–20,
  22, 210
Raemer, Roy, 19, 109
Ramsey, Randolph, 28–29, 30
Rankin, Marlene, 136, 166–167, 221
Ravenswood (Chicago), 17–20
Raymond, Dell, 35, 37
Reiner, Carl, 206
Rhodesia, 158–159
Rice, Grantland, 106
Rickey, Branch, 96–97, 101
Rio de Janeiro, Brazil, 119, 153,
  157, 186
Robertson, Oscar, 128
Robinson, Ermer,
  appears in 1951 film, 137
  laid off by Saperstein, 204
  origin of his nickname, 10
  performance in 1948 Lakers game,
    10–12
  roles with ABL teams, 183–184
Robinson, Jackie, 88, 96–98
Robinson, Sugar Ray, 111, 135, 165
Rochester, Minnesota, 42
Rochester (New York) Royals, 119
Rogers, Roy, 3

Romano Brothers, 140

Rome, Italy, 152, 170, 206

Roosevelt, Franklin D., 3, 44, 85

Rose Bowl, 109–110, 119

Rose, Frank, 4, 13–14, 38, 199

Rusan, Harry, 49, 54, 57, 73

Russell, Bill, 125–126, 170, 206

Russell, Charley, 126

Russia. *See* Soviet Union

Ryan, Bob, 217

St. Cloud, Minnesota, 44

St. Francis College, 193

St. John's University, 195

St. Louis Browns, 94–95, 121, 154

St. Louis Cardinals, 126

St. Louis, Missouri, ix, 66, 70, 182, 185

Sallaway, Pete, 8, 86

Salt Lake City, Utah, 209

Sand Springs, Oklahoma, 12

San Diego, California, 66

San Francisco 49ers, 122

San Francisco, California, 57, 66, 105, 128, 129, 180–181, 209

San Francisco Saints, 177, 181, 183–184

Saperstein, Abraham Michael, *16, 26, 48, 60, 92, 104, 114, 148, 164, 178, 200, 218, 222, 224*

   ability to count the crowd, 1

   acts as sportswriter, 58

   alleged relationship with Kapi Miller, 145

   approach to clowning, 6, 14, 41–43, 74–75, 80–81, 133

   attitudes toward Black athletes, 70, 82–83, 93

   birth of daughter Eloise, 58

   birth of son Jerry, 78

   business misfortunes, 140–141, 186–187, 203, 214

   business successes, 53, 69, 77, 99–100, 121, 140, 152–153, 206

   challenges other teams to play Globetrotters, 46, 55, 120, 204

   childhood of, 15, 19–21

   clashes with NBA commissioner, 177–180, 185

   criticizes quality of play in NBA, 129

   criticizes U.S. diplomats, 174–175

   death of, 210

   departs Soviet Union with furs and stamps, 160

   early jobs, 25–26

   embraces patriotic role, 85–86, 164–167, 170, 175–176

   falls out with Eddie Gottlieb, 127–128, 179

   falls out with Syd Pollock, 70

   favors physically aggressive play, 9

   financial ambitions, 53

   forms American Basketball League, 177–181

   forms West Coast Negro Baseball Association, 66

   friendship with Bill Veeck, 91–92

   friendship with Inman Jackson, 5, 50, 108–109, 209–210

   gifts to charity and the financially distressed, 105–106, 112

   greeted by Soviet leader, *164*, 169

   handles publicity for East-West games, 67–69

   illnesses and health conditions, 161, 207–210

   immigration of family to United States, 17–18

induction into Hall of Fame, 214
legacies of, 98–101, 189–197, 213, 217
managerial style and work habits of, 5, 12, 23, 47, 106, 108
marriage to Sylvia Franklin, *48*, 50
monitors team/player dynamics, 106
neighborhood/city of his birth, 15
establishes offices for his operations, 79, 118, 157
optimistic nature, 38, 76, 128, 203
owns shares of teams, 63–64, 67, 100, 121, 128, 154, 181
parents of, 15–17
personality away from work, 109
physical description of, 3, 21
plays in Globetrotters games, 44
ponders his successor, 206–207
promoter of arts and entertainment, 133, 139–143
promoter of boxing, lacrosse, and soccer, 58
provides leadership roles to Inman Jackson, 54, 79, 90, 183
reacts to losing games, 7–8, 56, 73
reacts to 1940 tournament win, 77
relations with wife and children, 109–112
relations with NBA, 117–118, 120–121, 128–129
relations with media, 49, 103–105, 141, 161
relations with players, 44, 106–108
religious practices of family, 19
respect for opponents' skills, 88
role in integration of professional baseball, 98–101
rumors of womanizing, 143–144

scouts Black baseball talent, 91, 98–100
seeks NBA franchise, 120, 128–129
seeks new gimmicks, 63, 187, 189, 192
seeks ties with celebrities, 135, 141, 205–206
sends his wife flowers each week, 111
serves as business agent for Satchel Paige, 61–63
soda-drinking habit, 199
suggests basketball rule changes, 190–195, 197
takes glitzy approach to salary/ bonus offers, 122, 126–127
target of anti-Semitism, 40
travel habits and opinions, 110, 157, 160
use of halftime performers, 110, 133-135
views on playing baseball games at night, 70
views on basketball's center jump, 190–191
views on basketball skills of foreign teams, 149, 157
views on foreign policy, 175
views on Jackie Robinson, 96 –98
views on race/racial barriers, 4, 82–83, 93, 172–173, 201–202
views on sports ticket pricing, 92
welcoming Black players to his home, 93
will and heirs, 108, 213-214
Saperstein, Anna, 15, *16*, 17, 19, 50
Saperstein, Fay, 18, 19, 118, 214
Saperstein, Gerald, 7, 109, 213
Saperstein, Guy, 18–19, 23, 110-111

Saperstein, Harry, 18–19, 22, 23, 35, 38, 86. 143
Saperstein, Jacob, *16*, 18
Saperstein, Jerry,
   birth of, 78
   comments on three-point shot, 193–194
   death of, 215
   decision to cancel Iowa game, 207
   enjoys lavish lifestyle as teenager, 111
   helps family of NBA player secure a pension, 107
   inheritance from his father's estate, 214
   receives gift of stamps from ambassador, 175
   relationship with his father, 111, 206
   roles in sports promotion, 215
   receives his mother's support to succeed his father, 213
Saperstein, Lanier, 23, 111, 206
Saperstein, Louis, 15, 17–19, 22, 50
Saperstein, Morry, 18, 58, 69, 90, 106, 128
Saperstein, Rocky, 18, 43, 86, 90, 124, 149, 207
Saperstein, Sylvia Franklin, 83, 209
   adolescence of, 50
   birth of daughter Eloise, 58
   birth of son Jerry, 78
   correspondence from her husband, 109, 111–112
   death of, 216
   enters beauty contests, 50
   inheritance from Abe Saperstein, 214

   lengthy absences of her husband, 111
   marriage to Abe Saperstein, *48*, 50
   personality of, 112
   physical description of, 50
   request she allegedly made of Marie Linehan, 143
   second marriage to George Kahn, 216
   seeks Jerry to succeed her husband, 213
   suggests comedy antic, 112
   traumatic winter trip with Globetrotters, 52
Savoy Big Five, 27–29, 39, 49, 79
Schiller's Florist, 22
Schissler, Paul, 129
Schreiber, Walter, 166
Sears, Kenny, 177
Seattle Steelheads, 66
Seattle, Washington, 32, 52, 66, 76, 106, 129, 133, 209
Sephus, Joe, 104
Servus Rubber Company, 41
Shamrock Capital Growth Fund, 216
Sharman, Bill, 182, 184, 193–194
Sheboygan Redskins, 57, 77
Sheboygan, Wisconsin, 77
Shelby, Don, 83–84, 204–205
Shelby, Montana, 40
Sherman, Eddie, 209
Siena College, 193
Sinatra, Frank, 3
Sinclair, Upton, 18
Singapore, 159, 161
Smith, Lyall, 181
Smith, Wendell, 56, 186
   criticizes Black baseball league, 69
   criticizes Ethiopian Clowns, 67

defends Saperstein as baseball promoter, 68

friendship with Saperstein, 97

moves to Chicago, 90

praises Saperstein's role in integrating baseball, 97

relationship with Jackie Robinson, 97

reports on All-Star Classic, 78

role as baseball scout, 98

views on the NBA, 113–115

Smith, Wyonella, 90, 97, 201, 210

South Africa, 159, 169

South Bend (Indiana) Studebakers, 63

"South Pacific" (musical), 110

Soviet Union, 157

1959 tour by Globetrotters, 160, 168–170

compensation paid to Globetrotters, 170

criticizes racial discrimination in U.S., 163

initial reaction to Globetrotters by Soviet fans, 168–169

prank pulled by Saperstein and player, 169–170

scalpers' prices for Globetrotter tickets, 170

Soviet leader greets Globetrotters, 169

struggle to arrange Globetrotter tour of, 168

Spain, 109, 153–154, 185

Spinning the Globe (book), 31

Spivey, Bill, 184

Spokane, Washington, 80

Spoor, George, 20

The Sporting News, 100, 152–153

SportsCentury: Most Influential People (TV), 217

Sports Illustrated, 117

Springfield, Massachusetts, 189

Stars of America, 152

Steinbrenner, George, 182, 184–185, 193

Stephens, Helen, 57

Straight, Hal, 82

Strauss, Michael, 29–30

Strong, Ted, Jr., 55–56, 65, 76, 79, 137

Sullivan, Ed, 143, 205

Sun Ra (a.k.a. Le Sony'r Ra), 142

Swanson, Gloria, 20-21

Swea City, Iowa, 42

Sweden, 135

"Sweet Georgia Brown" (song), 139–140, 153, 217

Sweetwater (film), 217

Switzerland, 151

Syracuse Nationals, 113, 184

Syracuse Reds, 76

Syria, 157, 167

Szukala, Stan, 78

Tacoma, Washington, 86

Take Your Choice: Separation or Mongrelization (book), 202

Tally-Ho (restaurant), 110

Taipei, Taiwan, 156

Tatum, Reece "Goose," 66, 74, 79, 88, 115, 124

appears in Globetrotter films, 137

baseball experience of, 6, 64

carries out eating-the-ball antic, 80

compensation of, 12, 123

disciplined by Saperstein, 123, 152

emerges as a star, 80

enters military service in World War
II, 85
exhibits tendency to disappear,
123, 152
hands that impressed the Pope, 154
induction into Hall of Fame, 214
joins the Globetrotters, 80
performance in 1948 Lakers game,
8–11
physical description of, 6,
plays last game with the
Globetrotters, 124
quits the Globetrotters, 124
relations with Saperstein, 106, 124
shows great rapport with children,
80, 155–156
suffers collision in Detroit, 9
Taylor, Willis Garner "Sec," 105
Technical Tape Corporation, x, 182
Temple Beth Israel (Chicago), 211
Tennessee State University (a.k.a.
Tennessee A&I State College), 89
Thailand, 171
Thomas, Damion L., 42, 163–164
Thomas, Danny, 141
Thomas, Isiah, 215
Thomas, Ron, 116
Thompson, Frank "Groundhog," 64
three-point shot in basketball,
adoption by ABA, 195–196
adoption by ABL, 189–195, *190*
adoption by college basketball, 196
adoption by NBA, 196
determination of the shooting arc,
193–194
efficiency of shots in ABL and
NBA, 195
impact on basketball, 196–197
origins of, 192–193

use of lights or noise to amplify, 195
views of coaches, referees, media,
and fans, 193–197
Tiberias, Israel, 109
Toledo, Ohio, 73
Toledo, Robert, 144–145
Tollefsen, Toralf, 140
Tong Brothers, 140
Trinidad, 154
Tripoli, Libya, 171–172
Tri-State Baseball League, 63–64
Truman, Harry, 13, 174
Tucker, Burt, 109–110, 112, 206, 208
Tunisia, 153
Turkey, 159
Turpin, Ben, 20
Tye, Larry, 62
Tygiel, Jules, 95

Uline Arena (Washington, D.C.), 118
United Farmers League, 39
United Kingdom, 149
United States Air Force, 166, 170
United States Department of State,
assesses 1951 Globetrotters-Owens
event, 167
cites Globetrotters as goodwill
ambassadors, xi, xiii, 164
concerns about impact of racial
discrimination in U.S., 163
financial/logistical assistance to
Globetrotters, 170–171
seeks to counter Soviet
messages, 164
suggests destinations for
Globetrotter tours, 171
support for proposed baseball
tour, 174

urges diplomats to facilitate
Globetrotter tours, 164
withdraws objection to Soviet tour
by Globetrotters, 168
United States Olympic team, 106
University of Arizona, 110, 206
University of California at Los
Angeles, 214
University of Cincinnati, 128
University of Illinois, ix, 21, 183
University of Kansas, 126, 191
University of Maryland, 195
University of Oregon, 192–193
University of San Francisco, 125,
128, 170
Uruguay, 153

Van Court, Albert, 139
Vancouver, British Columbia, 52, 209
Van Lier, Norm, 215
Vaughn, Govoner "Gov," ix
Veeck, Bill, *92*, 154, 210
background of, 91
develops theatrical ploys to draw
fans, 92
financial assistance from
Saperstein, 91
friendship with Saperstein, 91–92
plan to acquire Philadelphia Phillies
team, 91, 93–94
praises role of Saperstein, 100
signs Satchel Paige to contract, 99
Venezuela, 153
Victor Adding Machine Company, 22
Vienna, Austria, 160

Waldorf Cafe Five, 41
Walsh, Tom, 133
Walter Balls (baseball team), 26, 59

Wapp, Tony, 43
Ward, Arch, 7
Washington, Andy, 31
Washington Capitols, 117–118
Washington, Chester, 103
Washington, District of Columbia,
13, 45, 79, 86, 117–118, 168,
171–172, 181
Washington, Frank, 137, 174
Washington Generals, 108, 121, 206,
208, 210, 217
Washington Tapers, 181–182,
184, 187
Washington Wizards, 129
Waterloo, Iowa, 35
Waterloo (Iowa) Hawks, 113
Waters, Ethel, 30
Welch, Winfield, 65, 89, 121–122
Wembley Stadium (England), 150
Wenatchee, Washington, 103–104
West Berlin, Germany. *See* Berlin,
Germany
West Coast Negro Baseball
Association, 66, 136
West Germany. *See* Germany
West, Jerry, 183
Wheatland, Iowa, 37
Wheeler, Leon, 76
Wheeler, Sam, 9, 11
Whitechapel (London), 15, 17
White City (Chicago amusement park),
54–55
Wichita, Kansas, 80, 157
Wilcox, Robert, 144
Williamsburg, Iowa, 42
Wilson, Clarence "Cave," 137,
169–170
Wilson, C. W., 86
Wimbledon (tennis), 134

Winter, Max, 7, 209
Wirtz, Arthur, 186–187
Wolf, David, 214
Wong Howe, James, 138–139
Wooden, John, 214
Woodard, Lynette, 216
Woolpert, Phil, 170
World of Music (tour), 140
World Professional Basketball
  Tournament, 55–56, 73, 75–77, 79
World Series of Basketball. *See* College
  All-Stars
World Team Tennis, 215
Wright, Walter "Toots," *26*, 28–29,
  31, 45
Wrigley Field (Chicago), 3, 18, 125

Yale University, 27
Yankoff, Victor, 144
Yardley, George, 184
Young, Andrew Spurgeon "Doc,"
  91, 101
Young, Frank Albert "Fay," 28, 67, 68,
  76, 79, 101
Yugoslavia, 157

Zaharias, Babe Didrikson. *See*
  Didrikson
Zale, Tony, 3
Zeigler, Vertes, 9
Ziegler, Carol, 182
Zimbabwe. *See* Rhodesia
Zinkoff, Dave, 169
Zulu Cannibal Giants, 66–67

ABOUT THE AUTHORS

Mark Jacob, former metro editor at the *Chicago Tribune* and former Sunday editor of the *Chicago Sun-Times*, is the coauthor of nine other books, ranging from a celebration of Chicago's Wrigley Field to a biography of Benedict Arnold's wife, Peggy Shippen. He resides in Evanston, Illinois.

Matthew Jacob, a public health consultant, coauthored *What the Great Ate* with his brother Mark. He is a member of the Society for American Baseball Research. He lives in Arlington, Virginia.